WAITING FOR GONSKI

Tom Greenwell teaches history and politics in the ACT public education system. He writes about Australian education policy for *Inside Story* and *The Canberra Times*. He has explored a wide range of topics including growing segregation in Australian schooling, the history of Australian education, and contemporary trends and challenges. He previously worked as a research officer with the Australian Education Union.

Chris Bonnor AM is a former teacher and secondary school principal. He was a previous head of the NSW Secondary Principals' Council and is co-author, with Jane Caro, of *The Stupid Country* and *What Makes a Good School?* He has contributed to a range of publications and media, and has jointly authored papers on Australia's schools in association with the Centre for Policy Development and the Gonski Institute for Education.

'A forensic and gripping analysis of the power plays and vested interests that flipped Gonski from a needs-based, sector-blind funding scheme to its exact opposite. Greenwell and Bonnor even dare to float some ideas about how we might unravel the unholy mess that education funding has become.'

Jane Caro, novelist, writer and social commentator

'School funding arguments cut straight to core questions of national identity and this book is a tremendous feat of history and economics which privileges understanding over judgment. Greenwell and Bonnor present a definitive and clear account of how we got into this mess, and they offer bold ideas for how we might get out of it.'

Bri Lee, writer, journalist, activist and author of *Who Gets to be Smart* and *Eggshell Skull*

'*Waiting for Gonski* forensically maps the sweetheart deals, spin and threats that cynical vested interests have wielded over and over to maintain their own privilege, in the process damaging Australia's future and throwing our most vulnerable students under a metaphorical bus. Read it and weep. Then agitate.'

Marion Maddox, Honorary Professor of Politics, Macquarie University and author of *Taking God to School: The End of Australia's Egalitarian Education?*

'When Gough Whitlam broke the stalemate on "state aid" he hoped that the Schools Commission headed by my old mentor, Professor Peter Karmel, would provide equal opportunity for all students, particularly for "poor Catholic kids". Unfortunately, the powerful and greedy private and Church lobbyists have subverted that hope. They have lobbied all governments to protect the privileged at the expense of millions of children in public schools and some private schools. The virtue of this book is that it places the failure of the Gonski reforms within the larger story of state aid in Australia.'

John Menadue, publisher of *Pearls & Irritations*, who's had a distinguished career both in the private sector and in the Public Service

'Rigorous research compellingly presented, a sharp account of the highs and lows of the Gonski rollercoaster. This book offers both a cautionary tale and some excellent advice: we can do better for the nation's schoolchildren.'

Helen Proctor, Professor in Education History and Policy, Sydney School of Education and Social Work, University of Sydney

'Sometimes education systems need to choose a new way to address old problems. That remains Australia's challenge. *Waiting for Gonski* is a must-read for all policymakers, educators, and parents who want to know why we ended up having one of the most unequal school systems today and how we can rebuild it so that all children will have a fair go in education that they deserve.'

Pasi Sahlberg, Professor of Education, Gonski Institute for Education, University of New South Wales and author of *Finnish Lessons: What can the world learn from educational change in Finland*

WAITING FOR GONSKI

HOW AUSTRALIA FAILED ITS SCHOOLS

Tom Greenwell
& Chris Bonnor

UNSW PRESS

A UNSW Press book

Published by
NewSouth Publishing
University of New South Wales Press Ltd
University of New South Wales
Sydney NSW 2052
AUSTRALIA
http://unsw.press

First published 2022

10 9 8 7 6 5 4 3 2 1

NATIONAL LIBRARY OF AUSTRALIA

A catalogue record for this book is available from the National Library of Australia

ISBN: 9781742237268 (paperback)
9781742238326 (ebook)
9781742239224 (ePDF)

Design Josephine Pajor-Markus
Cover design Akiko Chan
Cover image istock by Getty Images
Printer Griffin Press, part of Ovato

This book is printed on paper using fibre supplied from plantation or sustainably managed forests.

UNSW
SYDNEY

Contents

Timeline

1866	Victorian Royal Commission recommends universal public schools teach a 'common Christianity'.
1872–93	The Australian colonies establish free, compulsory and secular primary schools. State aid is withdrawn from church schools.
1962	Goulburn Catholic schools 'strike': Catholic schools close for one week in a dramatic demonstration of the case for state aid.
1963	The Menzies Government initiates direct Commonwealth capital funding of Australian schools, providing grants for science blocks.
1969	The Gorton Government begins recurrent Commonwealth funding of non-government schools on a per capita basis.
1973	The Karmel report recommends the introduction of needs-based school funding. In response, the Whitlam Government introduces recurrent Commonwealth Government funding for both public and private schools.
1984	The Hawke Government is forced to back down after its proposal to reduce funding to Australia's 41 wealthiest private schools is denounced as a 'hit list'.
2004	The Labor Opposition's promise to introduce needs-based funding during the federal election campaign, including cuts to some schools, is

	labelled 'Latham's hit list' and comes to be viewed as an electoral negative.
2008	The Rudd Government extends the Howard Government's funding system for four more years.
2010	– 15 April, Julia Gillard announces a new school funding review and pledges no school will lose a dollar in nominal terms. – 23 June, Gillard replaces Kevin Rudd as prime minister. – 4 August, Gillard further extends the Howard Government's funding model for another year. – December, results from the OECD's Program of International Student Assessment (PISA) tests indicate Australian 15-year-olds are falling behind in reading and maths.
2011	In December, the Gonski panel hands its completed report to the Gillard Government.
2012	– 20 February, the Gonski Report is publicly released. – June, the 'I Give a Gonski' campaign is launched. – 20 August, Prime Minister Gillard pledges that every school will receive a funding increase. – 3 September, Prime Minister Gillard announces the National Plan for School Improvement, a commitment to deliver on the core recommendations of the Gonski Report. – November, the Australian Education Bill is introduced to parliament.
2013	– 23 April, the New South Wales Coalition Government signs up to the Gillard Government's school funding plan, the National Education Reform Agreement.

	– 4 August, Opposition Leader Tony Abbott announces a 'unity ticket' with the Rudd Government on Gonski funding. – November–December, the Abbott Government is forced to honour its pre-election commitment, but allows states to walk away from school funding obligations.
2016	– 30 September, Education Minister Simon Birmingham indicates that some schools should lose funding. – December, new PISA test results show that on average Australian 15-year-olds are a year of learning behind their predecessors in the year 2000.
2017	– 2 May, Prime Minister Turnbull and Minister Birmingham announce a new funding plan and a new review, again to be chaired by David Gonski. – 23 June, the *Australian Education Amendment Act* ('Gonski 2.0') is passed.
2018	The Morrison Government announces the Choice and Affordability package, an extra $4.6bn funding for non-government schools.
2019	New National School Reform Agreement defers delivery of needs-based funding to the end of the next decade.

Introduction

It was only after Julia Gillard invited him to review the funding of Australia's schools in 2010 that David Gonski realised how much education had transformed his own life. 'I remember sitting with Ken Boston and, I suspect, Kathryn Greiner in a subcommittee we were planning. And it suddenly hit me – it was like a bolt out of the blue – that my father was educationally disadvantaged', Gonski recalls almost a decade later. 'I hadn't … I hadn't thought that through before because my dad was a brain surgeon. And so I started to talk to my mother – my father was already dead – and it all came to me so clearly.'[1]

David Gonski's grandparents were dirt-poor migrants from Eastern Europe, who arrived in South Africa with little money and even less English. Their son, Gonski's father, was an extremely bright child, but it was only the assistance of philanthropic scholarships that enabled him to continue studies beyond school, eventually completing a degree in medicine. When David was still a boy, his parents left South Africa for Australia, where he would rise to become one of the country's leading businessmen, a famed networker among Sydney's rich and powerful, and a noted patron of the arts and philanthropist in his own right. 'Ultimately what happened because of that beneficence was that my father became a brain surgeon, and I had a great life', Gonski reflects. 'I had never focused on my dear dad until we started talking about this. And then I realised, actually this was the destiny of the review.'

One morning in early 2011, in the course of conducting the school funding review that would bear his name, Gonski left his Point Piper home to visit two primary schools, Villawood North Public School and Sacred Heart School, in Sydney's west. Upon arriving at the first school, he discovered the principal dealing with broken glass from a break-in the night before. As he sat waiting in the school's reception, Gonski observed the flow of children arriving for the school day: almost all were, like his father, the children of migrants from non-English-speaking backgrounds; many were from families as poor as his father's had been.

When the principal had finished dealing with the immediate issues, he and Gonski toured the school, discussing the challenges it faced. 'Most of his kids didn't see a book outside the school', Gonski recalls to us, his shock still apparent. 'I mean, we've had three kids. I've got two grandchildren. This is an absurd thing. No books!' 'I asked [the principal] the question: "what is the relationship between the school and the parents?" Because I was interested', Gonski says. '"What's the involvement of parents?"' It was a reasonable question and yet, as soon as he asked it, Gonski realised how removed he was from the realities facing this school. The principal looked at him, smiled and said, 'David, my job is to get the kids in here by 9am in the morning. Getting the parents in here at all is almost an impossibility', adding that 40 per cent of the student roll changed each year and his focus that year was on improving attendance.

Gonski's next destination was just down the road. He thought he would go on foot, but the principal advised him to drive. 'He was just not happy [with my assuming] that it was safe for me to walk – something I'd never thought of in my own city.' It is possible to imagine Gonski driving away from the school, pondering his father's story. How likely was it that a child of poor migrants with little English, growing up in these circumstances, would end up becoming a neurosurgeon? A growing body of evidence suggested it was increasingly improbable. NAPLAN (National Assessment Program – Literacy and Numeracy) results in 2009 showed that Year 9 students in hardscrabble areas of Sydney had poorer literacy and numeracy than Year 5 children in the wealthier parts of town that Gonski was more familiar with.[2] It seemed that our schools were merely reproducing inequalities that existed outside the school gate – and sometimes making them even worse.

Only a few minutes' drive away, Sacred Heart School seemed a world away. 'I saw just in that morning the difference between the way the schools were operating', Gonski reflects, almost a decade later. 'Every child was perfectly turned out in magnificent school uniforms. I was greeted by a concert which was a short one – beautiful singing by the kids. The headmaster was in total control of his buildings. They were perfect.' This school served a quite different group of children from the school down the road. Gonski asked the principal whether he faced the truancy problems experienced at the school he had just come from. 'Truancy?' the principal responded with surprise. 'I've got a waiting list for the school! If we have truancy, I tell the parents to take their kids away.'[3]

David Gonski believed that the opportunity his father had had to transform his lot should be the birthright of every Australian child; that 'differences in educational outcomes should not be the result of differences in wealth, income, power or possessions', in the words of the report that would take his name.[4] 'Julia Gillard made that wonderful speech, you may recall, in which she said a person's demography should not determine their destiny. You think about it in relation to my family: even though we were immigrants to this country, my father had a very good profession. He saved lives. I had a lovely life. Why? Because of education.'[5]

And yet that morning in 2011, visiting those two nearby schools in western Sydney, Gonski had witnessed close-up the growing divergence between the responsibilities Australian schools faced and the resources they had to meet them. The Gonski review found that in successful school systems internationally, students were able to achieve their best irrespective of their background or the school they attended. But that was less the case in Australia. The impact of family background on educational outcomes in Australia was much more pronounced than in comparable countries like Canada. And the gap in the learning outcomes between disadvantaged Australian children and their more privileged peers was growing.

In response to these challenges, the Gonski Report offered a seemingly compelling solution. First, identify the resourcing enjoyed by those schools where most students were achieving above-minimum national standards. Then, take that as the best guide to the necessary resourcing for a successful education and call it the baseline level of funding which *all* students should receive. A child with a severe disability, or low-English proficiency, or one who arrives at school without breakfast will likely need much more support to succeed. So a common resource standard would have to respond flexibly to each individual child's learning needs. Therefore it would be necessary to provide additional funding loadings on top of the baseline for those children who experience disadvantages that impede their learning, and for schools in remote or rural locations, or with small student populations, that face higher costs. Thirdly, set up an architecture to continuously verify and evaluate the calculations underpinning the first two steps. Even though the Gonski review commissioned rigorous research to assess the correct baseline amount and appropriate level of the funding loadings, it knew that the findings would always have to be reassessed in light of new evidence. So it recommended the appointment of a body of independent experts, one step removed from the political process, to perform this task.

Implementing Gonski's resource standard would require a substantial national investment – a 15 per cent increase on current expenditure. Modelling conducted by the review indicated that three-quarters of the additional spending would flow to public schools, reflecting the high levels of social disadvantage in that sector. But where disadvantaged students were enrolled in non-government schools, they too would receive additional resourcing. School funding would be needs-based and sector-blind.

The Gonski Report seemed like a simple but powerful response to Australia's educational ills. And unlike many previous attempts to reform school funding, it was welcomed by all school sectors. The Gonski panel seemed to have fixed on a formula that all sides of the often fractious school policy debate could realistically sign up to: a considered, rational approach to advancing the common good that had the potential to be more than just a triumph of one sectional interest over another. When in 2012 Gonski began to be championed by Adrian Piccoli, the National Party's Minister for Education in New South Wales, it became apparent that its appeal extended across the political divide. By April 2013, the Liberal New South Wales Premier, Barry O'Farrell, signed on to Gonski, providing further tangible confirmation of the bipartisan appeal of needs-based funding.

A month out from the 2013 federal election, the Coalition Leader, Tony Abbott, sensing the public debate had shifted, felt compelled to declare a 'unity ticket' with the Labor Government on the issue. Then, when he attempted to walk away from the promise after the election, an overwhelming public backlash confronted him, immediately forcing him to stage a retreat. It was definitive confirmation that needs-based funding now occupied the centre ground, enjoying the kind of widespread popular support that politicians would challenge at their peril.

Despite that, by the time Malcolm Turnbull ascended to the prime ministership in 2015, the momentum on school funding reform had seriously stalled. In a bid to recapture the political centre, Turnbull launched Gonski 2.0 in 2017. More than five years after it had been handed down, it seemed the Gonski Report had fundamentally changed the terrain on which school funding policy would be formulated. Everybody now claimed to 'give a Gonski'.

In proposing a sector-blind, needs-based funding system, the Gonski Report had appeared to achieve a breakthrough in discourse about school education policy in Australia. And in so doing, it seemed that it had found the key to unleashing the full potential of the nation's children, reducing the gaps between the haves and the have-nots, and improving the school experience of *all* young Australians – and, as a consequence, lifting Australia's school education outcomes. Embraced by politicians of all parties, David Gonski seemed to personify the possibility of achieving a national consensus where once there had only been rancorous division and vicious rivalry.

Why has Gonski failed?

And yet, despite all the optimism generated by the Gonski Report and the remarkable consensus that coalesced around it, the problems of Australian education have only worsened since the report was commissioned. International tests show that young Australians are getting less and less out of the education we are providing them.[6] The most recent round of the Program of International Student Assessment (PISA) tests, conducted by the Organisation for Economic Co-operation and Development (OECD), indicated that in reading, mathematics and science, Australian students are, on average, about a year of learning behind where they were at the start of this century.[7] Underlying the headline averages, we find the same old equity story in which social disadvantage is a powerful predictor of low educational achievement. On average, kids from the poorest quarter of the population are three years of learning behind children in the top quarter.[8] In 2010, Prime Minister Gillard insisted that demography should not determine destiny, but the reality for far too many Australian children in 2022 is that it still does.

The COVID-19 pandemic has only highlighted the predicament we face. In response to a succession of lockdowns, some schools have been able to provide high-class virtual learning experiences, safe in the knowledge that their students have access to computers and high-speed internet at home. For other schools, however, the immediate task has been to ensure all children have access to the basic infrastructure necessary for online learning. But the deepest divide has not been technological. Students who struggle to engage with – or even attend – school have been hit the hardest, as lockdowns have taken a toll on their motivation, sense of connectedness and relationships with their school community. And so the circumstances of the pandemic have only compounded the longer-term challenges.

A decade after the Gonski Report, Australia is further than ever from the vision of educational opportunity and attainment it espoused. Educational outcomes for Australian schoolchildren continue to decline, and there is a growing correlation between social disadvantage and educational underachievement. This book is an attempt to understand why. Why did Gonski inspire so much hope and even appear, for a time, to succeed? Has it ultimately failed? If so, do we need to revise our assessment of its policy prescriptions? Or were these never implemented? And if Gonski's recommendations have not been applied with much fidelity, why is that? What are the political interests and obstacles that have stood in the way?

As educators – Chris is a retired principal and Tom is a classroom teacher – we are deeply invested in these questions. Enriching the experience of learning, along with all the opportunities it brings, is what we have devoted our working lives to. In 2011, we each made our own submissions to the Gonski review because we believed that it could make a positive difference in the lives of the young people we work with. So we want to know where Australia has gone wrong. We do not think our nation's failure to realise its shared aspirations should be swept under the carpet.

We fear that if as a nation we do not confront these questions, we will continue to drift along in a kind of post-Gonski torpor, imagining ourselves to be closing in on needs-based funding – the supposed panacea for our educational ills – as it grows ever more elusive. And so our hope in telling this story is not only to provide insight into Australia's educational past, but to illuminate the possibilities – and pitfalls – that lie ahead of us.

To find the answers to these questions, we interviewed David Gonski, along with other members of the review's expert panel. We spoke to most of the major players, including Tanya Plibersek, Peter Garrett and Julia Gillard's top education advisor, Tom Bentley (although Gillard herself declined our request for an interview). We also talked to the protagonists on either side of the debate, from the president of the Australian Education Union at the time to the head of the National Catholic Education Commission.

To the extent that anyone thinks about why Gonski has failed, they're likely to respond in one of three ways. For those who were always unsympathetic to the whole Gonski project, it is taken as proof that money is nowhere near as important as it has been made out to be. For Labor 'true believers', the answer is the opposite. For them, Gonski hasn't worked because it has been systematically sabotaged ever since Labor lost office. The third response is that the review's prescriptions have been distorted and diluted by opportunistic, short-sighted politicians of all stripes – with Labor as guilty as the Coalition.

The problem with the first argument – that money doesn't matter – is that most disadvantaged schools continue to be significantly underfunded. In fact, under the Morrison

Government's plan, public schools overall will only ever be funded at 91 per cent of Gonski's school resource standard,[9] and they won't reach that level until around 2030. Money obviously can't work if it hasn't even arrived.

It is true that to improve student achievement additional money has to be spent effectively. The second Gonski review in 2018, the Review to Achieve Educational Excellence in Australian Schools, outlined how that can be done. But providing the right resourcing, allocating it appropriately and investing it effectively are not mutually exclusive. We need to do all these things to enhance educational outcomes.

As things stand, school funding is now even less needs-based than it was when David Gonski conducted his review ten years ago. Where Gonski said public schools with more disadvantaged children should receive the vast majority of additional funding, the opposite, in fact, has happened. Since 2009, taxpayer funding adjusted for inflation has increased by around $1600 per student in private schools, but only $300 in public schools.[10] By 2018, the ABC could report that over a third of non-government schools received more government recurrent funding than the average public school enrolling similar students.[11]

This evidence supports the argument that Gonski hasn't worked because it simply hasn't been implemented. However, unlike Labor folk, we think an impartial examination shows that some Coalition governments have made a real and lasting contribution to a better funding system. Moreover, we will argue, Labor bears a share of the responsibility for the delays and special deals which mean we are still so far from a needs-based funding system. One example, forcefully articulated by Gonski panellist Ken Boston, is that the Gillard Government ignored the third step in Gonski's argument, which called for an architecture of independent expertise – the machinery that would ensure an evidence-based approach to calculating the resourcing standard. Moreover, Labor's promises that no school would lose a dollar, and each sector would maintain its share of the funding pie, represented the antithesis of a needs-based approach.

For his part, David Gonski insists we should be patient, and that the reform clock only really started with the Turnbull Government. 'When people say to me today, "Oh this has been ten years since your report, and the disadvantaged educationally are still disadvantaged – it's all your fault", the first thing I would say is nothing happened until 2017. So you shouldn't judge us on ten years.'[12]

Part of the story we will tell in this book is how an admirable blueprint was not adhered to – by politicians on either side. But, we will argue, this story alone does not adequately explain our continued educational decline, or the problems that beset our schools. And nor is it very helpful in explaining *why* politicians have been unwilling or unable to put ostensibly good ideas into practice. To really understand why Gonski has not lived up to the hopes that were placed in it, we need to acknowledge that Australia has been trying and failing to introduce a needs-based school funding system for half a century. Forty years before the Gonski review, the Karmel report recommended a resource standard based on educational need that would apply to all schools irrespective of sector. And the mistakes and missteps of the last ten years have only repeated those of the preceding decades.

Gonski failed because our debate about school funding occurred within a framework of unchallenged and largely unconsidered assumptions that have proved to be fundamentally misguided. This framework of assumptions produced a contradiction at the heart of the Gonski Report. Despite rhetoric to the contrary, throughout the Gonski process it was always assumed that school funding would, in fact, continue to be sector-based and needs-blind in two critical and mutually dependent respects. Firstly, it was taken for granted that students in one school sector should benefit from a fully publicly funded, free education, while students in the other two should not. Correspondingly, it was assumed that public funding should help students in many non-government schools, which also charge fees, to enjoy advantages in *total* resourcing over other children in public schools with similar educational needs.

The Gonski review presented extraordinary evidence of the power of what educationalists call 'peer effects' – this refers to the impact on a child's learning of the other children in their class, year or school. The Gonski review found that if a child is in a class with a lot of disadvantaged children, this has a very negative impact on their learning. Indeed, it presented evidence that who you go to school with has an even stronger impact than who your parents are. This evidence came from numerous sources, including the premier research body, the Australian Council for Educational Research, and the country's largest education systems.

In Australia today, resource advantages make some schools more attractive, while high fees make them hard to enter. Enrolment tests in some schools, public and private, add a further barrier. As a result, kids from poor and disadvantaged families find themselves over-represented in free, comprehensive schools, much more than location alone can explain. This means that the odds, then, are being further stacked against the children who have the least luck in terms of the circumstances they are born into – the kids the Gonski reforms were meant to help.

Because these arrangements were assumed rather than examined, the Gonski review was unable to propose a solution adequate to the problem it identified. And in the ten years since, the problem has worsened: Australia now has one of the most socio-economically segregated school systems in the OECD, and our results continue to decline.[13] Whenever this system is sorely tested, as it has been by the pandemic and by teacher shortages in recent times, it emerges more divided than ever. The strugglers and their families are the last in the queue for help. They end up even further behind. And so does Australia.

Achieving a needs-based, sector-blind school funding system

Ultimately, the reasons why debate about school funding in Australia rests on the distinctive set of assumptions that it does are historical. When we created public schools in the late 19th century, we made a set of choices that have determined our attitudes to schools, religion and resourcing ever since. Sometimes laudable, often understandable, decisions have inevitably been reactions, we will argue, to the conflicts and contradictions that those foundational choices embodied. The impacts of these decisions are still with us.

In offering a critical assessment of the major players in the story of school funding in Australia over the last decade, we inevitably apportion praise and blame. But we are much more concerned to understand than to judge. The reality is that it is very difficult for any individual, even a prime minister or head of a review, to challenge assumptions that are pinned in place by the weight of history.

The argument of this book is that Gonski has failed because of flaws in conception as well as execution. Gonski has proved to be more a symptom of the troubled history that preceded it than a solution. To create a school system where differences in educational outcomes are the result of talent and hard work – and not the result of 'differences in wealth, income, power or possessions'[14] – we have to challenge the assumptions that Gonski itself didn't. In that sense, we believe it is time to stop waiting for Gonski.

As a country, we won't turn our results around until we level the playing field on which all taxpayer funded schools operate. That means that public funding has to come with commensurate public obligations, especially the responsibility to enrol children from all walks of life. This might seem politically impossible – even harder than delivering needs-based funding. But we argue that getting both the resourcing of schools right, and equalising the responsibilities they face, can be done. When we look to countries like Canada and New Zealand, there are examples we can learn from. We believe that we have to try, or else our nation's schools face the risk of further decades of decline and growing disadvantage.

So our criticisms of the Gonski review and the reforms that followed in its wake should not be read as an effort to discount or dismiss the achievements of the last decade. On the contrary, our purpose is to help revive the failed promise of Gonski, the realisation of a sector-blind and needs-based funding system. But in order to transcend our history, first we must understand it.

KIM AND MARIA, A 'FICTIONAL' STORY

There are many prepared to tell their version of the Gonski story, but what has been the experience of children and young people? We could tell multiple stories based on our experience, but instead we follow a couple of fictional students, Kim Armstrong and Maria Romano, who were in Year 3 in 2010, the year the Gonski review was announced, and left school after Year 12 in 2019. They lived in a small country town not far from the regional centre of Rivertown in the Riverina. 'Gonski' was supposed to be all about them. How did it work out? *(To be continued ...)*

1

The original sin: where did Gonski come from?

> We created a situation unique in the democratic world, it is very important to realise this. There were no rules about student selection and exclusion, no fee limitations, no shared governance, no public education accountability, no common curriculum requirements below upper secondary … We have now become a kind of wonder at which people [in other countries] gape. The reaction is always, 'What an extraordinary situation'.[1]
>
> *Jean Blackburn, Deputy Chair of the 1973 Interim Committee for the Australian Schools Commission, commenting in 1991*

In 2001, in the days leading up to the federal election, a Labor member of parliament released a fiery statement condemning the Howard Government's funding increases for wealthy private schools. These schools 'simply don't need the money', the MP declared. They 'get almost twice as much funding per student than public schools and to suggest that they're the ones that need extra funding most, is both ridiculous and unfair'.[2] The politician was Julia Gillard – elected to parliament three years before and still a backbencher, she would be appointed to the shadow cabinet in the wake of Labor's subsequent election loss.

By 2004, the Labor Opposition, now led by Mark Latham, had developed the criticisms voiced by Gillard, along with many others, into an ambitious alternative policy. Labor planned to introduce a national resource standard which would allocate funding 'to all schools on the basis of educational and financial need … taking into account funding from all sources'.[3] The effect of Labor's proposal would be to increase government funding for poorer private schools, but reduce the resourcing of the wealthiest – those schools already well above the proposed national standard, which Gillard had railed against three years earlier.

Labor's proposal was not welcomed, to put it mildly, by leaders of the non-government school sector; at least, not those with the loudest voices. Derided as a 'hit list', Latham Labor's attempt to advocate needs-based funding was met with a ferocious response that would become seared into the memory of every Labor politician. As *Inside Story* editor Peter Browne explained years later:

> The plan provoked a furore, particularly on talkback radio. The prime minister, John Howard, characterised it as 'old-fashioned class warfare', a phrase that appeared repeatedly – along with 'hit list' – in media coverage over subsequent days and weeks. The churches 'savaged' Latham (said a headline in the *Australian*), and the private schools warned of fee hikes and an exodus to government schools.[4]

When Labor lost the 2004 election, the schools funding policy was blamed. But the available polling evidence hardly suggests that the 'hit list' was the cause of Labor's downfall. Ten days after the Labor policy had been launched, an AC Nielsen survey of over 1400 voters reported 66 per cent in favour and only 27 per cent against.[5] Evidence from the Australian Election Study, based on a post-election survey, indicated education was, as always, an electoral plus for Labor.[6]

But even if the attitude of voters was much less hostile than came to be believed, the opponents of Labor's policy were vocal, and their voice was amplified by powerful lobby groups and championed by large sections of the Australian media. This provided plenty of material for those inside the Labor Party who had been opposed to taking on the private school sector in the first place. And the policy's unfortunate association with Mark Latham, who quickly evolved from Labor Leader to Labor's bête noire, damaged its reputation further.

At the next election in 2007, after 11 years of the Howard Government, the Labor Opposition, pursuing a 'son-of-Howard' strategy under the leadership of Kevin Rudd, was determined to play it safe. It was not going to attempt to launch a controversial schools funding policy from Opposition again. And so it made two commitments. The first was that it would maintain the Howard Government school funding system for the next five years. The second was that, prior to any changes for the funding period beginning in 2013, a review would be conducted. Thus was conceived what would eventually come to be known as the Gonski review, born of the twin desires to do nothing immediately, but something eventually.

On 15 April 2010, Julia Gillard, now Minister for Education, Minister for Employment and Workplace Relations, Minister for Social Inclusion and Deputy Prime Minister, announced a new review of funding for schooling.[7] It was a moment freighted with history. The tortuous path Labor had trod explained why the minister, two and a half years into government, was announcing not a new policy but a review, which would itself take 18 months to conduct – and even longer to implement. Everything about the announcement seemed designed to show that on the school funding issue Labor – and Julia Gillard herself – had changed.

The venue for the minister's speech was the Sydney Institute, the conservative think tank headed up by former Howard advisor Gerard Henderson. In her speech, Gillard struck a very different tone to the one she had adopted a decade earlier. Methodically outlining the case for a thorough, impartial and consultative review, she noted the passions in debates about school funding; debates which divided the community and pitted school against school, and school system against school system. 'My intention', she said, 'is not to follow this path, but to seek a constructive and open approach to the questions of school funding'.[8] The tone was conciliatory, and so was the message: no school would lose a dollar in funding as a result of the review the minister was announcing.

Gillard warned of those who would 'seek to misrepresent what I have set out today, to distort the implications of my argument, and to seek premature restriction and closure of this review's conclusions'. But as much as the minister tried to exorcise the demons of the past, the spectre of Mark Latham, armed with his 'hit list', hovered over proceedings at the Sydney Institute that evening. The next day, Shadow Education Minister Christopher Pyne immediately denounced the review, arguing that Gillard was 'right behind the Latham private schools hit-list'.[9] Opposition Leader Tony Abbott joined the attack, asserting that Labor could not be trusted to maintain private school funding because 'they don't like private education'.[10] Minister Gillard, in a further effort to reassure the private school sector, soon announced that the review would be headed up by David Gonski, who had only recently resigned after 17 years as chair of one of Australia's wealthiest independent schools, Sydney Grammar.

Like it or not, the review that Minister Gillard had announced would inevitably have to respond to a long history of disagreement and discord. The controversies that had given birth to the Gonski review were not new. Long before Labor proposed a needs-based funding model in 2004, the Whitlam Government had tried and failed to introduce one in 1973, and it had come a cropper on the same issue of planning to take funding off wealthy independent schools. In 1984, decades before Latham's policy had been reduced to a 'hit list', the Hawke Government education minister, Susan Ryan, had faced the same accusation when she proposed funding cuts to 41 very wealthy schools. Confronted with irate private school parents, as well as nervous colleagues in marginal seats and a displeased prime minister, Ryan backed down.[11]

This long history of controversy reflected deep divisions within the Australian community about how we resource our schools. While by the time of the Gonski review government funding of private schools had long since become a matter of bipartisan orthodoxy, Australians still did not agree on which private schools should receive taxpayer support, how much or on what basis. If the review that Minister Gillard was announcing in 2010 was going to offer a resolution that all sides could sign up to, it would have to understand where each side was coming from. Why was the controversy surrounding this topic so emotive and enduring? Before adjudicating a debate that had been going on for decades, the review would need to understand why so many disagreements remained unresolved. And that would require an understanding of the historical origins of the argument.

The first unlevel playing field: Church schools lose public funding

Between 1872 and 1893, each of the Australian colonies created public primary schools that were free, compulsory and secular, and abolished state aid to church schools. The decisions made in the late 19th century to cease funding to religious schools and to remove religion from public schools were equally controversial then as they would be later, and they provide the first key to the unresolved acrimony that Julia Gillard sought to address when she announced the school funding review that night in April 2010.

The first law to give effect to these changes was passed in the Colony of Victoria in December 1872. Victoria's Education Act stated that the school day of four hours should be devoted to secular instruction alone. Many educators and historians celebrate the establishment of public schools in the final decades of the 19th century as the moment when the Australian colonies finally succeeded in ensuring the universal provision of, and participation in, elementary education. In 1869, Sir Henry Parkes, who would later become premier of New South Wales and a father of federation, eloquently encapsulated this idealistic spirit:

> We are endeavouring to supply the means of sound instruction to those who, in a very few years, are to constitute the strength of the country … Let us by every means in our power take care that the children of the country grow up under such a sound and enlightened system of instruction, that they will consider the dearest of all possessions the free exercise of their own judgment in the secular affairs of life, and that each man will shrink from being subservient to any other man or earthly power.[12]

Others, however, remember a different Henry Parkes – a reflection of the intense divisions of the times. This is the Parkes who, according to Cardinal Moran in his *History of the Catholic Church in Australasia* published in 1896, waved a draft of the Public Instruction Bill in the air at a public meeting, declaring, 'I hold in my hand what will be death to the calling of the priesthood of the Church of Rome'.[13]

For Australia's Catholics, the education acts of the 1870s and 1880s represented a double injustice, establishing schools that Catholics could not, as a matter of conscience, attend, while withdrawing public funding from schools that they could and did.

Just prior to the passage of the *Education Act* in Victoria in 1872, the Bishop of Melbourne, James Goold, articulated the profound sense of injustice that Australian Catholics felt:

> They threaten the Catholics of this colony ... with religious persecution in the shape of a Godless and compulsory system of education. Taking our share of the public revenue, to which the Catholics contribute equally with all others, and applying as much of it as is deemed needful to any system of education in which the Church we belong to declares we can have no participation, is simply robbing the Catholics of so much of their public rights.[14]

Shortly before the 1880 *Public Instruction Act* passed in New South Wales, the Archbishop of Sydney, Roger Vaughan, expressed similar outrage, condemning:

> with marked emphasis, those schools, and that method of teaching in which the religious element is divorced from the secular ... This lavish expenditure on one section of the community, to the exclusion of others who cannot in conscience avail themselves of it, is, in a free community like our own, where all are equally taxed, a species of injustice which cannot be submitted to in silence.[15]

Reformers hoped that this intense opposition would subside in time and the Catholic laity would ignore the directions of the hierarchy to shun the new public schools. The decision that public schools would be secular had itself been a compromise solution, arrived at only after a series of failed attempts to accommodate the competing Christian denominations in one universal system of education.[16] In 1866, a Victorian Royal Commission had recommended that public schools teach a 'common Christianity', neither Catholic or Protestant in character, but this proposal had only united the churches in their opposition to it.

And so it was decided that the only workable solution was to remove religion from public schools – substantially if not entirely. While stipulating that the curriculum for school hours should be secular only, the Victorian act passed in 1872 did make allowance for religious teaching outside the hours of secular instruction. 'Nothing herein contained shall prevent the State school buildings from being used for any other purpose on days and at hours other than those used for secular instruction', the act stated.[17] That caveat would subsequently be repeated in the laws passed by many of the other Australian colonies. When, in 1880, the Colony of New South Wales passed the *Public Instruction Act*, it prescribed that secular instruction could include general religious teaching, 'as distinguished from dogmatical or polemical theology'.[18]

Secularism was an attempt to quell the rivalry and dissension between the Christian denominations, but it failed. The religious argument, already impassioned and emotional, was laced with ethnic, political and class enmities.[19] Irish Catholics – most of whom were working class – laboured under the Protestant ascendancy in Australia, just as the home country suffered under British rule. Irish Catholics in Australia feared that the new laws would make their children second-class citizens in de facto Protestant schools. And so they refused to enrol their children in public schools, paying instead out of their own pockets for separate Catholic schools.[20]

Rather than erasing divisions and fostering harmony, then, the establishment of secular public schools and the simultaneous withdrawal of state aid from Catholic schools became both the embodiment of sectarian division and the cause, among Catholics, of a deep sense of injustice. Two figures with immense experience in Australian education, Lyndsay Connors and Jim McMorrow, describe the regrettable result:

> [T]he seeds of discord were sown. The consequent withdrawal of public funding from non-government, largely Catholic, schools created a sense of grievance that simmered until the 1970s. It is hard for Australians today looking back at the 19th century and the first half of the 20th century to comprehend the bitter sectarianism that characterised the cultural and social milieu of that time. The relationship between parish Catholic schools and the public school community, but also the private schools that served the Protestant ascendancy was riddled with class and religious antipathies.[21]

In 1977, Labor speechwriter and historian Graham Freudenberg observed that 'the oldest, deepest, most poisonous debate in Australia has been about government aid to church schools'.[22]

We describe this moment as the 'original sin' of Australian education. In doing so, we are not pointing the finger of blame. We are not attempting to hold either Adam or Eve responsible, or even let God off the hook. Such judgments are beyond the scope of this book. But we do claim that the curse of this historical moment has been with us ever since. It was a critical juncture which would determine the path of Australian education, fundamentally shaping the arrangements that David Gonski and his colleagues would be asked to review and the problems they would be required to solve.

Our collective failure then meant that public education did not provide what one quarter of the public wanted from education. Mostly Irish Catholics had to pay fees for their children's schooling where their fellow citizens did not; they faced this imposition despite often being from the poorest part of the community. And the net result was that their children's schools were woefully

THE FIRST UNLEVEL PLAYING FIELD

The first unlevel playing field refers to the situation that resulted from the creation of public education systems across Australia in the 1870s and 1880s, and the simultaneous withdrawal of state aid from church schools.

As secular schools were not an acceptable option for much of Australia's Catholic population, they enrolled their children in schools run by the Church instead. But this meant that they had to pay fees where their (sometimes wealthier) neighbours did not, and their children's schools were much less well resourced.

Only in the 1960s did this situation begin to be redressed with the advent of state aid. It took many decades for Catholic schools to reach resourcing parity with the government sector. In the meantime, state aid was introduced in a way that allowed uneven resourcing and responsibilities to evolve and expand over time – a new unlevel playing field.

under-resourced, with overflowing classes, unqualified teachers and sub-standard infrastructure. This became more acute after the Second World War, but these basic dynamics were constant from the moment state aid was withdrawn from denominational schools. From the beginning, Australian schools operated on an unlevel playing field.

In time, the injustices of the first unlevel playing field of Australian schooling would begin to be redressed, as we will see.

But the schools that the Gonski review would encounter in 2010 still retained the imprint of these decisions made long ago. The Gonski panel visited Catholic schools in disadvantaged areas which were partly publicly funded and where the parents were required to pay fees. And it visited public schools in affluent areas where the relatively wealthy parent community did not have to pay any fees at all. While it was possible to take these incongruities for granted, to assume that's just how things are, they were in fact the end result of the path we had embarked on in the late 19th century. The distinctive turn we took then had produced the twin assumptions that religious schools must charge fees and only secular schools can be free. But many comparable countries, like Canada, had taken a quite different direction, and in many countries their church schools were fully publicly funded.

The original sin had given birth to what became a fixture in Australian school education: that, unrelated to any family means, some parents have to pay fees for their children's education while others do not. This would not only define the realities of the funding arrangements that the Gonski review would examine, but also significantly affected the attitudes and perspectives of the parties that had been at odds for so long. To see how exactly, we need to understand the second critical juncture in the story of Australian education: the return, after an absence of almost a century, of state aid.

The first unlevel playing field comes under siege: Menzies and Fraser restore state aid to church schools

Over the course of the first half of the 20th century, Catholic schools mostly survived on the modest fees their parent communities could afford and the free labour of brothers and nuns. But after the Second World War, the baby boom, increased immigration from

Europe and a growing tendency to stay on longer at school, coupled with the decline in teaching as a religious (and unpaid) vocation, brought the system of parish schools to the point of bankruptcy. For many baby boomers, the animating image of a Catholic school was the one they experienced as a child, with classes overflowing, controlled by the stern discipline meted out by often undertrained nuns and brothers.

In symbolic ways at least, the story of how the state came to the rescue began in 1962, with a crisis created by a school toilet block at St Brigid's Primary School in the largely Irish-Catholic New South Wales town of Goulburn. Half a century later, Father Dermid McDermott, a retired former parish priest in Goulburn, recalled availing himself of the urinals when he was a student at the school, 'never imagining the modest brick outhouse would one day become infamous'.[23] The spark was lit when the NSW Government determined that another toilet was needed if St Brigid's was to meet the occupational health and safety standards of the day. School inspectors ordered the cash-strapped school to build an 'additional sanitary convenience' or face closure.

In July 1962, around 700 people, mainly Catholic families, attended a public meeting which declared that governments had to 'recognise the justice of the claims of Catholics to a fair share of the public purse for its education system'.[24] Bishop John Cullinane, the Auxiliary Bishop of Canberra-Goulburn, promptly closed the six Goulburn Catholic schools and sent the 2000 students off to enrol in the nearby government schools.

The events in Goulburn in 1962 dramatised the longstanding Catholic arguments, going back to the 19th century, that taxpayer support was owed, as a matter of non-discrimination and fair treatment, to all sections of society. But the Goulburn strike also graphically demonstrated a new argument: not only should governments assume an obligation to help church schools stay solvent, but they also had a strong financial interest in doing so. By providing schools like St Brigid's Primary with enough public funding to stay open, and attractive, governments saved themselves the trouble of covering the entire cost of a child's education in a public school.

Catholic sources variously saw the Goulburn strike as 'the most spectacular demonstration of Catholic frustration in the history of state aid' and 'an explosion and a watershed in the state aid debate'.[25] But at the time, the action was intensely controversial. The media called the action 'demanding money with menaces', and insisted that the strike 'be broken, firmly and swiftly'.[26] Father McDermott, whose father was a local publican, as well as the town mayor and president of the local ALP branch, recalled how the strike divided the town and brought out high emotion.[27]

The Goulburn incident may have divided public opinion, but Prime Minister Menzies shrewdly observed that it divided the ALP, which was still reeling from the split with the heavily Catholic Democratic Labor Party (DLP), even more. And this was something Menzies was happy to exploit, especially as DLP preferences were critical to his prospects of remaining in government. In late 1963, the New South Wales Labor Government, belatedly responding to the events in Goulburn, announced a weekly payment to private school parents. But the national executive of the Labor Party, resolutely opposed to all forms of state aid, immediately forced the New South Wales Government to withdraw the policy. Menzies pounced, calling an early federal election and announcing a program of capital funding which would provide support for science blocks in both church and state government schools. Menzies won the 1963 election, while, in 1965, the New South Wales Labor Government was booted out after 24 years in office.

As a product of Melbourne's Wesley College, Prime Minister Menzies had no particular attachment to Catholic education. But he realised that support for Catholic schools could easily be packaged as a commitment to state-aided Liberal 'variety' in education, against Labor 'uniformity'. Commonwealth aid would be provided not only to poor Catholic schools that could not afford a new toilet block but also to wealthy Protestant schools. In Menzies' words:

> For us to discriminate in making a grant in aid for a purpose of high national significance, for us to discriminate between Government schools and non-Government schools, would open up a world of discrimination in other fields to my mind equally unjustifiable.[28]

Menzies' move was groundbreaking in precedent, but it was not until 1969 that Malcolm Fraser, education minister in the Gorton Government, introduced Commonwealth funding to schools on a recurrent basis, to assist with their annual operating expenses. Contrary to the principle articulated by Menzies, Fraser was willing to discriminate, by providing support to non-government schools only. In Fraser's view, resourcing of public schools was entirely a matter for the states – even though they faced many of the same financial pressures as the Catholic systems, and had lost the power to levy income taxes during the war.

Equally critically, Fraser prescribed that every non-government school would receive a uniform per capita amount – $50 per student for secondary schools, $35 per student at primary schools, irrespective of the private income enjoyed by the school or the circumstances of its parent community. In this manner, Fraser successfully subdued any residual Protestant resistance to state aid for Catholic schools. 'Till he left politics 15 years later', Gough Whitlam would reflect, 'Fraser's efforts were unremittingly directed to forging an alliance between the Catholic schools and the WASP grammar schools – between God and Mammon'.[29]

As the conservatives took the lead on state aid, the Labor Party almost tore itself apart. 'The most intense political debate in Australia during the 1960s was not about Vietnam; it was about education', Gough Whitlam reflected years later.[30] Like Menzies and Fraser, and unlike many in his own party, Whitlam supported state aid for non-government schools. 'One of my most poignant memories', Whitlam would recall:

> is the interview I had with Archbishop Mannix in 1962, the year before he died at 99 ... 'For forty years', he said, 'I have fought for justice for our schools. I am no nearer than when I started'. He used the sole argument of justice.[31]

Whitlam supported state aid on the basis of educational need, recognising the acute circumstances faced by schools like St Brigid's in Goulburn.

But unlike Malcolm Fraser, Whitlam believed that Commonwealth funding should be provided to public schools as well as private schools. In Whitlam's view, under post-war conditions, the Commonwealth alone could 'ensure that an equal opportunity was given to pupils to develop their natural talents irrespective of their parents' locality, religion, means and occupation'.[32] And unlike Malcolm Fraser, Whitlam believed Commonwealth funding should be distributed to schools according to need rather than on a per capita basis.

In time, these two competing visions of the Commonwealth's role in funding schools would define the conflicts and controversies of the next half century. The two visions would still be unreconciled when in 2010 Julia Gillard announced a review of school funding, having given rise to many of the problems the review would have to solve. But in the 1960s Gough Whitlam had a more immediate battle on his hands. In attacking the twin shibboleths of state aid and states' rights, the Deputy Labor Leader had pitted himself against the old guard of his own party. The official Labor Party position was that parents were welcome to send their children to non-government schools, 'provided they do so at their own cost'.[33] In keeping with this stance, in early 1966 the national executive of the Labor Party launched a constitutional challenge against the Menzies Government's grants for science blocks.

Whitlam was apoplectic, and publicly rebuked his own party in the most damning terms. Attacking the national executive, he did not leave anything unsaid: 'No country with our resources should tolerate the present standard of our schools; no socialist party should tolerate the present inequality of opportunity for our school children'.[34] In response, Whitlam was subject to charges of disloyalty, and the future prime minister came within two votes of expulsion from his own party.

Fraser versus Whitlam: the first failed attempt to introduce needs-based funding

Not only did Whitlam survive, he became Leader of the Labor Party the following year, and from 1967 onwards it was clear that Labor was committed to the provision of federal aid to non-government schools. From this point on, the most ardent voice of opposition to state aid was the lobby group, the Council for the Defence of Government Schools (DOGS), which even contested state and federal elections in the late 60s and early 70s, although without success. Additionally, unions representing public school teachers continued to actively oppose state aid into the 1980s, before shifting to a begrudging acceptance that it had become a fact of life, buttressed by bipartisan support.

At the 1969 ALP Federal Conference, Whitlam's proposal for a Schools Commission to oversee Commonwealth funding became

Labor policy.[35] The education minister, Malcolm Fraser, dismissed the Labor proposal as bureaucratic overreach and a Canberra power grab – language that would echo down the decades.[36] By this point, the debate had shifted rapidly, becoming less about whether to provide state aid than about how, how much and to whom.

Upon election to office in 1972, Whitlam established an interim committee of his proposed Schools Commission to report on just these questions. Under the leadership of Professor Peter Karmel, an economist with a special interest in education, the Interim Committee conducted an exhaustive review, handing down its report *Schools in Australia* in May 1973. Karmel and his committee were candid about what they had found: 'In both the government and non-government sectors there are schools where the quality of personnel, buildings and equipment reflects an attitude towards children which, whether it arises from public indifference or ignorance, is incompatible with the manifest values of our society'.[37]

In response, almost four decades before the Gonski review, the Karmel report proposed that the government introduce a needs-based funding system. This would be achieved by funding schools, regardless of sector, to a common resource standard – something that involved differential funding. 'There are many schools where the proportion of children needing intensive educational care is greater than average', the report explained. 'In recognition of these cases, the Committee has formulated a scheme of special supplementary grants to schools having a high proportion of children who are likely to require a greater-than-average share of educational effort, and hence of expenditure.[38]

In proposing funding according to need, the Karmel report explicitly rejected the Fraser model of uniform, per capita grants to non-government schools, irrespective of their circumstances. 'Given the limited funds available and the wide differences existing among non-government schools', the report stated, 'uniform per capita grants would be an expensive way of bringing about acceptable standards in all schools and would unduly delay their attainment'.[39] The committee was quite clear about where funding should and should not be directed. It believed that 'government aid could not be justified in maintaining or raising standards beyond those which publicly supported schools can hope to achieve by the end of the decade'.[40]

Accordingly, the Karmel report placed non-government schools into eight categories, A through to H, on the basis of their existing resource levels. The Karmel plan would mean that poorer non-government schools, the ones below the resourcing target, would receive a significant funding boost. But it would also mean the phasing out of financial support for schools already above the resource standard. For the second-highest category, the committee recommended continued Commonwealth support but at lower levels than previously. For the wealthiest schools in Category A, it proposed abolishing Commonwealth aid altogether. 'Category A schools already use a volume of resources that well exceeds the 1979 targets; and the Committee believes that government assistance to these schools cannot be justified.'[41] In this way, all schools would be placed on a trajectory towards a common resource standard.

Recognising the potential for difficulties to arise from the sudden termination of Commonwealth funding, the Karmel report recommended phasing out financial support to Category A schools over 1974 and 1975. But in keeping with the temper of the times, the Whitlam Government decided against delay. On 6 August 1973, the Minister for Education, Kim Beazley senior, released a list of non-government schools in their respective funding categories, including the 105 schools placed in Category A that would no longer receive Commonwealth financial support.[42]

Inevitably, the wealthy independent schools resisted this

proposal fiercely, defending the existing program of per capita grants[43] on the grounds that citizens and taxpayers should be treated equally.[44] More surprisingly, perhaps, they were joined in opposition to the needs-based funding plan by the Catholic systems that would be among its chief beneficiaries. Almost immediately upon the release of the Karmel report, the Central Commission of Catholic Bishops released a statement maintaining that 'it was imperative that per capita grants were equal for all children',[45] and decrying the idea of unequal treatment of children in different circumstances.

Influential conservative Catholic BA Santamaria took the argument even further, calling the needs-based funding plan a 'bribe with barbs'. Santamaria even suggested that Catholics return the money that had been allocated to Catholic schools but which 'justly belongs to children in Protestant schools'. Santamaria set out the logic which would define Catholic opposition to needs-based funding for the next half century:

> If Catholic schools, and the bishops and religious orders … condone this outright political bribery and the clear discrimination against children in the eliminated Protestant schools, they will get a sectarian backlash which will be thoroughly deserved; and they will be responsible for the consequences that will inevitably follow. The entire Protestant community will feel a very deep sense of injustice … The Liberal and Country parties … will gradually turn against the principle of State aid.[46]

For the previous century, funding of Australian schools had been defined by sectarian enmity between Protestants and Catholics. Now the churches had formed a new powerful political coalition – what Whitlam called an alliance between God and Mammon

– which would shape Australian schools for the next half century. It was precisely in order to placate this political coalition that Julia Gillard went to the Sydney Institute that evening in April 2010, armed with a conciliatory message.

The argument about whether schools should be funded on the basis of needs or per capita (equality of opportunity versus equality of treatment) culminated in December 1973, when the government found itself without the numbers to pass legislation in the Senate. The result would be an awkward hybrid which contained the seeds of enduring conflict. Liberal senators, implacably opposed to the government's plan, were unwilling to negotiate.[47] However, the Country Party, prefiguring the role of Adrian Piccoli 40 years later, agreed to cross the floor and support the legislation if the government agreed to phase out funding to Category A private schools, rather than immediately abolish it.

A dual-system of publicly funded schools: when the solution creates new problems

In December 1973, the Karmel plan became law. But as the DLP Leader Frank McManus said when he reluctantly voted for the Whitlam legislation, along with the Country Party, 'This is only an armistice – the fight will continue in the years to come'.[48] Indeed it did. It is no overstatement to claim that when Julia Gillard announced a funding review in 2010, it was yet another attempt to finally resolve the disagreements that had echoed down the decades from that point on. In responding to the bitter debates of the last century, the introduction of state aid had only opened a new plane of disagreement.

In time, state aid began to address the inequities of the first unlevel playing field. Poor non-government schools began to receive much-needed assistance from the Commonwealth

Government. But progress was slow. In 1970, there were around 23 students for every teacher in a Catholic school, compared to 17 students for every teacher in public schools. It was only by 2007 that rough parity in the ratio of students to teachers between the two systems was achieved.[49] The Gonski Report recorded that in 2009 the average income from all sources per student in Catholic schools was $10 000 – much lower than independent schools, but also lower than public schools ($11 100).[50] By this point, public schools enrolled many more disadvantaged students, and there were a lot more remote, rural and small public schools, further inflating average costs. Comparing schools in similar circumstances, by 2011 the Catholic sector had finally reached rough resourcing parity with the government sector (that was the average picture at least – there was still lots of variation from school to school).

But while some poor non-government schools were catching up, other wealthy schools were getting ahead. The dismissal of the Whitlam Government in November 1975, and the installation of Malcolm Fraser in the Lodge, saved the funding of Category A schools before it could be phased out. But it did much more for wealthy non-government schools than that. Over the course of the Fraser Government's term in office, annual Commonwealth funding to private schools doubled, while support to public schools was reduced.[51] Between 1996 and 2007, this pattern would be repeated under the Howard Government, during which federal funding of private schools doubled once again.[52]

In 1976, the non-government school share of Commonwealth funding had been 35 per cent. By the end of the Howard Government in 2007, it was 64 per cent. So in the decades that followed the Karmel report, taxpayer funding did not only help the wealthiest private schools expand their financial advantage, it also eventually created a much larger group of non-government schools with a substantial resource edge over comparable public schools. These schools were mostly from the independent sector (private schools that, unlike Catholic parish schools, are not part of any system). The Gonski Report would record that by 2009, these schools, on average, enjoyed thousands of dollars more per student in average total resources than public schools.[53] Even this figure substantially understated the gap, because many more public schools enrolled higher cost students in higher cost places.

Australia's dual system of publicly funded schools not only produced dramatic disparities in resourcing, but also in the way schools were regulated and the responsibilities they faced. The solution to the first unlevel playing field had opened a uniquely Australian Pandora's box: governments were now increasingly funding private schools to operate alongside, and compete with, public schools – but on very different terms.

Public schools had been pitted in competition with private schools that were not only better resourced but could select (and expel) students at will, and offer the appeal of exclusivity. The inevitable resulted: private school fees, and selective enrolment practices, meant non-government schools were often inaccessible for low-income families and educationally disadvantaged children. Figure 1 shows the increasing sector separation of school enrolments, when measured by family income. We were increasingly sorting children into different schools on the basis of their social background, dramatically exacerbating variations in social geography, leaving many public schools with increasing concentrations of social disadvantage.

The funding arrangements that the Gonski review would be called on to examine in 2010 could only be understood as the outcome of the long and tortured path Australia had trod since public schools were established in the 19th century. They were defined by a series of contradictions, each accompanied by attendant conflicts and controversies. As Dean Ashenden, a seasoned commentator

FIGURE 1

Ratios of low/high family income in government and non-government schools for all secondary schools in each census year from 1986 to 2016

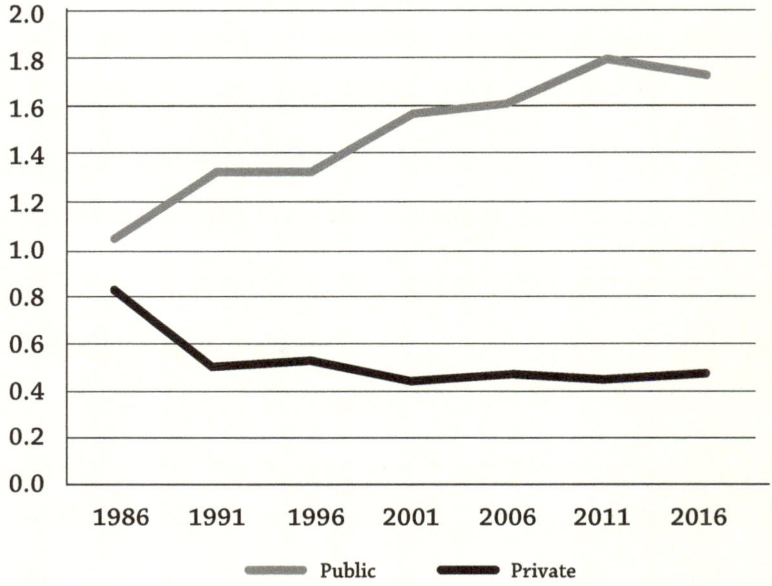

Barbara Preston, 'The social make-up of schools: A report prepared for the Australian Education Union', Barbara Preston Research, Canberra, 2018.

with a long view of the history of Australia's schools, observed, the Fraser/Whitlam settlement:

> [G]ave Australia both free *and* publicly subsidised fee-charging schools; schools lavishly funded *and* schools relatively impoverished; schools permitted to select on grounds of capacity to pay and/or religious affiliation and/or academic performance *and* schools prohibited from doing any of those things; parents who are required to pay when often they can't afford it *and* parents who aren't and can; and parents who are offered the full menu *and* others who must take whatever is put on their plate.[54]

Jean Blackburn was the Deputy Chair of the 1973 Interim Committee of the Schools Commission, created by Whitlam, and co-author of the Karmel report. A quarter of a century later, she would describe the result as 'a situation unique in the democratic world', and 'a kind of wonder at which people [in other countries] gape'.[55] Neither observation was meant as a compliment.

If the new review headed by Gonski was to succeed, it would need to attend to the fault lines that had been opened up by the uneasy settlement that had followed the introduction of state aid, and never resolved. The Gonski review would hear considerable concern from public school parents and educators that they could see the funding which would help them meet their increasing challenges being allocated elsewhere to support choice, for some. And meanwhile, they were left with universal obligations which non-government schools did not face. Arguably all we had done was create one unlevel playing field of winners and losers among schools in the 19th century, and proceeded to reverse it with another a century later. Since the advent of state aid, the playing field had changed, but it had only become unlevel in new ways.

However, inevitably private school parents and educators did not see it like this. They regarded increasing levels of state aid as an entitlement owed to parents as citizens and taxpayers. 'Every child and his parents are entitled to equal treatment in educational matters', as the headmaster of Geelong Grammar and head of the Independent Schools Council put it.[56] And it continued to be argued, in the same manner as it had been since Goulburn in 1962, that Commonwealth investment in private schools delivered overall savings for taxpayers by attracting students away from the public system. As a consequence, monies were freed up to fund the public system, so the argument went. And, it was claimed, disproportionate Commonwealth funding for private schools was justified because state governments predominantly funded public schools, as was their constitutional responsibility.

The review Julia Gillard announced in 2010 would inevitably have to respond to these duelling perspectives and adjudicate between them. But the controversy was not only about how much funding governments should provide to different schools but what taxpayers should require in return. By the end of the Howard era, Australia's school system looked very different to what it had in the early 1970s. Sixty-five per cent of students were in public schools in 2011, down from 78 per cent in 1972. Catholic schools enrolled 21 per cent, up from 17 per cent. Independent schools enrolled 14 per cent, well up from just 4 per cent in 1972.[57]

For private school advocates, parents had voted with their feet and found the school that best suited their child. For many parents, religion was no longer the sole or even primary motivation. In 2015, journalist Ross Gittins noted that the shift to mostly religious schools occurred at a time of ever declining religious observance.[58] Instead, private schools embodied the benefits of choice and competition. As one parent told researchers in 2009, the attraction of the private schools was their perceived responsiveness to parents as consumers. 'They're in the business of providing an education for my daughter ... and I'm treated, and she's treated, as a customer getting that service. But I certainly didn't get that feeling when I was looking in the government system. And I think that's part of the big bureaucracy that they're under.'[59] Among the many champions of this market ethos was none other than Minister Gillard, who launched the My School website, designed to facilitate parental choice, just months before she announced the funding review.

But for public education advocates, the story of the decades preceding the Gonski review was not so much one of increasing choice as growing segregation, and the exodus from public schools was evidence of the corrosive nature of successive government policies. We now had two kinds of taxpayer funded schools with quite different funding, obligations, operations, purposes. It was inevitable that private schools would be more attractive to many when they were often better resourced and could select students according to their academic ability as well as their parents' capacity to pay.

The irreconcilable differences about how we resourced and regulated our schools were the ultimate reason why there was a Gonski review at all. But as much as Australia's school funding arrangements were the subject of intense controversy, in the decades since the Karmel report the terms of debate had narrowed. The most significant attempts to reverse the inexorable expansion of Commonwealth funding to private schools occurred under the Hawke Government in 1984, and with the policy the Latham Opposition took to the 2004 election. Both caused great controversy, but only seemed to confirm the political impossibility of winding back what had been previously granted. And yet both policies were much less bold than the original vision articulated in the Karmel report. They sought only to reduce funding to the wealthiest private schools, not abolish it outright. The role of public funding in accentuating resource disparities between schools had become accepted as a fact of life. The argument was only over the extent.

Another unstated assumption concerned the different responsibilities and obligations faced by the sectors. In 1973, the Karmel report recommended 'joint planning and operation of facilities' across school sectors and wondered out loud where this might lead: 'Such developments when taken together with changed patterns of funding open up the possibility of the eventual development of a school system itself diverse, where all schools supported by public money can operate without charging fees'.[60] Alternatively, it countenanced the possibility of the provision of government assistance 'specifically to enable the reduction of fees' and to make 'a designated proportion of free places available'.[61]

However, these aspects of the Karmel report were fleeting and largely hypothetical. As it turned out, fee regulation was never seriously countenanced in the ensuing decades, let alone the possibility of a free and fully publicly funded system of non-government schools. Private schools saw their independence as integral to the alternative they offered to government systems. In the decades following the introduction of state aid, governments, for the most part, accepted this view.

Political debate inevitably occurs within a tacitly agreed framework of assumptions. There is a sphere where ideas are contested: in election campaigns, in opinion columns, in parliament. Outside that sphere there are beliefs deemed to be so obviously wrong they are not worthy of serious consideration, or so obviously true that they do not need to be justified.[62] What was striking about the framework of assumptions that had come to characterise debate about school funding in Australia was how different it was to those of other countries, even ones similar to our own.

In places like Canada, the Netherlands or the UK, the existence of fully publicly funded, free religious schools was taken for granted. But in Australia, it was simply obvious you could not do that. Australians did not so much disagree with *full* public funding of church schools as we did not even think about it. Meanwhile, in Australia, it was assumed that non-government schools should have unconditional autonomy over the fees they charge, and who they enrol and expel – despite significant taxpayer support. In most comparable countries this was regarded as anathema. One overseas observer who gaped in wonder at the Australian model was Margaret Thatcher. When the great free marketeer visited Australia in 1988, she was heard to express outrage upon learning that even the country's wealthiest private schools were subsidised by the state.[63] The question for the Gonski review was whether it would work within the framework of assumptions that had coalesced around school funding policy – or seek to critically examine them.

THE KARMEL PARADIGM

We call the framework that defined mainstream debate about school funding during the Gonski review and reforms the 'Karmel paradigm', because it reflected the policy terrain that evolved in the wake of the 1973 Karmel report. Characteristic of this framework is the belief that all schools are entitled to some public funding, but only some schools should be fully publicly funded, as it would be unaffordable to do otherwise. The subsidised schools should retain autonomy in setting fees and defining enrolment policies, and the parents who have to cover part of the cost of school education out of their own pockets are entitled to expect their children will enjoy an overall resource advantage. So, in the Karmel paradigm, resource disparities between schools are assumed; debate focuses on how large the gaps are, and how much public funding should contribute to them. It is also taken for granted that free, comprehensive schools will enrol a disproportionate share of disadvantaged students. Debate occurs about whether to provide those schools with additional resources or to increase subsidies to the other schools to help make them more affordable.

A new beginning? Julia Gillard launches the Gonski review

The review Julia Gillard announced in April 2010 was born in no small part from Labor's desire to make the school funding issue go away, at least temporarily. But now the review had arrived. And by its nature, it had the potential to challenge tacit assumptions, interrogate past practice and compare our own path with that taken by other countries. Announcing the review that evening at the Sydney Institute, Gillard insisted that 'we must be prepared to examine the funding of all schools from all sources', adding that 'the funding review can only do the full job properly if it examines how we fund every school, government and non-government'. When the review's draft terms of reference were released in subsequent weeks, it indicated that the review would need to find out: 'What lessons can be learnt from overseas and domestic funding models, particularly in systems and nations that deliver world class, high-equity outcomes in cost-effective ways?'[64]

The discussion paper accompanying the draft terms of reference noted that Australian students performed well in international standardised tests, but that our results had declined in recent years, partly due to the relatively poor performance of students from disadvantaged backgrounds. Referring to results from the 2006 Program of International Student Assessment (PISA) run by the OECD, the paper commented that 'the difference between students from the poorest backgrounds and the richest was, on average, more than two years of schooling in both reading literacy and mathematics'.[65] The discussion paper observed that the influence of social background on student performance was more marked than in other comparable countries.

All this only underscored the potential for the review to stir up the intense emotions and animosities that had characterised debate about Australian schools for the previous 150 years. In this respect, the selection of David Gonski to chair the review was a political masterstroke. Given his ties with the independent schools sector, his appointment immediately reassured those who felt they had most to lose. And yet Gonski's charm, his evident empathy and his considered, thoughtful approach would prove to be enough to win the trust of the other side, the public sector. Gonski offered just the kind of political cover Julia Gillard needed.

And so, too, did the other figures chosen to join Gonski on the expert panel. All highly capable people, with decades of experience and expertise, they also collectively represented the most powerful interests in Australian education. Kathryn Greiner, an old girl of Loreto Kirribilli and member of the school's council, added another independent sector perspective, as well as her links to the Liberal Party. Peter Tannock was a giant of Catholic education in Australia, having served as chairman of the National Catholic Education Commission, as well as director of Catholic Education in Western Australia. Tannock had even been a member of the Interim Committee of the Schools Commission that had delivered the Karmel report all those years ago. Ken Boston was best known as a previous Director General of the New South Wales Department of Education, who brought a public education perspective to the panel. So, too, did Carmen Lawrence, in so far as she had served as a state education minister as well as premier of Western Australia, in addition to her association with the Labor Party. When economist Bill Scales was appointed to the panel later in 2010, he assumed that the reason was to provide a perspective that was entirely independent of those of the entrenched interest groups.[66]

David Gonski was on the Gold Coast taking a holiday when his phone rang and the caller announced it was Julia Gillard.[67] His first reaction was to wonder which friend with a wicked sense of humour it could be. But the female voice on the other end of the line explained that she was the Minister for Education and would like to do a review of funding of schools. 'I would like you to chair the review, David', Julia Gillard said. Gonski collected his thoughts. 'Why?' he asked. 'I fully understand why you would like to do the review. Why would you like me?' The minister explained that, given the review was about funding, she was looking for a person with experience in business and public policy rather than an educationalist. Gonski's experience as a university chancellor and the chair of an independent boys school, in addition to his background in business and previous roles on government reviews made him the ideal candidate. Gonski told Gillard he wanted to think about it. How long did he have? 'She's an amazingly focused person. She said, "How about 24 hours?"'

Walking on the beach with his wife, Orli Wargon, Gonski contemplated the education minister's offer. 'I don't know whether I'm the right person for this. I'm not an educator, and if I get it wrong I'm going to be really scorned', he said. 'And I remember my wife said to me, "This could be the biggest thing you do in your life". And I think in a way she was right'. Gonski rang Julia Gillard back and told her, 'I'll do it'.

2010: A SMALL COUNTRY SCHOOL

Julia Gillard's announcement in 2010 of the review into school funding did not make much of a splash in the scattered small towns of the Riverina. The weather and grain and livestock prices usually squeezed out other topics of conversation.

As far as education was concerned, the local public school in their little town served Kim Armstrong and her best friend Maria Romano very well. The little town once had two schools, but the small Catholic school had closed a few years back. Some of their students travelled to school in the nearby regional centre, Rivertown, as did most of the high school kids, except for those attending boarding schools in Sydney or Melbourne. (*To be continued ...*)

2

Needs-blind and sector-based: the 'no school loses a dollar' saga

> Today I make a commitment that, following the conclusions of this funding review, the same funding guarantee will apply to any school. It will continue to receive the same funding as before until its new funding allocation reaches that level and begins to overtake it.[1]
>
> *Julia Gillard, announcing the Gonski review to the Sydney Institute, 15 April 2010*

> Every independent school in Australia will see their funding increase under our plan.[2]
>
> *Julia Gillard, Independent Schools Council of Australia National Forum, 20 August 2012*

Julia Gillard went to the Sydney Institute in April 2010 to make a peace offering: she was going to reform school funding, but she wanted to establish that she was not interested in taking money away from schools. Gillard was no longer the fiery backbencher she had been in 2001. She certainly wasn't Mark Latham. So, she made it clear: no school would lose a dollar as a result of the review.

But the private school lobbyists Gillard had hoped to placate did not receive her announcement as an olive branch. On the contrary, they regarded it as a declaration of war. They focused on the fact that the minister's promise still permitted the possibility of a funding freeze. If funding to some private schools was frozen at current levels, while teachers' salaries ticked up each year, they would no longer be able to hire as many teachers. So over time, the schools' purchasing power would be reduced. This would amount to a loss of funding in real terms.

The private school lobbyists were right, and Gillard had been quite clear. She stated that 'no school will lose a dollar of funding, in the sense that their school budget per student will not reduce in dollar terms'.[3] That would mean, she explained, that if the review decided a private school was receiving excessive taxpayer support, and the government agreed, 'it will continue to receive the same funding as before until its new funding allocation reaches that level and begins to overtake it'.

So Julia Gillard was making a commitment about the transition to a new funding scheme. As for what the destination would look like – the new funding formula that schools would transition to – that would be up to David Gonski and his colleagues to determine. The Gonski panel remained free to recommend a funding system in which some schools had a reduced funding entitlement. And Minister Gillard had not ruled out the possibility that the government could accept such a recommendation.

The non-government school representatives immediately made it clear that they viewed such an outcome as absolutely unacceptable. The director of Catholic Education Commission in Victoria, Stephen Elder, said parents and schools would not be reassured by Minister Gillard's statements because she had not guaranteed to maintain funding in real terms. Independent Schools Victoria chief executive Michelle Green welcomed some of Gillard's assurances, but not if funding was to be frozen indefinitely at current levels.

And she rejected the prime minister's intention to examine the funding of all schools from all sources.[4] The private school lobbies demanded a guarantee that no school would lose a dollar *in real terms*, ensuring existing funding would not only be maintained, but annually increased in line with inflation.

If Minister Gillard stuck to her guns and refused to provide this guarantee, she would have a serious political battle on her hands. This was the kind of fight that had not ended well for her predecessors. And yet one of the main reasons Gillard was launching a review was that the Howard Government itself had made this concession, and its 'funding maintained' deals had produced a situation in which private schools in exactly the same circumstances received very different levels of funding.

David Gonski and his co-panellist Kathryn Greiner knew this from firsthand experience. Both had attended and served on the boards of wealthy Sydney independent schools that charged very high fees and served extremely privileged student populations. Gonski's school (Sydney Grammar) received less than \$3000 per student per year in public support; Greiner's school (Loreto Kirribilli) – a major beneficiary of Howard's special deals – received more than \$7000.[5]

If no school was going to lose funding in real terms, these arbitrary differences would have to be preserved. Otherwise, the funding at a school like Gonski's would have to be brought up to at least the level of Greiner's. Not only would this be extraordinarily expensive when implemented across the board, it would be no more logical than before, because it would still be the product of past practice rather than a coherent policy rationale.

So to bow to the private school lobbies' demand, and guarantee no school would lose a dollar in real terms, would be to fatally compromise the review before it had even begun. Not for the first or last time, Julia Gillard found herself between a rock and a hard place. And while this quarrel was bubbling away, the Member for Lalor had also been attending to some other matters. Barely two months after the school funding review had been announced, the education minister became the prime minister. On the evening of 23 June 2010, ABC 24 reported that Gillard was challenging Kevin Rudd for the prime ministership, and she had the numbers. Labor backbenchers decried the story as another beat-up, and yet the next day Australia's first female prime minister was sworn in at Government House in Canberra.

At one level, the school funding review's status had suddenly been elevated, along with the political fortunes of its progenitor. But the leadership change also raised questions about whether the Labor Government was capable of prevailing over – or even presenting a united front against – the powerful forces arrayed against it. Rudd's overthrow had been precipitated by his capitulation on climate change and would immediately result in his successor surrendering on the mining tax. Every interest group in Australia could see that a divided Labor Government was uniquely susceptible to pressure.

In addition to the challenges posed by the aftermath of the Global Financial Crisis, an Opposition Leader on steroids, and an increasingly hostile media environment, school funding was one of the most divisive and heavily contested issues of the modern political era. Would Prime Minister Gillard be able to advance the common good in the face of these intense pressures?

The first test would occur immediately upon Gillard's ascension to the top job. During the 2010 election campaign, as the new prime minister, still in the shadow of her seriously bitter predecessor, stumbled from misstep to misstep, Christopher Pyne pounced. The Opposition Education spokesperson wrote to the Catholic bishops, promising that a Coalition government would give them what they wanted: a guarantee that all non-government schools would have their funding maintained in real terms.[6] There would be no more threat of a funding freeze if the Coalition was elected. In receipt of Pyne's letter, and at a moment of maximum political vulnerability for Gillard, the bishops sought the same assurance from Labor. Foreshadowing the attacks that awaited the government if it refused to relent, Bishop Greg O'Kelly claimed the potential funding freeze threatened the viability of hundreds of Catholic parish schools.[7]

Labor's bid for re-election was already complicated enough, and this stoush had the potential to blow up into a major blue. The new prime minister was trying to neutralise attacks on carbon pricing, asylum seeker arrivals and the mining tax, as well as explain why she had replaced Kevin Rudd. She did not need another fight on her hands. The day before going to Yarralumla to call the election, Gillard sent Simon Crean, who had succeeded her in the education portfolio, to meet with Bishop O'Kelly and work out a compromise deal.[8]

Gillard describes what happened next in her memoir:

> Suddenly negotiation with some figures in Catholic education proved inexplicably difficult. Such was the level of agitation that in the second week of the election campaign, I met with a delegation of senior Catholic education figures in Melbourne, including Cardinal [George] Pell. In this mood they were not going to accept blanket reassurances of any nature.[9]

Confronted with the threat of escalation, in an election campaign rapidly careening out of control, Gillard blinked. On 4 August, just over two weeks out from election day, she announced a compromise.[10] The current funding quadrennium, due to expire at the end of 2012, would be extended for one year. The new funding system would not begin until the start of 2014. Guaranteeing that nothing would change in nearly four years was a fast way to take the heat out of the issue. And now the findings of the funding review would not be implemented until after the next federal election in 2013, meaning that the whole review process would have to be relitigated during an election campaign. This was of course exactly what the non-government sector lobby groups wanted – and why they agreed to the terms of the truce.

Angelo Gavrielatos, the head of the powerful public school teachers union, the Australian Education Union, was out to dinner in Melbourne when Julia Gillard's advisor, Tom Bentley, called to break the news. Gavrielatos was furious. Labor had justified renewing the Howard funding arrangements when it got into government because it did not want to take on the contentious school funding issue at the 2007 election. Now they would be fighting the same issue out at the 2013 election, after having preserved Howard's funding system for six years.

Stepping outside the restaurant, Gavrielatos let rip. 'You've got to be joking, Tom. You have got to be fucking joking', Gavrielatos remembers bellowing down the phone. 'The whole idea was to take the review outside the electoral cycle', he fumed. 'Don't you realise you just brought it back in?'[11]

Julia Gillard didn't need to be convinced. 'It hurt me to make this concession', Gillard recalled. 'I felt like I was ducking a big debate, an education reform central to treating all of our children fairly. But the politics of living to fight another day descended on me. We were at risk of losing the 2010 campaign. I could not afford to be fighting with the powerful Catholic education lobby.'[12]

Because that's what we've always done: the Gonski review meets the private school lobbies

With this drama unfolding around them, the Gonski panel got down to business. As Julia Gillard and Tony Abbott duked it out through July and August 2010, the panel embarked on a nationwide listening tour, meeting with 71 key stakeholders across the country. Among these organisations were state education departments, Catholic education commissions, the associations of independent schools in each jurisdiction, and the teacher unions in every state and territory.[13] Taken together, they represented the interests underpinning Australia's unique three-sector system, each supported by two levels of government, replicated in each state and territory. Gonski and his colleagues knew they would have to please all these groups, or at least placate them, if they were going to offer the government a politically plausible set of recommendations.

As for what was discussed behind closed doors, it is impossible to believe that the concerns that had almost boiled over into open confrontation in the election campaign were not conveyed to the expert panel directly. The private school lobbies' core demand was still that no school would lose a dollar in real terms as a result of the review. Prime Minister Gillard had only delayed the beginning of a new funding system, managing to ensure the controversy had not become an election issue, but she had not conceded the essence of the argument. It was still open to the Gonski panel to recommend a reduction in the taxpayer contribution – a funding freeze, in practice – for some private schools. Such a possibility was still unacceptable to the private school lobbyists.

If Gonski and his colleagues remained in any doubt about this, it was spelt out in black and white in the Catholic and independent submissions to the review. On the first page of the Independent Schools Council submission it read: 'The independent schools sector's key outcome for the Review of Funding for Schooling is that no independent school or student should receive less funding in real terms'.[14] The National Catholic Education Commission likewise left no room for doubt that it would not accept any reduction without a fight: 'As part of any new funding model

Catholic schools require the current level of total funding in real terms from the Australian Government and State/Territory Governments.'[15]

The showdown with Julia Gillard had now metastasised to the review, presenting the expert panel with a profound dilemma: any set of principles *consistently* applied in the development of a new funding system would produce *some* losers.

If the purpose of public funding was to ensure all non-government schools were adequately resourced to meet the educational needs of the children in their care, there was a strong case for increasing it in some instances. Some private schools were scraping by, under-resourced compared to public schools serving similar students, even when taxpayer support and modest fees were combined. Four decades after the Karmel report had first articulated the case for needs-based funding, these were the schools where it still had not arrived.

But other non-government schools were more than adequately resourced without any government funding. If educational need was the basis for taxpayer support, the same principle that justified increases to some private schools warranted reductions at others. Even when taxpayer support contributed to a level of resourcing above what could be justified by educational need, there were other well-rehearsed arguments for continued funding of non-government schools. Many of these arguments advanced a cogent case that the public interest was served by providing taxpayer funding to some schools in this category. But none could justify no school losing a dollar. Let's look at them, one by one.

Take the argument that had been successfully prosecuted ever since the famous Goulburn strike in 1962: that subsidising private education created a net saving for the public purse. Between February and May 2011, the Gonski panellists visited 39 schools across the country. It was clear from even this small sample that the budget savings argument did not apply in many cases. At schools like SCEGGS Darlinghurst and St Andrew's Cathedral School in Sydney, parents paid well over $20 000 per year. Their readiness to do so would hardly be affected by the withdrawal of a few thousand dollars per student in taxpayer funding. The fiscal argument supported funding reductions. At the other end of the spectrum, the panel visited private schools receiving more public funding than nearby public schools (which served greater numbers of disadvantaged students).

In Western Australia, the Gonski panel visited Holy Cross College, a K–12 Catholic school in the northeastern suburbs of Perth, where combined state and Commonwealth government funding added up to $11 600 per student. This was $400 more than at the public school down the road, Ellenbrook Secondary College. In Bendigo, Victoria, the Catholic school visited by the panel received hundreds of dollars more per student in government funding than the government school they toured. In both Perth and Bendigo, the private schools received more public funding despite enrolling a smaller proportion of disadvantaged students than the neighbouring public school. This was hardly saving the taxpayer money.

Independent Schools Victoria argued for a Milton Friedman-style voucher scheme, in which all students, at public and private schools, received the same level of government funding irrespective of the fees charged at the latter.[16] But even if the panel had gone out on a limb and adopted this extreme position, they would still have had to recommend that some private schools should lose funding – because under the status quo they were getting even more than similar public schools. The overfunded schools the panel visited were not typical but nor were they outliers either. In 2009, 5 per cent of Australia's private schools received more public funding than the typical similar public school.[17]

When the Howard Government had boosted public funding of non-government schools at the turn of the 21st century, it made much of how its new arrangements would increase school choice. 'The new arrangements will particularly extend choice to low income families', claimed Education Minister David Kemp. 'This is a significant step forward for educational equity.'[18] And yet throughout the subsequent decade, private school fees had continued to grow, well ahead of inflation. In 2000, the principal of Melbourne's Wesley College claimed the school would cut fees under Howard's new funding system. But in reality the school's fees doubled over the subsequent decade.[19] At schools visited by the Gonski panel, such as SCEGGS and Geelong Grammar, exactly the same thing had happened. If expanding choice for low-income families was really the purpose of increasing public funding to schools like these, it was simply not working.

The fact that non-government schools were funded so inconsistently also prevented the panel from logically recommending that no school should have their funding entitlement reduced. The Independent Schools Council of Australia called for a minimum entitlement for all private schools of at least 25 per cent of average public school funding. But even extremely wealthy schools that had been the beneficiaries of historical deals were receiving much more than this. The school that Kathryn Greiner had attended and would ultimately chair, Loreto Kirribilli, was receiving around 60 per cent of the resourcing standard.[20] So to apply the Independent Schools Council's own principle would necessitate that some schools would lose funding.

Because some private schools were receiving much more than others, and some were receiving more than public schools, as soon as the panel developed a logical, coherent rationale for the new funding system, it would involve some private schools losing funding. The only way the expert panel could deliver the outcome the private school lobbies were demanding was this: accept that the fact that a school had received a certain level of funding in the past was itself a reason for it to continue to do so in the future.

But this is not a reason so much as a refusal to offer one; an insistence that private school funding be exempt from critical scrutiny. In effect, the private school lobbies were telling the expert panel, 'review as much as you like, just don't do it around here'. In demanding that no school lost a dollar in real terms, they were not submitting a substantial case about what the review should find, but insisting that taxpayer funding of private schools should not be the subject of review. At its heart, their demand was a refusal to accept that a common set of rules could be agreed through a fair, independent process, guided by expertise and extensive consultation, and that such rules should be applied equally to all, without fear or favour.

In effect, then, the threshold question for the review became not whether funding should go up or down or stay the same, but whether they would assert their jurisdiction over the issue. They would have to if they were going to do the job they had been given. The expert panel had been tasked with reviewing 'the funding of all schools from all sources'.[21] To do this required that they critically examine the purposes of publicly funding private schools and the most efficient and effective way of achieving those objectives. In other words, the panel would have to revisit the basic assumptions that had characterised school funding since the Karmel report, including the belief that taxpayers should provide funding to schools which were already better resourced than their neighbours.

Writing in the *Australian Economic Review* as the work of the review proceeded, economists Chris Ryan and Luke Sibieta commented that 'one area where the [Gonski] report could make a useful contribution to public debate will be if it can set out a coherent, contemporary rationale for the public funding of private schools in Australia'.[22] Ryan and Sibieta were making the simple point that it is important for governments to have clear reasons for how they spend money. 'In the absence of a clear, contemporary policy goal', they observed, 'it is impossible to measure the extent to which the private schools funding program is achieving its purpose'. 'Accountability for the expenditure of public funds of the magnitude involved requires a clear, contemporary statement of the purpose of funding for private schooling, so that its impact can be properly evaluated.'[23]

Normally this would be setting a pretty low bar for a public policy review. If we don't know why we're doing something, we can't know when or how. But the politics surrounding school funding presented the expert panel with an enormous challenge. The dilemma came to a head during the review in a debate about the most exclusive schools where fees were two or three times the average funding per student at public schools, with the taxpayer contribution further extending their resource advantage. David Gonski and his colleagues vigorously debated where to set the level of public funding that would be provided to the wealthiest non-government schools. Should the wealthiest private schools receive 25 per cent of the schooling resource standard they were developing, as the national Independent Schools Council called for?[24] Or should the level be set at 15 per cent, as one eminent figure had submitted? Or at 13.7 per cent, as it was in the existing funding system?[25]

External pressures aside, the members of the expert panel were inevitably going to bring very different perspectives to this question. After all, they had been chosen in significant part because of their longstanding associations with the three school sectors and two major political parties. At least one panellist had close links with the figures who had shirtfronted Julia Gillard on the issue during the election. But some panel members believed that the most exclusive private schools should get no government funding at all. 'It was only those of us who had worked in education systems in our previous lives, who said that would be inviting World War Three with some very wealthy people', recalls Gonski panel member Carmen Lawrence.[26] Debate gave way to a pragmatic acceptance of the political realities.

The residue of this debate can be seen in the Gonski Report, in a remarkable passage that is worth quoting at length. First, the report recounts a series of seemingly weighty arguments against the provision of any taxpayer support to high-fee non-government schools:

> Those against a minimum public contribution argued that some schools already have a level of resources, which they have raised from parents and their communities over a period of time, significantly above that required to meet reasonable resource needs. Providing public funding to these schools was criticised as unnecessary and a poor use of limited public funds when needs are higher elsewhere. High fees in these schools may be an indicator of the willingness and capacity of some parents to invest very heavily in their children's schooling, as well as a preference for private schooling that is unlikely to be affected by reduced public funding.[27]

These arguments seemed to invite a substantial reply, an explanation of how a public purpose was served by such funding. But here the Gonski Report makes clear that the rationale for public funding of private schools will remain unexamined and unreviewed, stating that the principal or, indeed, sole argument for providing some public funding to all non-government schools is that 'the Australian Government has for many decades provided an entitlement to every student in every school'.[28]

This is the point where it becomes apparent that the private school lobbies had prevailed; the fact that something had been done in the past was being taken as the reason for doing it in the future. The Gonski review would not present 'a coherent, contemporary rationale for the public funding of private schools in Australia', or, indeed, any rationale at all. It would not argue that this funding should continue because it was necessary, fair, effective, efficient or smart, but because that is what we have always done, at least in modern political memory. An explanation of the purpose of funding private schools, and the place of taxpayer subsidies in a funding system based on educational need, had been banished beyond the borders of the review. This is the moment when it was decided that the Karmel paradigm which had defined our thinking for the last 40 years was going to shape it for the next ten.

Instead of providing a justification for the arrangements they endorsed, the reviewers went to great lengths to convey the impression that their hands were tied. The ultimate recommendation about the minimum public contribution to all non-government schools was explicitly linked with Julia Gillard's 'no losers' promise:

> To meet the Australian Government's announcement that no school will lose a dollar per student as a result of this review, a minimum public contribution towards the cost of schooling should apply to non-government schools at a level between 20 to 25 per cent of the resource standard per student amounts without loadings.[29]

This approach, the report explained, would ensure the wealthiest private schools were entitled to at least the level of funding they were currently enjoying.[30]

'To meet the Australian Government's announcement' is an oft-repeated refrain in the Gonski Report. And by making a great show of Julia Gillard's public commitment, the panel was able to not-so-subtly imply that the review's recommendations were made under sufferance. But the panel did have room to move, and it knew it. Because Julia Gillard had not ruled out the possibility that some schools would have a reduced entitlement, and have their funding frozen, her public statements did not prevent the panel determining the minimum contribution as it saw fit. Which is why they had a debate about it. It was true that the implication of Julia Gillard's promise was that all private schools would continue to receive *some* level of public funding – a reduction to zero would require a cut, which she had ruled out. But even so, it was possible for this course of action to be countenanced in the review's deliberations because it was an independent review, responsible only to its terms of reference. Nothing in the terms of reference prevented them from making this recommendation.

It is telling in this respect that days after the public release of the Gonski Report in February 2012, David Gonski told the *Australian Financial Review* that 'we were instructed as part of our terms of reference that no school will lose a dollar on a per student basis on our proposals'.[31] But that claim is simply incorrect. The 'no school loses a dollar' commitment was not included in the review's terms of reference, and these did not impose a constraint on what the panel could recommend in this regard.

The real constraints on the expert panel were not in the terms of reference or even in the Prime Minister's promises. Having witnessed the events of the 2010 election and the subsequent extension of existing funding arrangements to 2014, and having seen and heard the submissions of the Catholic and independent sectors, it was clear to the Gonski panel that reducing the level of funding to private schools would seriously undermine the prospects of a consensus in support of the report. If the Gonski review ignored the private schools' red line, their report would likely be politically unpalatable, a document the government would almost certainly disregard. The review would end up becoming little more than an interesting intellectual exercise, changing little. The expert panel, with David Gonski in the lead, was understandably determined to avoid such an outcome. They wanted to produce a blueprint for action. A report that elicited vehement opposition from major stakeholders would likely have been dead upon arrival.

And so, the prevailing view on the panel was that pragmatism was in order. Whatever they believed were the optimal settings in terms of good public policy, they would also need to recognise the key demands of the most powerful interests in school education. The panel's pragmatism paid off – in the short term, at least.

When the Gonski Report was publicly released in February 2012 it was greeted with remarkably widespread support. Even those who had heavily resisted the whole process greeted it enthusiastically. The Independent Schools Council Executive Director, Bill Daniels, congratulated Gonski on 'achieving the seemingly impossible task of recommending a funding model which has been met with general support from across the education sector'.[32] His New South Wales counterpart, Head of the NSW Association of Independent Schools, Geoff Newcombe, likewise commended the Gonski panel on a job well done, describing its proposals as 'balanced, fair and good news for school education as a whole'.[33] The Head of the National Catholic Education Commission, Therese Temby, described the report as 'a major piece of work and a roadmap for a way forward'.[34]

Less than two hours after receiving the report, Christopher Pyne attempted to sabotage this apparent outbreak of school funding peace, claiming that 'every non-government school is on a private school hit list'.[35] But he failed to get any traction in the first instance. Paul Kelly dismissed Pyne's claims in *The Australian* as a 'ludicrous scare', pointing to the fact that even the private school lobbyists were refusing to back them.[36]

There was no magic trick involved. The Gonski Report had ostensibly observed the bottom line of the major stakeholders. The response of a headmaster at an exclusive Melbourne private school, where fees were as high as $35 000 a year, illustrated the reality of the moment. He explained to *The Age* that his school would be eligible for about 30 to 35 per cent of the schooling resource standard, which meant funding at his school would be unaffected. 'I think it's a very fair report', the headmaster said.[37]

But in successfully negotiating the realpolitik, the Gonski review had paid an enormous price in terms of public policy. The report that was being so enthusiastically welcomed effectively endorsed arrangements for which it offered no rationale, and advocated contradictory outcomes without explanation. While arguing that a needs-based funding system was critical to addressing Australia's educational ills, the new funding system it proposed would not itself *be* needs-based. Finding 10 of the report stated that 'Public funding arrangements need to reflect the nature of the educational challenges faced by a system or school given its characteristics and student population, regardless of whether it is in the government or non-government sector'.[38] At the same time, the report endorsed the status quo in which public funding was often unrelated to the circumstances and challenges faced by schools. Schools that already charged fees well in excess of the resource standard would receive more still from the taxpayer. More pervasively, combined public and private income would give some lower-fee non-government schools a resource advantage over comparable public schools.

The Gonski Report failed to offer any rigorous rationale for the ongoing resource disparities that it tacitly endorsed. If they were justified by savings to the public purse, for instance, then logic suggests that an essential step would have been to quantify how much governments were saving. Without some idea of how much, we could not know how significant this supposed benefit was.

Once the benefit had been identified it would have to be carefully weighed against potential costs – fiscal, economic and educational – of using public funding to encourage families to enrol their children in private schools. But the claim was not argued, it was assumed; taken as an article of faith.

The Gonski panel wagered that they could renovate Australia's school funding system while leaving assumptions like this one unexamined. The Gonski review and reforms would take place firmly within the Karmel paradigm, and would not question the disparities in resourcing or responsibilities it entailed. The risk of this approach was that they had waved through the very problems they had been summoned to solve, and their reforms would be gradually distorted and deformed by the sinking foundations on which they were built – the inconsistency, inequity and inefficiency of the Karmel paradigm.

But for the time being, Gonski and his colleagues basked in the glowing reviews that met the public release of their report. Over-egging the constraints imposed by Julia Gillard's 'no losers' promise did not only disarm the private school lobbyists, it helped head off any potential disquiet from the other side of the debate. The Prime Minister could take the heat for the political compromises, while the report preserved the impression that the panel remained firmly above the fray.

And then there was a twist: Gonski's secret modelling

The Gonski Report is 286 pages long, and not all of its implications were immediately apparent. While it left the minimum public contribution to private schools unquestioned, it did recommend that all schools be funded consistently. As 2012 unfolded, it became clear that this would have consequences for schools that had been overfunded by the Howard Government.

The Gonski Report was scathing about Howard's 'funding maintained' policy. When, in 2001, the Howard Government had introduced a new school funding model, it guaranteed that any private school negatively affected by the changes would have its funding maintained in real terms. A secret internal review conducted by the Commonwealth Education Department in 2006 found that even though the arrangements were supposedly transitional 'there is no mechanism that would naturally unwind its effect'.[39] When, in 2008, *Sydney Morning Herald* journalist Anna Patty broke the story of the damaging secret report, it was revealed that private schools had been overfunded by more than $2 billion over four years and some were set to be overpaid by as much as $23 million each in the next funding cycle.[40]

By 2010, over 1000 non-government schools were funded above their actual entitlement. In the issues paper released in December 2010, the Gonski panel had commented: 'The Funding Maintained arrangements seemed to operate as a separate and second funding model that applied to a prescribed group of non-government schools, which provided a secure and favourable funding environment, but one that was not consistent with the equal application of the SES [socio-economic status] funding model'.[41]

During the review process, even figures responsible for the 'funding maintained' deals had disowned them, including the former Howard Government education minister, Brendan Nelson.[42] So it was little surprise that the Gonski Report recommended their termination, and that all non-government schools should be funded on a consistent basis. Recommendation 4 of the report stated: 'From 2014, non-government schools should be funded by the Australian Government on the basis of a common measure of need that is applied fairly and consistently to all'.[43]

The Gonski Report hinted that this meant there would have

to be cuts at overfunded schools. 'It would be difficult', the report stated, 'to completely address the funding anomalies associated with Funding Maintenance by recalibrating the existing funding model in a way that did not disadvantage any school and also retained a reasonable degree of targeting of assistance to schools in need'.[44] But the report stopped short of explicitly stating that the resolution of the existing anomalies meant some private schools would have to lose funding, remaining coy about exactly what its recommendation would mean in practice. Would the funding at an overfunded school, like the one Kathryn Greiner had attended, be trimmed back to the level of David Gonski's old school? Or did the report's apparent assurance that no school would lose a dollar mean that the funding at a school like Gonski's would have to be brought up to at least the level of Greiner's?

The Gonski Report did not say. The review had commissioned modelling to test the precise impacts of its recommendations, but the modelling itself was not published (and remains under wraps to this day, impervious to freedom of information requests). The Gonski Report stated that the modelling showed that 'all sectors would have received increased government funding' under its formula.[45] But it notably omitted to mention whether those increases would have applied to all schools or whether the modelling indicated that the recommended abolition of 'funding maintained' would have caused some of the beneficiaries to lose funding.

After the report was publicly released in February 2012, and the news cycle had moved on, the private school lobby groups burrowed into the detailed implications of Gonski's proposals. It was not long before their initial enthusiasm faded, and the public positioning shifted. In March, they called for the publication of Gonski's modelling. Inside the Gillard Government, an argument broke out about how to respond. The main antagonists were the education minister, Peter Garrett, and the Prime Minister's communications director, John McTernan. 'The nub of the dispute between me and Peter Garrett is a very simple one', John McTernan told us. 'He wanted to publish the workings of Gonski which I refused to do.'[46] McTernan believed that the revelation that some schools would lose out financially under Gonski's proposals would be hugely damaging. 'That was never going to be announced by any government in the history of Australia', he said.

According to McTernan, Garrett argued for the release of Gonski's modelling on the basis that the government's proposals would be seen in a more positive light by virtue of their contrast with Gonski's. '[Garrett] wanted to publish that modelling and I didn't. And I was right, and he was wrong', McTernan says. 'I won on that one.' Instead of releasing Gonski's modelling, Minister Garrett provided stakeholders with 2009 and 2010 funding data, enabling them to conduct their own modelling of Gonski's proposals.[47]

By May, the peace pipes had been put away. The independent schools lobbyist Geoff Newcombe argued that their analysis suggested Julia Gillard's promise that no school would lose a dollar now looked 'hollow'.[48] He not only reiterated earlier calls for Minister Garrett to release Gonski's modelling, but also demanded a two-year extension of the existing funding system.[49]

Then on 19 August 2012, an explosive report by Samantha Maiden appeared in the *Herald Sun*. Half a year had now passed since the public release of the Gonski Report, and the government was preparing to finally announce in-principle support for the review's major recommendations. But Maiden's story torpedoed that plan. Private school modelling, the report revealed, indicated that thousands of schools would lose funding under Gonski's plan. Under the headline '3000 schools face funding cuts', a table set out a list of schools allegedly in the firing line. 'Is your school on the list?' the pull-quote asked. 'Search our online database.' A picture of a forlorn-looking mother, along with her two children, accompanied the story. 'It would be a tragedy if the government were to take money away from them', the mother commented. 'I'm sure parents are feeling the same across Victoria', she said. Maiden's report did not make clear which organisation had conducted the contentious modelling, but Stephen Elder, the head of the Catholic Education Commission of Victoria, was quoted liberally.

The real significance of the story, however, was not the private school modelling, the veracity of which was questionable. It was that it elicited a major revelation from the Prime Minister, who finally conceded what had been kept secret until this point: some schools *did* lose out in the modelling commissioned by the Gonski panel, contradicting the Gonski Report's apparent affirmation that no school would lose out under the new funding formula. 'While the original modelling from the panel had some schools missing out, there was no way we were going to let that happen', Prime Minister Gillard told Maiden.[50] The Prime Minister had been forced to concede what the Gonski Report had obscured: it was impossible to create a consistent new funding system, and end the special deals, without reducing funding to some schools.

Much of the Gonski Report gave the impression that it had been forced to ensure that no school would lose a dollar. David Gonski had even claimed that the edict had been in the terms of reference. Now the Prime Minister was claiming that the Gonski review's own modelling indicated some schools would lose funding as a result of its recommendations. What was going on? It appears that, under Gonski's recommendations, the abolition of 'funding maintained' would have reduced the funding entitlement of some schools. But to avoid causing offence, the Gonski Report only intimated this, stopping short of stating the result of its recommendations explicitly. The political challenge of delivering the bad news was left to the government.

In August 2012, the Prime Minister was finally forced to

disclose the reality of the report. Following this, Tony Abbott immediately went on the attack. In a speech to a private school conference in Canberra, he trumpeted the unverified claims about the number of losers being in the thousands: 'The problem, ladies and gentlemen – as all of you would know because I'm sure all of you were conscious of the material in the papers on the weekend – is that even if Gonski is fully funded to the tune of some $5 billion more a year, it seems that some one in three schools would be worse off', the Opposition Leader crowed.[51]

No school loses a dollar mark II, August 2012: Prime Minister Gillard promises every school will get more money

In response to the heightened agitation, the Prime Minister immediately delayed the government's formal response to the Gonski Report.[52] Conscious that years of patient work was at risk of falling apart, Gillard finally capitulated. Instead of declaring her government's support for the recommendations of the Gonski review, she used her address to the same private school conference in Canberra where Tony Abbott spoke to grant the ultimate concession: 'Every independent school in Australia will see their funding increase under our plan', Prime Minister Gillard promised her audience.[53] No private school would lose funding, none would have their funding frozen, not even the most overfunded.

For over two and a half years, the private school representatives had doggedly defended the status quo; sometimes holding back, while at other times they emerged into open confrontation. Now they had finally triumphed. Their core demand – that not even one school could lose any funding in real terms – was secure. First, in April 2010, Julia Gillard had promised no school would lose a dollar in nominal terms. But, they had argued, this posed the threat of a funding freeze. In the midst of the 2010 election, Gillard buckled and extended the existing funding system until the start of 2014. Aware of the political realities, the Gonski review made a show of preserving the minimum taxpayer contribution to all private schools. But, more surreptitiously, it recommended that some schools which had been overfunded by the Howard Government should experience reductions in taxpayer support. But the lobbyists did not rest. They again turned up the pressure on Julia Gillard, this time extracting the ultimate concession. Even the most extremely overfunded schools would still receive a 3 per cent increase in taxpayer support each year.

The reaction from the non-government schools lobbies to Gillard's announcement was predictably enthusiastic.[54] But it was not only the private schools that the Prime Minister had mollified. Almost a decade earlier, the Murdoch tabloids had loudly broadcast their condemnation of Mark Latham's proposal to reallocate public funding from high-fee to low-fee non-government schools, calling it class warfare. Now Murdoch's organs oozed praise for the Prime Minister's obeisance to the private school lobbies. 'Prime Minister Julia Gillard has learnt from Mr Latham's error', the *Daily Telegraph* editorialised, 'and now promises, as part of the government's response to the Gonski review, to take an approach that is the very opposite of Mr Latham's'.[55]

The immediate consequence of Gillard's move was that the cost of school funding reform ballooned. And, as a result, two-thirds of additional funding for needy schools was delayed until 2018 and 2019 – beyond the forward estimates. This made the commitment to fully deliver needs-based funding extremely vulnerable to the vicissitudes of the electoral cycle. The decision to provide even more money to overfunded schools is a significant part of the reason why disadvantaged schools remain underfunded today – and will remain so for the next decade.

The concession also meant abandoning a coherent funding system in which all schools would be funded on a consistent basis. Instead, some schools would remain overfunded in perpetuity, with distinct sets of arrangements applying to different schools in the same circumstances. The terrible irony was that one of the most widely acknowledged flaws in the old funding system was that it was inconsistent and illogical because it was peppered with special deals. And yet, after years of exhaustive effort, a new 'funding maintained' deal had produced the same result, with the old funding formula baked into the new one.

Peter Garrett, the minister who oversaw the implementation of the reform, describes the consequences of the backdown: 'It's hurting you in terms of delivering something which is robust financially, where it could have been more robust. And it's a maintenance of … special deals or sweetheart provisions sort of hanging off the scaffolding of something which, at its best, was a great deal more rigorous than that'.[56]

For these and other reasons, Julia Gillard has been roundly criticised for the 'no losers' promise. But before making a final assessment of Gillard's decision, it is essential to acknowledge a number of salient points. Firstly, it is necessary to distinguish between two very different commitments: the one made in April 2010 and the other in August 2012. The April 2010 announcement that no school would lose nominal funding involved an element of compromise. But Angelo Gavrielatos, now president of the New South Wales Teachers Federation, describes it as 'realpolitik, and the assessment that we made was without it, nothing would have happened'.[57] If that was the assessment of the teacher unions, it is hardly surprising that it was the position of Labor in government. It did not substantially constrain what the Gonski review could recommend.

Julia Gillard's real concession came only after two and a

half years of intense pressure, in August 2012. The costs of that capitulation were massive. But even then, it was an extremely difficult call. Failing to placate her opponents in that moment would have risked sinking the whole reform project entirely. The Prime Minister knew she would have to persuade the six states and two territories to sign up to school funding reform. That would prove incredibly difficult anyway; if the private school lobby groups had been openly trashing the government's proposal, it would almost certainly have been a non-starter.

Gillard might have hoped that the review itself – a highly consultative and comprehensive 18-month process, headed by a former private school chair – would persuade the intransigents that change was necessary, and that some schools would have to lose funding. For a time it seemed the Gonski review had worked some magic, but ultimately it hadn't been enough. So in August 2012, some time after the Gonski review had been completed, Julia Gillard ruled out a funding freeze and promised that all private schools would have their funding maintained in real terms – after the review, not before it.

One of the reasons so much of the opprobrium was directed at Gillard was that Gonski and his fellow panellists had effectively shifted responsibility for their own pragmatic political calculations onto her. Both in the report, and after the review was handed down, the panellists conveyed the impression they had arrived at their position on funding wealthy private schools only because of constraints imposed by Gillard. In a 2014 speech to the New South Wales Teachers Federation, Gonski panellist Ken Boston stated that 'the Labor Government, not Gonski, said no school should lose a dollar, and to satisfy that requirement we included in the model a base grant for all schools'.[58] Warming to the theme, Boston described the undertaking that no school should lose a dollar as 'the albatross around the neck of the Gonski Panel'.[59]

This was a very successful framing. It quickly evolved into something of an orthodoxy that by promising that no school would lose a dollar, Gillard had fatally compromised the review before it had even begun. In 2016, former Howard Government Education Minister Amanda Vanstone summed up the received view: 'I feel a bit sorry for Gonski ... not everybody appreciates that Gonski's view, is as expressed within his terms of reference, which had a clause that had "No losers"', she claimed – falsely, but without challenge.[60] Meanwhile, on the other side of the political divide, public education advocate Trevor Cobbold wrote in 2018 that the review 'was shackled by Julia Gillard's edict that "no school will lose a dollar of funding" under the new model. It meant that the over-funding had to be folded into the new model'.[61]

In reality, the constraints on the Gonski panel were the same as those faced by Julia Gillard; it had to keep the powerful private school lobbies in the tent. That was the real albatross around everybody's neck. And in response to that common constraint, the Gonski panel engaged in its share of pragmatic political compromise, largely leaving existing private school funding untouched. It preserved the minimum taxpayer contribution to all private schools, it maintained the resource advantages enjoyed by many, and it refrained from seriously scrutinising the purposes of public funding. These positions were produced by the panel's view about what would be palatable to major stakeholders, not by Julia Gillard's commitment that no school would lose a dollar in nominal terms.

However furtively, the Gonski review did defy the non-government school lobbies in recommending that school funding should be consistent, and that the egregious anomalies should end. A funding review could hardly recommend anything else while still retaining any self-respect. But even this minimal requirement was fiercely – and successfully – resisted, confirmation of the profound political challenge faced by both Gillard and Gonski. Like Julia Gillard, the Gonski panel made deeply problematic compromises, and yet the historical record seems to suggest they had little choice.

As it would turn out, there would be moments in the years ahead where it would appear that, despite everything, pragmatism had prevailed and Gillard and Gonski's unwavering focus on the art of the possible had succeeded in permanently transforming school funding. The question was whether, after all the compromises, the solution would be adequate to the problem. But to answer this question, first we need to return to 2010 and 2011 and take a closer look at the schools the Gonski panel encountered and exactly what the Gonski Report recommended.

2010: YEAR 3

Being in Year 3, Kim and Maria could now walk to and from school. They knew most of the kids in their town of 900 people. Kim's parents owned a small shop and her mum taught at the school. Maria's mum was a cleaner and her dad worked on a property just out of town. Regardless of their income, background, religion, almost all the kids went to the local school.

Kim and Maria were good friends. Kim was a higher achiever, and both sets of parents appreciated how she helped Maria get through her schoolwork. She had a good influence on Maria. The girls' teachers appreciated it, too; Maria was one of a few who really needed extra support. The parents felt that help was on the way, they were quite excited about a new review of schools which might see their little school get the resources, particularly the specialist support that students like Maria needed. (*To be continued ...*)

3

The unlevel playing field: what Gonski found

> Many international studies ... confirm that concentrations of students from certain socioeconomic groups within a school has a strong impact on the educational outcomes achieved by all students at the school. Importantly, research also suggests that this impact is more significant than the effect of an individual student's own socioeconomic status on outcomes.[1]
>
> *Final report of the Review of Funding for Schooling ('The Gonski Report') 2011*

Almost as soon as the Gonski panel got down to work, they were confronted with the sheer scale of the problem they had been tasked to solve. In December 2010, results from the latest round of the OECD's Programme for International Student Assessment (PISA) were published. Since PISA's inception at the start of the century, the tests in reading, maths and science taken by a random sample of 15-year-olds every three years had rapidly become one of the most important measures of how a nation's schools were faring.

The discussion paper released by then Minister Gillard when the Gonski review was launched had pointed to the signs of decline, closely linked to social disadvantage, in Australia's 2006 results.[2] Now the situation was even worse. In maths, Australian students were about six months of learning below the level they had been at in 2000, and Australia was one of few countries to record a decline in reading levels over the first decade of the century.[3]

The disconcerting drop in average results was closely associated with a long tail of underperformance. By 2009, one in seven Australian 15-year-olds were not meeting the basic standard of achievement needed for full participation in society, in any of the learning areas tested – up from one in eight in 2000.[4] That meant around half a million young Australians were leaving school each year without the most basic skills needed to succeed in life, the Gonski Report would conclude. On average, 15-year-olds from the most disadvantaged quarter of Australian families were three years behind children from the top quarter.[5] Powerfully summarising the situation, *The Australian*'s education editor, Justine Ferrari, wrote, 'The latest results from the OECD's testing program show that demography is still destiny in Australia'.[6]

The PISA results came on top of a range of other evidence all pointing to the same conclusion.[7] The circumstances into which Australian children were born – their parents' income, employment status and educational attainment – were a powerful predictor of their fortunes at school. 'Achievement in NAPLAN from 2008 to 2010 demonstrates that lower levels of parental education are strongly and consistently associated with lower student performance, and this holds across all the year levels tested (Years 3, 5, 7 and 9)', the Gonski Report would observe.[8] Indigenous children, kids from poor families, those with low-English proficiency, or a disability, and those who lived in rural and remote locations were all starting school behind their peers, falling further behind with each year at school, and completing secondary education at much lower rates.[9]

Just a week after the PISA results were published, the Gonski panel released an 'emerging issues' paper, summarising the major themes that arose in its conversations with stakeholders. The panel felt it needed to define what it meant by equity. 'The panel believes that a commitment to equity means that differences in educational outcomes should not be the result of differences in wealth, income, power or possessions; it is not meant to suggest that all students are the same or will achieve the same outcomes', the paper stated.[10] Bold in its clarity, this statement raised the hopes of those who believed demography should not be destiny. In conservative circles, it raised eyebrows and elicited mutterings of 'socialism' and questions about what David Gonski was up to.

Whatever ideological significance could be attributed to the expert panel's statement, it reflected a pragmatic recognition that so long as we allowed social disadvantage to play an outsized role in determining educational outcomes, we were simply failing to tap our full potential as a community. Gonski panellist Ken Boston put the matter simply: 'David Gonski believed that the key was to drive up the performance of Australian education; that the problem with the performance was disadvantage; that if we got more equity we'd get greater performance'.[11]

The power of peer effects

The 2009 PISA results graphically portrayed the social chasm dividing children in Australian schools; now the Gonski panel clearly articulated that it intended to address it. But to solve the problem, the panel had to understand its causes. Why was Australia witnessing a decline in educational outcomes, and why was social disadvantage playing a more pronounced role than it had done previously (and more than in other parts of the world)? The Gonski Report did not purport to be able to fully answer these immensely complex questions, but it did provide some critical insights.[12]

It would be natural to assume that differences between the school sectors play a role in performance and, indeed, that is what many parents believe. Equally, it is possible that some states or territories were doing a better job of running their school systems, generating better results. But, in fact, it turned out that there was little support for either of these explanations of student outcomes in the data.

In standardised tests like PISA and NAPLAN, students in the independent sector outperformed those in the Catholic sector, who, in turn, got better results, on average, than children in public schools.[13] But in its report on PISA 2009, the Australian Council for Educational Research (ACER) concluded that 'the average performance differences between sectors disappear once student and average school-level socioeconomic background is accounted for'.[14] In the same manner, a jurisdiction like the ACT outperformed one like the Northern Territory, but the differences disappeared after accounting for the contrasting circumstances of young people in those places.[15] Thus the apparent differences in outcomes between the sectors and jurisdictions did not offer any obvious insights into the country's educational predicament, other than to confirm the decisive influence of a child's social background on their success at school.

While the review was not able to provide a definitive diagnosis, over the course of 2011 a hitherto underappreciated driver of student results came into focus. A body of evidence emerged which indicated that a child's educational prospects were not only related to their parents' educational attainment, occupation and income level, but also to the socio-economic circumstances of their classmates.

In early 2011, as part of its submission to the Gonski review, the New South Wales Department of Education issued a discussion paper, which included an analysis of student achievement. Like My School, the New South Wales analysis divided students into quarters, where Quarter 1 (Q1) represented the most disadvantaged quarter of the population and Quarter 4 (Q4) was the most

Figure 2

Year 9 Department of Education and Communities students – average performance in literacy and numeracy by student and school socio-economic status quarters

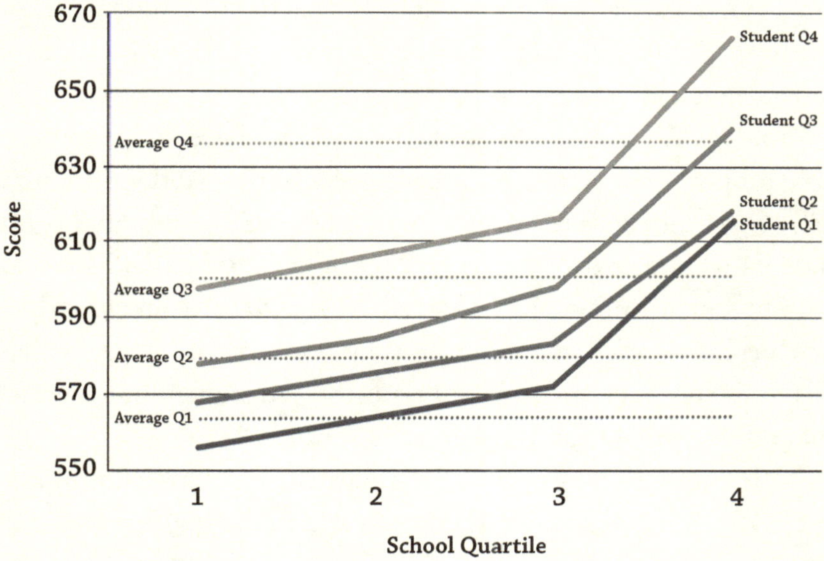

New South Wales Department of Education and Communities, *Discussion Paper: Australian School Funding Arrangements*, NSW DEC, 2011, p. 12. <drive.google.com/file/d/1cEUu9FUlTsmJHD2nGSDUdBK_dodkgLN0/view>.

privileged.[16] Examining Year 3 reading results, the New South Wales Government found that children in the most disadvantaged quarter of the population (Q1) were significantly behind their peers. But if the same children attended a school where most of their classmates were from the most advantaged quarter of the population (Q4), they averaged 30 points higher in the reading test. An eight-year-old's family situation mattered a whole lot, but so too did the social circumstances of their classmates.[17]

This research demonstrated a phenomenon that educationalists variously call the compositional effect, the neighbourhood effect or the peer effect. These terms refer to the collective effect of all the other kids at a school on a student's educational outcomes, over and above the impact of their own family circumstances. As the New South Wales Department of Education research indicated, negative peer effects are associated with students from disadvantaged social backgrounds; positive effects with students from advantaged backgrounds.

The NSW data showed that by Year 9, the effect was even more pronounced. So much so that low SES (Q1) students in high SES (Q4) schools were on average outperforming high SES (Q4) students who attended low SES (Q1) schools.[18] The data showed that student learning was impacted by the social background of their peers, represented in Figure 2 by the unbroken lines which start in School Quarter 1 (most disadvantaged student population) and end in School Quarter 4 (most advantaged).

Why does a child's peer group have such a powerful impact on their learning at school? There are various reasons. For one, it is a question of the teacher's attention. If a student is in a class with a large number of strugglers, then there is much more intensive demand for time with the teacher and they are likely to receive correspondingly less individual attention. If the strugglers also tend to be disruptive, they are then likely to absorb even more of the teacher's time and that of the class as a whole.

More subtly, the social environment can profoundly shape a child's sense of identity and motivation. Academically motivated students can bring a wealth of background knowledge to a class, contribute to a shared sense of the value of education and spur each other on to new heights. Conversely, a significant number of students who are disengaged from learning, or poorly behaved, can readily influence those around them and undermine a shared sense of purpose. And what applies to a lesson is equally resonant over a longer time horizon. If a young person is in a school where none of their classmates is considering further study as a post-school option, it becomes that much harder to imagine it as a possibility, let alone a goal to strive for.

Additionally, the profile of a class, a year group or a school will profoundly influence the curriculum. As much as teachers seek to differentiate learning experiences for individual students, they ultimately teach a group. Assessments of a group's overall ability will affect which texts are chosen, how lessons are pitched and how units are designed. Given the repeated finding that numerous years of learning can separate the highest and lowest performing students, the mix of students in a class can lead learning in very different directions.

As research discussed in the Gonski Report found, where there are lots of high-SES children, students tend to benefit from 'rigorous and demanding academic programs oriented toward university entrance exams'. For a child who might aspire to university but is at a school characterised by overwhelming disadvantage, such programs are often entirely absent.[19] In addition, the composition of a class or school also has implications for teacher recruitment and retention. Concentrating a large group of disadvantaged and low-achieving students together will also make it harder for a school to recruit and retain teachers, because teaching and learning conditions are inevitably so much more difficult. The Gonski Report found that 'concentrations of disadvantage have been demonstrated not only to impact on student performance, but also to impact on teacher morale and community alienation from the school, and result in difficulties in attracting and retaining good teachers and students'.[20]

These issues are not difficult to discern. While parents do not use the term 'peer effects' when they are chatting at the school gate or over a barbecue, the basic concept is very intuitive – and widely understood. When education researchers Craig Campbell,

VOICES FROM THE STAFFROOM: THE IMPACT OF PEERS ON STUDENT LEARNING

The power of peer effects is part of the everyday experience of educators. Retired principal Bernie Roebuck recalls how 'fellow rural principals talked about the absolute need, almost above all else, of fighting tooth and nail to try and retain as many capable, motivated students as possible. We did this because it was blatantly clear of the effect that "good kids" had on the peer group. Unquestionably, in year groups where you had a good core of such kids you could be almost guaranteed of getting better outcomes.'

A teacher in a regional New South Wales public school explains what happens when there is a large number of disadvantaged students in one class: 'You spend so much time trying to manage behaviours that you often do not have the time to attend to each student's learning needs or interests'. Another educator recalls a class in which 'three boys, in particular, had the ability, collectively or independently, to sink a lesson with disruption. The disruption coming from these three boys alone I would say conservatively took up 75 per cent of my time, hence limiting my ability to help other students'. Betty Harper, a principal in Western Sydney for many years, says: 'In a school populated with students who come to high school still far below the literacy and numeracy national benchmarks, the few who are intellectually able battle for attention'.

Another teacher in a highly disadvantaged context explains the situation his students face and what it means for his classes: 'Trauma backgrounds are common, and we often

> hear stories of domestic violence, alcoholism, and neglect at home. This often manifests in the classroom as intense emotional dysregulation: unpredictable outbursts of swearing or violence, wandering in and out of the classroom, or sullen, withdrawn, hostile behavior. Attendance is intermittent so establishing classroom routines is hard'.
>
> Peter Morgan, a school leader for a quarter of a century, relates what he found on arrival at one highly disadvantaged school: 'Verbal abuse was a more than daily occurrence, physical violence frequent. Across the school, teachers were in survival mode with low expectations, low support, employing busy work to avoid a blow up'. A teacher in a disadvantaged public school explains how the student cohort impacts on expectations: 'The majority of our students do not end up with university entrance scores, and general engagement is quite low in many classes. Attendance is patchy, and we plan our assessments around the assumption that a significant number of students will not complete all required work'. Another educator reflects on the challenge she faces in this regard: 'A common experience for me is feeling like I am never able to extend students. I feel very guilty when I can see that the work is well below their level. But if you don't cater to the students with lower academic ability, their disillusionment or frustrations have a much greater impact on the whole class'.[21]

Helen Proctor and Geoffrey Sherington interviewed parents for their 2009 book *School Choice: How parents negotiate the new school market in Australia*, the importance of peer effects was often mentioned. 'A student who is not willing to learn … can disturb the class so much that the learning of your child can be affected', one parent told the researchers. 'So you try and make sure that you take your child to a school where that is minimised as much as possible'.[22] Another parent attributed her choice of an out-of-area school for her children to the ethnic mix at the local school. 'There is predominately one element at the school that was our feeder school that I didn't want them to mix with. I am not racist by any stretch of the imagination but there is a certain element that – I don't feel that they're safe with.'[23]

Researchers have placed different emphases on the various reasons for peer effects,[24] but there is no doubt about their impact on student learning. The NSW Department of Education findings were confirmed by other state-based analyses of NAPLAN results[25] as well as analysis conducted by ACER of national PISA data. ACER found that, in fact, the social background of the other kids in the class had a bigger impact on learning than a child's own family circumstances.[26] The advantage from attending a school with a high socio-economic intake amounted to an average 33 score points – equivalent to almost a full school year of learning. As significant as this finding was, it was not new. ACER's conclusions repeated almost verbatim its report on the 2006 PISA results.

The Gonski Report neatly summarised what a wide array of research comprehensively demonstrated: 'Many international studies, as well as research using PISA and NAPLAN data, confirm that concentrations of students from certain socioeconomic groups within a school has a strong impact on the educational outcomes achieved by all students at the school. Importantly, research also suggests that this impact is more significant than the effect of an individual student's own socioeconomic status on outcomes'.[27] Finding 21 of the Gonski Report concluded that 'increased concentration of disadvantaged students in certain schools is having a significant impact on educational outcomes, particularly, but not only, in the government sector'.[28] The question facing the review was how to design a school funding system that mitigated the impacts of concentrated disadvantage on children's learning.

The second unlevel playing field: how fees, entrance tests and resourcing separated Australia's schools

To address the problem of peer effects, the Gonski review would have to frankly acknowledge the differences between the school sectors. While recognising the great diversity within each of the three school sectors, the Gonski Report observed, 'there is a disproportional number of students from the most disadvantaged backgrounds attending government schools'.[29] Public schools enrolled almost 80 per cent of students in the lowest quarter of socio-educational advantage; 85 per cent of all Indigenous students; 78 per cent of students with a funded disability; and 83 per cent of students in remote schools.[30]

The Index of Community Socio-Educational Advantage (ICSEA), used on My School, effectively places Australia's approximately 10 000 schools in a long line according to the social backgrounds of the students they serve. At one end, there are schools like Sydney Grammar where no children come from the most disadvantaged quarter of the population. At the other, there are schools in remote communities where everyone lives in poverty. Of the 3480 schools in the bottom four ICSEA deciles, 89 per cent were public schools, enrolling 94 per cent of the students at those schools.[31] The overwhelming majority of schools serving disadvantaged student communities, where the negative impact of peer effects on student outcomes was most pronounced, were public schools.

Our schools did not simply mirror the towns and suburbs in which they were located. Australia's unique hybrid education system

– some free schools, some fee-charging; some selective, others comprehensive – was sorting Australian children from the same neighbourhoods into different schools, making the concentrations of poverty or privilege much more pronounced. Australia's schools operated on an unlevel playing field: resourced and regulated in inconsistent, sharply varying and often illogical ways.

Nowhere could this have been more piercingly apparent to the Gonski panel than in Geelong, southwest of Melbourne, which they visited as part of the review. At Geelong Grammar, one of Australia's most famous and prestigious independent schools (which numbers the Prince of Wales among its alumni), over half of the children (57 per cent) came from the most advantaged quarter of Australia's student population.[32] This would have come as little surprise to the visitors from the school funding review. Meanwhile, at the neighbouring school, Northern Bay College, the proportion of children from the most advantaged quarter of Australia's student population sat at just 2 per cent. When the dux of Northern Bay, Emma Henderson, took a wrong turn shortly after getting her driver's licence, she was brought face to face with the blatant differences between the facilities offered at these two nearby schools. Approaching the grounds of Geelong Grammar, Henderson was confronted with the sight of a school that seemed to belong to another world. Geelong Grammar seemed 'like Hogwarts out of a *Harry Potter* movie', she told *The Age* newspaper in 2012. 'I felt sad because … there was clearly a lot they had that I didn't.'[33]

The differences between the two Geelong schools were not any result of their locations – they were barely seven minutes' drive apart. The chief reason that they served such dramatically different student populations was that fees at Geelong Grammar averaged over $16 000, compared to the non-compulsory annual payment of around $200 at Northern Bay College.[34] For poor families in Corio,

Geelong Grammar wasn't too far away geographically, it was simply unaffordable. As a result, nearly half (46 per cent) of the students at Northern Bay College – right next door to Geelong Grammar – came from the most disadvantaged quarter of Australian families.

By the time of the Gonski review, the exclusion of low-income and disadvantaged families from non-government schools had been publicly acknowledged by the private school authorities themselves. As early as 2004, the Executive Director of the NSW Catholic Education Commission, Brian Croke, was quite candid about the reality of the situation. Responding to research that found that two-thirds of poor Catholic students went to public schools,[35] he said: 'The Catholic school share of the poorest Catholics in the community is declining. More and more of them are going to government schools rather than Catholic schools. That is a statistical fact. What is driving that? It's affordability. Even though we think our school fees are relatively low, for many [parents] increasingly they are too high'.

In 2006, the Catholic Archbishop of Sydney, George Pell, delivered an address to the National Catholic Education Conference in which he reflected on the growing exclusion of poor Catholics from Catholic schools. 'Catholic schools are not educating most of our poor, especially at the primary level', Pell said. 'Seventy-two per cent of Catholic students from families with the lowest third of family income attend government infant/primary schools and only 19 per cent attend Catholic schools … Predominantly our schools now cater for the huge Australian middle class.'[36]

The Gonski panel witnessed what this looked like close-up when they visited Alice Springs in early 2011. At Bradshaw Primary, in the shadow of the MacDonnell Ranges, half the students were Indigenous, and on the Index of Community Socio-Educational Advantage (ICSEA), the school was in the third percentile. In the long line of Australia's schools the ICSEA represented, Bradshaw was right near the end. And when the kids at Bradshaw finished Year 6, most ended up at Centralian Middle School, where the level of disadvantage was even starker.

Alice Springs' Catholic school, Our Lady of the Sacred Heart (OLSH), ran from Kinder to Year 12. Fees at OLSH were a far cry away from the exclusive private schools in the capital cities. But they averaged a little under $3000 a year, and the difference in its student body was striking. Only a four-minute drive from Bradshaw, it placed in the 50th ICSEA percentile, making it an average Australian school in socio-economic terms. Only 13 per cent of children were Indigenous.[37] While OLSH might have been a medium-fee Catholic school, the barrier to entry was still too high for many, an obstacle that was engendering concentrations of disadvantage elsewhere. This was precisely the phenomenon that the Gonski review had identified as having such a negative impact on educational outcomes. Because few poor and disadvantaged children attended the Catholic school, and even fewer were enrolled in the town's other private school, St Philip's College, they made up a very large proportion of the students at the public school. And the evidence before the Gonski panel indicated that the character of this group of students would, in itself, have a profoundly negative impact on the educational outcomes of each individual child.

As George Pell and Brian Croke had effectively acknowledged, the Alice Springs example was broadly representative of the role of Catholic schools across Australia. In terms of the index that measured students' family backgrounds, just 7 per cent of Australia's Catholic schools were in the bottom three ICSEA deciles.

If the Gonski review was going to address the profound impact peer effects were having on student learning, it would need to examine the policy settings that were producing concentrations of disadvantaged children in some schools. While acknowledging arguments in favour of school choice, the Gonski Report pointed out that alternatives were often inaccessible: 'not all Australian parents are able to access or afford such choice in schooling, particularly those from low socioeconomic backgrounds. While some non-government schools may offer parents scholarships covering all or part of a student's fees, or may discount or waive fees due to financial hardship, these benefits are not available to all'.[38]

Like the Catholic authorities, the independent schools' peak bodies had themselves presented evidence that fees made their schools unaffordable for many Australian families. In early 2011, Geoff Newcombe, the chief executive of the Association of Independent Schools of New South Wales, reported on private polling which showed more students would have attended independent schools if fees were not an issue.[39] Because fees made them prohibitively expensive, independent schools overwhelmingly served students from well-off families. In 2010, 47 per cent of students at independent schools came from the highest SES quarter, compared to 29 per cent at Catholic schools and only 22 per cent at public schools.[40] On My School's Index of Socio-Educational Advantage, 64 per cent of independent schools were in the top three deciles, while only 7 per cent were in the bottom three deciles.[41]

The Gonski panel saw this reality in microcosm when they visited a number of schools in Bendigo, Victoria. At Girton Grammar School, only 4 per cent of the school's students came from the most disadvantaged quarter of the population. As in Alice Springs, fees were serving as a barrier that poor families sometimes struggled but mostly failed to surmount. At the same time, fees and government funding combined to give Girton Grammar a substantial advantage in total resourcing per student, adding to its allure for those who could afford the entry price. At the public school the panel visited, the total income per student was around $10 000 a year. Girton Grammar's fees were around $11 000, already giving it a financial edge of about $1000 per student. But on top of that, taxpayer support for Girton of around $7000 per student served to dramatically extend its advantage in recurrent resourcing.[42]

As the Gonski panellists contemplated this scenario, and the questions about fairness, effectiveness and efficiency it raised, it was evident that the power of peer effects added another dimension to the problem. A financial edge was inherently advantageous, but it also provided schools with a greater capacity to accrue an equally critical resource: high-performing and educationally advantaged students. Funding did not just affect a school's capacity to serve the students attending in the present year, but also its ability to attract new enrolments for the following ones. The funding advantage enjoyed by Girton Grammar gave it a greater capacity to attract enrolments through smaller class sizes, flashier buildings and a larger marketing budget. And so differences in financial resources were helping schools like Girton pull in more advantaged or academically able students, just as fees pushed others away. Fifty-four per cent of the private school's students came from the most advantaged quarter of the population, where only 22 per cent did at the public school the panel visited.[43]

Academic research suggested the link between better resourcing and enrolment growth applied generally. In a study of the impact of public funding of private schools since the 1970s, economists Chris Ryan and Louise Watson found a direct correlation between growing taxpayer funding, reduced class sizes and increased enrolments. 'Improvements in private school student:teacher ratios relative to public schools after 1979', they concluded, 'were associated with steady improvements in the enrolment share of both Catholic and independent schools'.[44]

The research on the power of peer effects had dramatic implications for the Gonski review, because what it really showed was that a student's classmates were a critical resource in their education. So truly understanding how a school was resourced would require paying attention to its human resources – students as well as staff – in addition to its financial resources. As the Gonski Report explained, 'school concentrations of high socioeconomic status students appear to be a valuable resource in terms of individual student performance, while concentrations of low socioeconomic status students are a disadvantage'.[45]

From this, it then followed that funding relativities also mattered. As long as a school like Girton had *more* resources, it could advertise smaller class sizes with more individualised attention, a greater variety of curricula and co-curricular offerings, and so on. And that would help it recruit students away from competing schools, often leaving those schools with the concentrations of disadvantage that the panel had found were so injurious to student learning. In the competition for students, the combination of public and private funding was giving a school like Girton Grammar a huge advantage in the marketplace.

If the panellists were troubled by this dynamic, their unease can only have been heightened when they visited Catherine McAuley College in Bendigo. This Catholic school was one of the examples the panel encountered of a non-government school that received more government funding (state and Commonwealth combined) than the nearby public school. The fees charged by Catherine McAuley – around $3500 a year – only served to increase this resource advantage, further enhancing the school's capacity to attract new enrolments.

While resource advantages were making some schools more attractive, and fees were making the attractive schools inaccessible to many, evidence presented to the Gonski panel also indicated that selective enrolment practices were further exacerbating the uneven spread of students across Australia's schools. Some schools

THE SECOND UNLEVEL PLAYING FIELD

The performance of schools is heavily dependent on the students they enrol, both because some children start ahead and progress faster, and because a child's learning is influenced by their peers. This means that the performance of a school is heavily impacted by the operations and behaviours of surrounding schools. If one school is able to attract most of the high-performing and educationally advantaged children in a community, another school has to enrol most of the strugglers. That school's headline academic results – and very possibly its character and morale – will be affected accordingly.

The second unlevel playing field is the term we use to refer to the uneven power of Australian schools to attract high-performing students. While **resource advantages** help some schools attract new enrolments, **unregulated fees** are often prohibitive for low-income and disadvantaged families. **Selective enrolment practices** employed by some schools, both private and public, contrast with other schools that have a set of **public obligations** that mean they are legally required to be open and free for every child from every family. These factors, which are all produced by public policy, interact with **location**. Schools very broadly reflect their location, but better-off families in poorer communities tend to seek out higher SES schools elsewhere – or relocate into the catchment of those schools. This boosts the SES of schools they seek, with a reverse impact on those they leave behind. Ninety-five per cent of students are in a school that is in competition with at least one other school.[46]

Historically, the second unlevel playing field was a consequence of – often understandable – efforts to resolve the injustices of the first unlevel playing field. Tragically, state aid was introduced in a way that allowed uneven resourcing and responsibilities to evolve and expand over time. We argue that the second unlevel playing field is a major cause of negative **peer effects** and, therefore, the decline in the educational outcomes of young Australians witnessed over the course of the 21st century.

---

were comprehensive, with a legal obligation to enrol all children in the local area, but others had complete autonomy over the entry criteria they applied.

In his submission to the review, Chris Bonnor examined how these dynamics played out in the southern New South Wales town of Wagga Wagga. At one extreme, the Riverina Anglican College ranked in the 90th percentile of Australian schools in socio-economic terms, with just 9 per cent of students from highly disadvantaged families. At the other extreme, Mount Austin High School was in the 5th percentile, with over half of its kids from highly disadvantaged backgrounds and just 2 per cent of enrolments from the most advantaged quarter of the population. In between the two extremes, Wagga Wagga Christian College was in the 69th percentile. Fees of around $5000 at Riverina Anglican College and $3000 at the Christian College were part of the reason why their student profiles looked so different to those at the public school. But fees were not only the driver of exclusion, as Bonnor pointed out in a 2011 article. 'The enrolment form for Wagga Wagga Christian College runs to fifteen pages,' he noted.

'The Riverina Anglican College, established in 1999, requires two referees, previous school reports, payment of various amounts (in addition to fees) and a parent interview. Schools such as Mount Austin High, which cannot or will not apply discriminators, have a disproportionate enrolment of low-achieving students'.[47]

Governments were funding some schools on the basis that they would enrol every child in the local area without charge, and they were funding others on the basis that they had complete autonomy over which students they would enrol and how much they would charge. The imbalance in enrolment obligations primarily existed between public and private schools. However, academically selective public schools were also drawing in a high proportion of advantaged students, compounding the concentrations of the strugglers in comprehensive public schools.

This was mostly the case in New South Wales, where around 10 per cent of secondary schools were selective – of these, half were fully selective; the other half, partially selective. In other states, selective public schools were less prevalent or did not exist at all. But where selective public schools did exist, their students came predominantly from very advantaged socio-economic backgrounds, with an average ICSEA at selective schools of 1150.[48]

As researcher Jack Keating eloquently explained, selective public schools could be understood as a response to the competition government schools faced from selective and often better-resourced non-government schools. 'The sectoral isolation and different governance, accountability and financing arrangements', Keating wrote, 'have resulted in an unequal distribution of market power between the sectors, especially in a context of rising middle class affluence. As a consequence the government sectors, that have the poorest market deal, have attempted to deliver market power internally. The means of achieving this invariably is to allow the government systems to become more internally selective ... the cost is to internally concentrate educational disadvantage and under achievement'.[49]

The consequence of selective schools acting as a magnet for gifted and advantaged students was that it was pulling those students away from local comprehensive and low-fee non-government schools, often exacerbating concentrations of disadvantage in those contexts. While selective state schools were primarily a New South Wales phenomenon, some public schools in other jurisdictions were sometimes able to exercise informal discretion over enrolments. Where highly sought-after public schools, generally located in affluent suburbs, had an excess of out-of-area applicants, they were often able to pick and choose who they would accept.

As students, as parents and even as teachers, we tend to think about schools as self-contained communities. And to some extent they are. But what the evidence before the Gonski review illustrated was that schools are also very sensitive elements in a much larger ecosystem. Changes at one school can quickly have consequences at another.

In conducting the review, the Gonski panellists were presented with an aerial view of Australia's schools in which these consequences could be discerned. Many years after their work was complete, the reality they witnessed was compellingly articulated by Julia Gillard's top education advisor, Tom Bentley. 'The combined impact of school funding and school behaviour', Bentley wrote, 'is deeply interconnected and interdependent, even when they are governed separately. The recurrent funding levels of public schools affect the way the recurrent funding levels of Catholic systemic schools are perceived. In turn, the enrolment practices of local Catholic schools influence the demographic mix of students enrolled in their neighbouring state schools. The marketing and competition for students of independent schools, whatever their quality, in turn influences the pressures and incentives experienced by local state schools. In other words, changes in resourcing, enrolment and behaviour in individual schools or sectors will affect not just each school but also on each other'.[50]

Across Australia, the under-representation of disadvantaged children in some schools was producing an over-representation at others. And this dynamic was self-perpetuating. In the 1980s, Barbara Preston, a research officer with the Victorian Secondary Teachers Association, observed that uneven resourcing and regulation was leading to a process she described as 'residualisation'.[51] Free, comprehensive schools were serving very large groups of children with acute educational needs, often with insufficient resources to meet them and adequately cope with significant social dysfunction. As a consequence, when they were able to, families would start to leave the school, moving to nearby non-government schools or, possibly, out-of-area government schools, thus heightening the over-representation of very disadvantaged children at the school. Over time, this would likely undermine the shared expectations around learning and student engagement, and chip away at teacher morale and retention. Additionally, the smaller student population would reduce economies of scale, increasing costs on a per student basis, as well as making it harder to offer a diverse curriculum. These developments would likely cause enrolments to dwindle even further, thus catalysing a vicious cycle of decline.

Over the subsequent quarter of a century, Preston's analysis could be seen playing out, gradually but inexorably, on a sectoral level. The Gonski panel found that socio-economically average students had left the government sector for Catholic schools, while high-SES students had migrated from both public and Catholic schools to independent schools.[52] Since the late 1970s, the Gonski review found, the 'tendency for parents from higher socioeconomic backgrounds to move their children from government schools to non-government schools or select-entry government schools' had produced very different student profiles across the three sectors.[53]

As students from both the middle and the top of the socio-economic ladder had gone to the non-government sector, public schools were left with an increased concentration of social disadvantage. In 1996 there had been 13 low-income children for every ten high-income kids in Australian public schools.[54] By 2006, that ratio had increased to 16 for every ten. The majority of students in public secondary schools were at a school with a below-average ICSEA score.[55]

As the Gonski panellists considered this dynamic in places like Geelong, Bendigo, Wagga Wagga and Alice Springs, it was evident that one of the main attractions of schools like Geelong Grammar, Girton Grammar, Riverina Anglican College or Our Lady of the Sacred Heart was the presence of an affluent and educated peer group. The successful schools in the competition for the 'right' students would almost certainly succeed more generally, with high academic results and further enrolment growth. Thus Australian schools competed intensely to attract high-SES students. But by its nature, this meant that Australian schools were not competing for the expensive-to-educate students – the kids who started school behind their peers, the Year 9 students who were working at a Year 5 level – in order to turn their lives around. They were not competing on their ability to progress the learning of the most disadvantaged children, but rather to attract the custom of the most advantaged.

A successful strategy of attracting high-SES students at the individual school level, applied over and over again throughout the country, added up to a recipe for national disaster. The most urgent work – the most challenging and important work – was left to the 'losers' in the competition for students: the schools that had to serve all children because that was their mission and legal obligation. Not only did those schools have to bear this burden alone, their work was all the more difficult because of the scale of social disadvantage they had to cope with.

And governments were adding fuel to the fire. By allowing some publicly funded schools to pick and choose which students they served, to set fees as they please and to enjoy resource advantages over their competitors, they were helping some schools recruit the 'right' students and thereby compounding the problems of the others. The Gonski Report summarised the problem the expert panel faced in the following terms:

> Some parts of the community have voiced concern about the consequence of Australia's competitive market for school education. These concerns centre on the alleged segregation of students into schools with markedly differing socioeconomic compositions, largely based on the ability and willingness of parents to pay fees. This segregation is considered to have been exacerbated by the government sector's gradual loss in market share to the non-government sector, resulting in the government sector educating an increasing proportion of educationally disadvantaged students. It is suggested that this has impacted on the capacity of some government schools to provide a quality education for all students.[56]

If the Gonski review was going to get to the root causes of our educational malaise, it would have to revisit the series of unexamined assumptions that had prevailed ever since the Karmel report in 1973.

Levelling the playing field? Gonski links resourcing and regulation

In late December 2010, David Gonski gave a remarkable interview to the *Sydney Morning Herald*. In it, he reported an argument that had been put to the expert panel: that strict obligations should be imposed on non-government schools in receipt of significant levels of public funding. Specifically, the case had been made that governments should regulate private school fees. 'There have been questions as to (a) whether schools that receive government funding should be giving full details of their activities and (b) some have asked, if they are getting government funding, should they have some sort of regulatory environment in terms of their fee structure', Gonski told the *Herald*. 'There is a (c)', he added, 'and that is: does the level of funding to the school maybe have different grades? … If you get only a small amount of funding, maybe you don't have all of those requirements. If you get a lot of funding, maybe you do'.[57]

The Gonski review had found that concentrations of social disadvantage were having a profoundly negative effect on student outcomes. What the panel had seen suggested that they needed to find a way of levelling the playing field on which Australian schools operated. And this would involve challenging the basic assumptions of the Karmel paradigm: the autonomy of private schools over fee and enrolment policies; and the role of public funding in producing large variations in the resources that schools had at their disposal.

In the 2010 *SMH* interview, Gonski made it clear that he was not endorsing any of the options that he was floating. The panel, after all, was still a year away from completing its report. But it is inconceivable that an operator as formidable and as experienced as David Gonski did not know what he was doing. He was not going to articulate an idea in public unless he was giving it serious consideration, especially a proposal such as this which had the potential to spark significant controversy. What was David Gonski thinking? Where did these ideas come from?

Gonski did not tell the newspaper who had put these views to the panel. But following his appointment to chair the funding review, he met with the Secretary of the Department of Prime Minister and Cabinet, Terry Moran.[58] In the early 2000s, Moran had headed up the Victorian Department of Premier and Cabinet under the Labor Premier, Steve Bracks, where he had commissioned a report called *Governments Working Together* which proposed significant changes to how schools were funded. Moran pointed to this report and advocated for its prescriptions when he met with David Gonski. Among the proposals laid out in that report was the following:

> Schools receiving the highest levels of government funding would be required to provide open access to students from the whole community, or a substantial group in the community (e.g. to those of a particular religion), on a non-exclusive basis – that is, no prospective student would be barred by school-instituted academic prerequisites, fees (schools would need to put in place arrangements for exempting families with limited resources from paying fees), or other restrictions.[59]

In other words, non-government schools that were mostly funded by taxpayers would be obligated to enrol all comers in the local area, as public schools did, with allowances made in accordance with the school's special ethos.

Moran's model sounded a lot like what Gonski would float publicly a couple of days before Christmas, 2010. The Victorian proposal even included variations in public obligations corresponding to different levels of public funding. 'Schools receiving lower levels of government funding', it stated, 'would be required to hold a significant proportion of their places for students who would otherwise be excluded because of an inability to pay fees or other restrictions; selection for these places would be on the basis of an approved access policy'.[60]

In addition to the proposals to regulate school fees, the *Governments Working Together* report proposed a funding model that the Gonski review would ultimately replicate: a baseline per student amount; funding loadings for disadvantaged students; additional loadings for schools which face greater costs because of location or size; and adjustment of actual government funding for private schools in inverse proportion to their fee income.[61]

But the Bracks Government report was not the only resource that offered the Gonski panel possible solutions to the problem of the unlevel playing field. A diverse range of researchers, stakeholders and policymakers also challenged them to think along these lines. In July 2010, at the third meeting of the Gonski review panel, the panellists received a briefing from Lyndsay Connors and Jim McMorrow, two figures with enormous experience in Australian education. McMorrow had served in very senior roles in both the New South Wales Department of Education and the National Catholic Education Commission, while Connors had been on the Commonwealth Schools Commission in the 1980s and chaired the Schools Council that replaced it.[62] Connors and McMorrow brought a 100-page report to the Gonski review meeting, setting out an entirely new funding model for Australian schools, which took as its starting point a simple but striking observation: government funding to private schools had increased to the point that governments fully covered the costs of the teaching workforce in 95 per cent of all Australian schools. Connors and McMorrow saw in this reality grounds for establishing 'a common framework for determining schools' entitlement to such teachers, as assessed against their relative workloads, in order to provide quality teaching and learning for the students they enrol'.[63]

The approach advocated by Connors and McMorrow would mean that teachers – whose salaries were all paid by the taxpayer, in public and private schools alike – would be allocated to schools according to the nature and scale of the educational task they faced. The two veterans of Australian education proposed that non-government schools should continue to be free to operate according to their particular religious or philosophical ethos, but that access would be regulated by 'agreements with governments on fee levels'.[64] Fee increases would have to be demonstrated to be necessary. The model also envisaged increased cooperation and coordination across sectors to ensure that the establishment of new schools, and closure of old ones, would respond to demographic changes efficiently and effectively, maximising economies of scale.

At the same meeting in July 2010, the panel also heard from Professor Jack Keating. Keating mattered. Not only was he one of the pre-eminent scholars in Australia when it came to the resourcing and regulation of schools, he was very well connected in Labor circles, a close friend of Steve Bracks. Also in attendance for Keating's presentation were Simon Crean, who became education minister when Julia Gillard became Prime Minister, and Tom Bentley, the Prime Minister's top education advisor.[65] Keating spoke to the panel about his report 'Resourcing Schools in Australia',[66] which explained that although substantial public funding of church schools was typical across OECD countries, Australia was unique in giving those schools complete autonomy in relation to fees and enrolment practices. Pointing to the example of the Netherlands, where 'the majority of schools are under the legal ownership of the churches, but are subject to the same levels of government direction as the publicly owned schools', as well as countries like Canada and New Zealand, Keating highlighted that the international norm was for public funding to be accompanied by reciprocal obligations.[67] Keating's perspective was especially pertinent as the review's terms of reference invited the panel to consider relevant overseas examples.[68]

As the Gonski panel continued its work, questions about the unique autonomy of Australia's non-government school sector were raised from other directions. For its part, in 2008 the Australian Secondary Principals' Association had advocated a model with two types of non-government school. Non-government schools that received taxpayer funding would have their fees capped and face a range of other accountabilities. Alternatively, non-government schools could continue to set fees as they wished and enrol students as they pleased but would receive no government funding.[69]

Meanwhile, Christian Schools Australia (the peak body for around 130 mostly low-fee independent schools) called for free, fully publicly funded religious schools, stating that 'We believe it is time to consider "fully funded" non-government schools as part of the funding mix'.[70] Acknowledging that 'even with an affordable fee structure faith-based schooling is beyond the financial capacity of many families',[71] and that there are limits on the capacity of non-government schools to provide fee concessions for families in challenging financial circumstances, Christian Schools Australia's submission proposed that 'community-based non-profit organisations could be licensed by government to provide educational services to meet specific needs in an identified location, with funding equivalent to that provided for educational services in government run (state) schools in a similar situation'.[72] For inspiration on how full public funding could be reconciled with a schools' religious ethos, the submission suggested that the panel look to places like New Zealand, where compromises had been found.[73]

Having pinpointed the problem of peer effects, the Gonski review had now been presented with a range of possible solutions.

What these arguments and alternatives all had in common was an ambition to alleviate the very uneven spread of students across Australian schools, reducing the tendency for disadvantaged kids to be crowded into the same classrooms as each other. Thus each of these solutions sought to address the root cause of the problem by revisiting the basic assumptions underlying Australia's dual system of schools, some fee-charging and exclusive, others free and comprehensive. They offered ways of levelling the playing field on which Australian schools operate.

A renovation of the Karmel paradigm: Gonski recommends more money where it is needed most

In the final result, the Gonski Report did not address the contradictions at the heart of our education system. The centrepiece of the report was the recommendation that recurrent funding of schools be based on a new schooling resource standard, a rigorous measure of the educational needs of individual students. This was a vitally important proposal, and it included increased funding to address the challenges created by peer effects. But the Gonski Report left the structural elements of the unlevel playing field largely unexamined and unchallenged, and instead advocated additional expenditure to mitigate and ameliorate their unfortunate consequences. What the Gonski Report was proposing was a renovation, but the Karmel paradigm would be left in place.

The signature reform and central argument of the report was elegantly encapsulated by panellist Ken Boston, a former Director-General of the New South Wales Department of Education. Boston described 'the schools at the lower end of both the scale of aggregated social disadvantage and the scale of educational performance' as 'the emergency wards of Australian education'.[74] As with medical conditions left untreated, education problems if allowed to persist will only grow worse. With social disadvantage comes acute learning difficulties which, if left unaddressed, will go on to produce a whole host of new challenges. Therefore, diagnosis and intervention are required to ensure all children have the opportunity to succeed at school. The immediate costs of the requisite investment are far outweighed by the long-term benefits, both for the young people directly affected and for society as a whole.

The proposed schooling resource standard would be comprised of a baseline per capita amount for all students, accompanied by funding loadings to meet the additional costs associated with school size and location and student characteristics including socio-economic status, Indigeneity, disability and English language proficiency. The funding loadings meant that additional resourcing would automatically follow students who were in one or more categories of disadvantage demonstrated to have a negative impact on student outcomes.

This additional support would be built into recurrent funding rather than based on special purpose and time-limited programs. The 'base plus loading' model offered a consistent and comprehensive basis for responding to educational need, a way of ensuring that the emergency wards of Australian education would be adequately equipped for the task they faced. The design of the loadings responded to the reality that many young Australians experience compounded disadvantage across multiple categories of disadvantage. An Aboriginal child in a remote location would likely come from a low-income family, and very possibly would have a disability and low English proficiency. Each form of disadvantage represented an impediment to success at school, and the Gonski panel's resource standard recognised this.

This was an urgent and essential reform. Additional expenditure was absolutely critical to meeting the needs of children across

Table 1

Schooling resource standard loadings – indicative ranges

	From (lower end of range)	to (upper end of range)
School size and location	**10%** for medium-sized schools in remote locations	**100%** for very small schools in very remote locations
Low socioeconomic status	**10%** for each low SES student in schools with under 10% of students in the lowest SES quarter	**50%** for each low SES student in schools with more than 75% of students in the lowest SES quarter
Indigeneity	**40%** for each Indigenous student in schools with between 5% and 25% of students who are Indigenous	**100%** for each Indigenous student in schools with more than 75% of students who are Indigenous
Limited English and language proficiency	**15%** for each student with limited English proficiency	**25%** for each student with limited English proficiency (for example, recently arrived refugees)

SOURCE D Gonski et al., *Review of Funding for Schooling: Final report*, Federal Department of Education, Employment and Workplace Relations, Canberra, December 2011, p. 169.

Australia. But the resource standard also broke new ground in policy terms, embedding a response to the power of peer effects in the design of Australia's school funding system. The Gonski panel not only recommended funding loadings for various categories of disadvantage, but that the size of the loading should expand as the population of disadvantaged students in a school increases. For instance, the panel proposed that the additional funding loading for students from low socio-economic status backgrounds should range from 10 to 50 per cent of the baseline per capita amount, growing along with the number of other low SES students at the school. The size of the loading would expand in recognition of the acute challenges associated with concentrations of disadvantage. Schools where half or more of the students were from disadvantaged backgrounds needed resources to accomplish things which other schools could take for granted: to establish norms around attendance and a culture of positive behaviour; to create community connections with the school; to help students make strong links with post-school possibilities; to recruit and retain staff, and to train them for the intense challenges they would respond to day in, day out.

The Gonski panel's proposal was a superb recommendation, reflecting nuanced consideration of educational research, the realities on the ground, and what governments could do to address them. But it was a palliative response, not a cure. If mostly tacitly, the Gonski Report endorsed the core elements of the unlevel playing field that had defined Australian schooling for the previous half century. The forces that were increasingly isolating students from different backgrounds from each other were not challenged. Quite the opposite. In ways, they were further consolidated. Under the report's recommendations, there would continue to be great disparities in the total resources available at schools that were otherwise alike (and often pitted in competition with each other). Those schools would continue to be subject to very different regulations, and face sharply contrasting responsibilities and obligations. While some schools would be legally required to be open to all comers, others would face no rules regarding student selection and exclusion. While all schools received public funding, some would be free and others would face no limit on the fees that they could charge.

Taxpayer funding with no strings attached: Gonski endorses the policies that had produced the unlevel playing field

When private schools receive money from governments, they have a choice: they can use the money to make their school more accessible (by reducing fees) or more attractive (by buying more teachers and better buildings). Governments, in turn, can influence that choice: they can, if they so decide, help to ensure that non-government schools use funding that is drawn *from* the whole community to make their schools more accessible *to* the whole community. In their review, the Gonski panel heard a range of proposals to regulate private school fees to achieve this purpose. The panel appeared to give these arguments a sympathetic hearing and extend them serious consideration. Indeed David Gonski himself even floated the possibility publicly. And yet when the final report ultimately appeared in February 2012, all sign of these deliberations had vanished without a trace. It turned out that the Gonski panel had embraced and endorsed the Howard Government policy that had been responsible for soaring school fees across the country over the previous decade.

There was no missing what was happening. An internal review by the Department of Education conducted under the Howard Government in 2006 found that even the beneficiaries of the especially generous 'funding maintained' (FM) arrangements were hiking fees at an astronomical rate. The analysis revealed that '42 per cent of FM schools increased their fees by more than 40 per cent during the period 2000–2004', while 'the number of FM schools with annual fees below $2,500 fell by 24 per cent'.[75]

Reports about soaring school fees were a fixture of the nation's newspapers. Shortly before the Gonski review was announced, in December 2009, *Sydney Morning Herald* reporter Anna Patty revealed that 'Private schools are raising their fees by as much as five times the inflation rate of 1.3 per cent. This despite a 32 per cent increase in federal funding, which will exceed $26 billion over four years.'[76] A year later, Patty found that private schools just kept on getting more expensive: 'Of NSW's 20 most expensive schools, the 17 that provided full details lifted fees by an average of 102 per cent between 2001 and 2011'.[77] That compared to inflation of 37 per cent over the same period, and was over double the rate of growth in teachers' salaries.[78]

The Gonski panel saw this phenomenon of ever-increasing fees in the schools they visited around the country. At Geelong Grammar and SCEGGS Darlinghurst, fees had averaged around $14 000 in the year 2000.[79] By the time the Gonski panel visited, they were double that at both schools. Fees were rising much faster than inflation, and private schools were becoming less and less affordable for low-income families. And none of this was a coincidence. It was the direct result of changes introduced by the Howard Government at the turn of the century.

Before John Howard came to power, private school funding had been based on a measure of a school's actual private income (from fees and other sources) called the Education Resources Index (ERI). The ERI meant that when a school received more income from fees, it would move into a higher category and receive less taxpayer funding. Independent schools disliked the ERI because it presented them with a trade-off: private schools could increase fees, but as their private income grew they would eventually move into a new funding category at which point taxpayer funding decreased. This reduced the benefit from raising fees, so fees grew more slowly than they would have done otherwise. But it also placed a limit on the total funding – from both public and private sources – potentially available to non-government schools. This is what independent schools disliked.

When Howard Government Education Minister David Kemp announced his school funding reforms in 1999, hedeclared he would 'remove disincentives to private investment in education'.[80] Abstract and technical-sounding, with a double negative thrown in, the meaning of this phrase was easy to miss. But what Kemp meant was that his new system would remove the trade-off presented by the ERI. Now private schools could raise fees as much as they liked without losing any government funding. Kemp's new scheme was called the Socio-economic Status (SES) model. It replaced the ERI's measure of actual school income with a measure of what the parents at a given non-government school were capable of paying (based on census data about income and occupation). Like the ERI, public funding still tapered away as the parent community grew wealthier. But the new SES model allowed private schools to increase fees as high as the market was willing to bear – without incurring a corresponding reduction in public funding. And so, as the 20th century came to a close, the auction began, and over the course of a decade parents had been bidding up the price of a private school education higher and higher. And for low- and medium-income families these schools had become more out of reach than ever.

In early 2011, as the Gonski review was underway, *The Australian*'s Justine Ferrari conducted a survey of fee increases in the wealthiest private schools across the country and found that they were once again going up by 5 to 6 per cent for the next school year.[81] Instead of using extra taxpayer funding to reduce fees, private schools were offering an ever more abundantly resourced educational experience for those who could afford it. This could be seen in the explanations school principals were offering for their ever-increasing fees. Parents of students at the exclusive Sydney school Ascham, for instance, received a letter telling them: 'At Ascham, we are committed to attracting and retaining the best teachers for your daughters, to keep our pupil–teacher ratio low and to offer students a wide choice of subjects'. The letter was accompanied by a notice that there would be a $1600 increase in tuition fees for the new school year.[82]

When Adelaide's Scotch College raised its fees by almost 7 per cent at the end of 2010, the school's finance manager, Trevor Johnson, told *The Australian* that 'the key is we pride ourselves on having, if not the best, then most of the best teachers in South Australia, and we want to keep them'.[83] The principal of Prince Alfred College, also in Adelaide, attributed a similar jump in fees to capital works, as well as teacher salaries. 'The redevelopment of our music and technology areas over the vacation period', the principal explained, 'will significantly improve the learning experience for boys'.[84]

The Gonski panel had no illusions about what was going on. 'The shift to the SES funding model', the report stated, 'and with it funding need based on capacity to contribute, occurred because it was believed that it would … minimis[e] disincentives for parents to invest in their childrens' [*sic*] schools'.[85] The report also recorded that private schools wanted the Howard policy to stay in place, so they could continue to raise fees as they pleased. 'Many submissions from the independent sector supported the continued use of SES. In particular, it was said to minimise disincentives for private investment in schooling.'[86]

The panel understood the policy and could see the consequences. And, it turned out, it liked what it saw. The overriding priority expressed in the report was that public funding continue to be provided to non-government schools in a manner that did not artificially constrain the fees they were able to charge. A funding formula should 'preserve incentives for parents to invest in the education of their children where they choose to and are able to do so', the report declared, echoing the language of David Kemp and the independent schools sector.[87] An SES-style measure of capacity to contribute, the report argued, 'provides stronger incentives for private investment by parents and others'. Conversely, 'linking public funding to the actual private contribution [as the ERI did] would distort these incentives'.[88]

The Gonski review had ensured the level of taxpayer contribution to private schools remained untouched. Now it had delivered on another major demand of the non-government sector. In the words of Geoff Newcombe, following the report's release, 'Gonski's model would also allow schools to raise private income through fees, donations and fundraising without suffering any penalty through loss of government funding'.[89]

This raised questions about the basic goals of government funding of non-government schools. Wasn't the purpose of government funding of private schools to improve affordability? Wasn't the objective to increase the choices families had available to them? It seemed not. The Gonski panel appeared to recognise that there was a tension between its endorsement of unrestrained fee growth and its ambition that educational outcomes would not be the result of differences in income, wealth, power or possessions. But, although the final report acknowledges the tension, the panel did not resolve it in any meaningful way.

It was as though the part of the report that highlighted the power of peer effects, and the part on private school fees, were written by two different panels. Public funding, combined with growing fee income, was providing some schools with net resource advantages, helping them attract children from middle- and high-income backgrounds, while ever-increasing fees put those schools further and further beyond the reach of low-income families. In recommending more of the same, the Gonski Report offered a prescription that would serve to compound the concentrations of social disadvantage that it had elsewhere identified as a major driver of declining educational outcomes.

The same pragmatism that had led the Gonski panel to largely adhere to the 'no school loses a dollar' demand could also explain its support of no-strings-attached subsidies. But, in reality, it appears that the laissez-faire approach to private school fees resulted more from a failure to join the dots. When asked about this, David Gonski commented that 'I don't even know that anybody actually argued the question that the government money would make these independent or non-government schools more accessible to students'. He went on to say: 'I'm not even sure that anybody made it, and I don't really believe in it'.[90]

The Gonski Report's failure to address the policies that had created an unlevel playing field was also evident in its defence of non-government sector autonomy over enrolment practices. The report did not question the right of non-government schools to expel troublesome students, suggesting only that they 'should have welfare policies that seek to find the most appropriate learning environment' for 'students who are unable to remain'.[91] For the principals and teachers who ended up being responsible for the challenging students other schools did not want, it might not have been clear whether the report was offering a band-aid solution, or rubbing salt in the wound.

'The panel does not advocate for incentives that encourage students to move between schools to "even out" the distribution of disadvantage', the report declared.[92] The relevant question concerned how fees, enrolment practices and resource disparities – all heavily influenced by public policy – had been inducing students to move between schools for decades. The report's statement, with its implicit rejection of affirmative action and the busing programs associated with desegregation in the United States, reflected its failure to grapple with how existing policies were producing concentrations of disadvantage in Australian schools.

Taking concentrations of disadvantage as a given, the Gonski panel hoped only to ameliorate their consequences.[93] While the additional resourcing was urgently needed, it also represented a contradiction in terms of both education and fiscal policy: a contradiction that had been pointed out while the review was still underway. In September 2011, Professor Richard Teese summed it up succinctly: 'Firstly, there is the cost of migrating students out of local catchments (financing choice). Secondly, there is the cost of seeking to compensate children who are "left behind" (financing equity)'.[94]

Based on economic modelling of the review's recommendations, implementation of the schooling resource standard in 2009 would have involved an additional cost to governments, both state and federal, of $5 billion – a 15 per cent increase in recurrent expenditure.[95] The risk of publishing the $5 billion figure in the final report was that the big bucks would overshadow the principles and methodology behind a needs-based resourcing standard. The report would be viewed as just being about more money rather than what it was really about: basing expenditure on an explicit educational rationale. But the modelling had been done, and there would be an inevitable demand to know how much was needed to implement the recommendations. As things turned out, media attention immediately zeroed in on the extra billions the report was calling for. And yet the confusion about the report's true meaning went beyond its presentation.

A benign modification of the status quo

There was a dissonance at the heart of the Gonski Report. On the one hand, it acknowledged that to concentrate disadvantaged children together in the same schools and classrooms was to undermine their educational prospects. On the other, it endorsed policy settings that were generating those concentrations or exacerbating them. Those aspects concerning how schools were resourced and regulated, which were making them even more separate and segregated than the communities in which they were situated, remained unaddressed.

The schooling resource standard recommended by the Gonski Report would be applied across sectors and schools with very different obligations to enrol all children and very different capacities to raise additional revenue from private sources. That meant that the forces which were increasingly driving disadvantaged young Australians into the same schools and classrooms, with such negative effects on their learning, would continue unabated. The report envisaged the possibility of fully publicly funded private schools but only in very rare circumstances, such as remote Indigenous schools.[96] It was not a recommendation concerning Australian schools in general.

There was one significant exception to Gonski's endorsement of the status quo. Following the proposals made in the 2004 *Governments Working Together* report,[97] and in line with recommendations advanced by Connors and McMorrow and others, the Gonski Report recommended the establishment of school planning authorities in each state. These bodies would ensure cross-sectoral collaboration and planning concerning school openings, closures and infrastructure expenditure. 'School Planning Authorities with government and non-government sector representation should be established within each jurisdiction and work to develop a coordinated approach to planning for new schools and school growth', the report recommended.[98] The goal was to respond to demographic change and community demand in an efficient and educationally effective manner, thereby minimising the harmful effects on school communities of untrammelled and uncoordinated competition.

But by and large there was little ambition to level the playing field. The optimistic scenario was that a speedy and significant injection of resources could help. The Gonski Report included a fleeting reference to the possibility that adequately resourcing schools for the students they served could help them attract new enrolments. 'Increased investment in schools with concentrations of disadvantage can also be used to help schools introduce programs that will make them more attractive to higher socioeconomic status families', the report noted.[99]

But the other possibility was that the implementation of Gonski's recommendations would preserve arbitrary differences in enrolment practices across sectors; consolidate and expand the advantages in net resourcing at some non-government schools; and allow private school fees to continue to grow and become more prohibitive. In so doing, its prescriptions would allow our schools to become increasingly defined by either poverty or privilege, and the root causes of educational underachievement would remain unaddressed.

2011: YEAR 4

Looking back on their time at primary school many years later, Kim and Maria saw these as the golden years. They loved their country town primary school. What was not to like? Some classrooms were even air-conditioned. Their teachers were pretty good and most lived in the town. This was an extra bonus for the locals and for community life.

The teachers were conscious of the challenges faced by many of the kids at school. There wasn't much extra support for those falling behind. Extra funding would have been a bonus, but even getting teachers, and support teachers, to more distant and disadvantaged schools was getting harder. Maybe that review announced last year might make sure they got the teachers they needed? As it was, half a dozen parents were worried that their children might be held back by the strugglers, and they sent their kids on the bus each day to school in Rivertown, half an hour away. *(To be continued ...)*

4

A troubled birth (2012)

> I had a strong conviction that we needed to have a well-resourced and expanding public education system, and I was surprised to find that to some extent that wasn't shared universally in the Cabinet.[1]
>
> *Peter Garrett, Minister for School Education, Early Childhood and Youth (2010–13), 2020*

'There were moments during that period when [the Gonski Report] came out that I couldn't walk down the street in the centre of Sydney without somebody tapping me on the shoulder and saying "bravo"', reflects David Gonski a decade later. 'People loved the idea of the formula. They loved the idea of state and federal governments coming together, and they loved the idea of looking after the disadvantaged.'[2]

David Gonski's argument that what we were doing wasn't working quickly ascended to the level of orthodoxy, and the spotlight that the report placed on the troubling and growing gap in the educational outcomes of Australian children soon became the starting point for discussion. 'Even if nothing else happens', wrote the educational historian Helen Proctor in late February 2012, 'the Gonski review panel has already achieved a minor miracle. As someone who has been following the school-funding debate for years, I have been amazed by the outbreak of goodwill since the report's release – it's been nearly universal'.[3]

When in April 2012 the Liberal premier of New South Wales, Barry O'Farrell, endorsed the report, he provided the strongest indication yet of Gonski's potential to transcend hardened partisan divisions. 'I think it's a formula that both benefits public education and non-government education', O'Farrell said. 'And it's a formula that we would dismiss at our own peril.'[4]

The head of the Australian Education Union, Angelo Gavrielatos, had met with David Gonski before the review's findings were announced. 'Angelo', Gonski had asked him, 'what if I told you that the cost is somewhere in the order of five billion, and that you will get 75 per cent of it?' 'I said to him,' recalls Gavrielatos, '"Well, if you told me that, I'd kiss you"'. The official statement from the Australian Education Union was less exuberant, but no less enthusiastic: 'We now have a once in a generation chance to get school funding right ... the greatest need is in public schools where the required investment is around $3.8 billion a year'.[5]

The Gonski Report was finally published on 20 February 2012. As chance would have it, this was Gavrielatos' birthday. 'It was my birthday present', Gavrielatos says. But the celebrations were short-lived. 'That morning I was doing radio – talking it right up, so there's no rewriting of it', comments Gavrielatos. 'All of a sudden, when [Julia Gillard] releases the report – what just happened? Nothing, nothing! We were scrambling, saying, "Look, what's happening here?"'[6]

At a joint press conference with David Gonski and Peter Garrett to launch the report, Prime Minister Gillard declined to offer even in-principle support for its recommendations. 'We think that this is a good insight into a new approach to school funding', the Prime Minister observed half-heartedly, adding that funding loadings for disadvantaged students offered 'a good insight, too'.[7] Three months after David Gonski had handed the Prime Minister the final report of an 18-month-long review, it was hardly a ringing endorsement.

'Gillard fails to back school funding recommendations' ran the headline in *The Australian* – a write-up that could hardly have surprised the Prime Minister's media team.[8] A bemused Justine Ferrari wrote that 'Gillard refused to be drawn on any details, refused to rule anything in or out, refused to support any of the review's recommendations even in principle'.[9]

The next day, Prime Minister Gillard and Minister Garrett went to Our Lady of the Rosary Primary School in Western Sydney to spruik the government's vision for school funding. But after a few comments about slipping standards and doing more than throwing money at the problem, the assembled press pack quickly turned to murmurings of a leadership challenge: 'Will you be holding talks with Kevin Rudd about the leadership?' one journalist asked Gillard. 'Do you want a pledge of loyalty from the Foreign Minister?' inquired another.[10]

The following day, in an early morning press conference in New York, perfectly timed for the evening news back in Australia, Rudd announced his resignation as foreign minister. By the time he made his first bid to return to the prime ministership a week later, Julia Gillard, the government and the headlines had well and truly moved on, leaving the Gonski Report behind. The elaborate machinery for further consultation, including Council of Australian Government working groups, a ministerial reference group and forums across the country with families, teachers, principals and the wider community, soon came to be seen as a review of the review – and a substitute for action.[11]

As education minister, Peter Garrett was in charge of this process. But it was not a gig the Midnight Oil frontman was excited about: 'The problem with this approach was that extending the negotiations almost indefinitely gave space to those who wanted to sabotage the reform', he reflected later. 'It also gave rise to the impression that the government wasn't fully committed and risked jeopardising the effort if Rudd should take the leadership again and abandon the model, as he had, in private conversations, suggested could happen. And what if', Garrett fretted, 'we lost government before the new arrangements had been sufficiently bedded down?'[12]

By May, when there was still little sign of concrete action, Gonski panellist Ken Boston spoke out publicly, calling for legislation to turn the report's recommendations into reality.[13] He was soon joined by fellow Gonski panel member, and former ALP national president, Carmen Lawrence, who warned that any further delay would stall the momentum that had been created by the review. 'This will eventually mean the Gonski Report will disappear unfortunately', Lawrence told an audience at La Trobe University the same month, noting that the panel had continuously liaised with the Gillard Government over the previous two years. Lawrence didn't pull any punches in expressing her frustration: 'I'm mystified. I was disappointed the government didn't say on day one: "This is what we are going to do" and step it out over five to 10 years'.[14]

Overshadowed by the Rudd–Gillard wars, the Gonski Report had been knocked off the front pages. Now, as the government continued to delay, the teachers' unions grew increasingly concerned that the report would be left on the shelf to gather dust. The question was quickly becoming not when, but if any of the report's recommendations would be taken up. Angelo Gavrielatos and his comrades were concerned that the vacuum created by the government's inaction would allow others to set the agenda.

When the Australian Education Union commissioned research, it found that although public awareness of the Gonski Report was low, there was significant support for the recommendations once they were explained. Gavrielatos spoke with his media advisor, Mark Robinson. They agreed they needed a big campaign that would make the findings of the Gonski Report famous. 'We knew it would have to be reheated in a big way as an issue', Robinson says, 'and it would take a comprehensive national campaign to do that and build the support necessary to convince the ALP to deliver the funding recommended'.[15] Gavrielatos agreed that Robinson would talk to some creative agencies about how to brand the campaign. 'So he came back after a week or two', recounts Gavrielatos. 'And he says, "Mate, they've come up with some material: 'I Give a Gonski.'" And I said, "We pay for this? Are you serious? Are you serious? No. It's not happening". He said, "Mate, just calm down. Don't rule it out". For about a two-week period, I don't know how many walks around the block we had. And he … he convinced me.'[16]

'Look, if his name was Smith, it wouldn't have worked', says Gavrielatos. '"I Give a Smithie" wouldn't have worked. But it was quirky. And these things are good luck, good fortune as much as anything else. And, you know, it worked. Gonski became a name, a verb, an adjective.' Later on, Gavrielatos would raise the union's campaign in a telephone conversation with David Gonski. 'By the way, I should apologise that I've besmirched your family name,' the union chief told the head of the funding review. But David Gonski was untroubled by all the attention – 'Angelo, I think it's marvellous', was his reply.[17]

The 'I Give a Gonski' campaign was launched in June 2012.[18] As television ads began running in prime time, tens of thousands of people joined up online and education union members began letterboxing voters in marginal seats. The campaign enjoyed an early win when crossbench MPs Andrew Wilkie, Tony Windsor and Rob Oakeshott came out in public support.[19] It was now clear the government had the numbers to get the reforms through parliament. All that was needed was the will.

Some Labor MPs were starting to get restless, beginning to question why the government was taking so long.[20] Backbencher

Steve Georganas declared he 'Gave a Gonski' on Facebook, while Queensland MP Shayne Neumann spoke in parliament in support of the reforms, and half a dozen other Labor MPs did likewise. 'There would be a significant number of MPs who think this is core Labor business and should have been legislated', said Labor MP Stephen Jones.[21] In mid-July, the NSW ALP State Conference passed a resolution, moved and seconded by former state education ministers Carmel Tebbutt and Verity Firth, calling on the federal government to enact the Gonski reforms as a matter of priority.[22]

Adding to the pressure, the heads of the Smith Family and Australian Council of Social Services teamed up with the CEOs of Westpac and the Business Council of Australia in a joint call for the government to deliver school funding reform.[23] And the Prime Minister began to find herself accosted by Gonski supporters demanding action. At a community cabinet meeting in Brisbane in July 2012, there were three questions posed about the review in the space of an hour: 'What is stopping the implementation of the Gonski Report?' one woman asked the Prime Minister. 'It's so important, we need you guys to get on board.'[24]

'What is stopping the implementation of the Gonski Report?' What the Prime Minister thought but did not say

In response, Gillard could point out that additional technical work was required, as the Gonski Report itself had stated. It was also true that the extension of the existing funding arrangements, announced during the heat of the 2010 election, meant that the new funding system would not begin until 2014, giving the government time to play with. But none of this explained why Prime Minister Gillard still refused to offer even in-principle support for the review she had commissioned. Nor did it explain why the government was so reluctant to vocally make the case for increasing funding to disadvantaged schools.

The real reason that the government was delaying was the budget situation. 'Internally … there was turmoil over where the money would come from to pay for all this', Julia Gillard explained in her memoir. 'The government was in full fiscal-consolidation mode. Government revenues were plummeting against Treasury's predictions. The aftermath of the GFC and the strong Australian dollar put our nation into new economic terrain and the consequences for the budget were both large and unpredictable.'[25] To complicate matters further, the Gillard Government was also committed to another social reform with a big price tag: the National Disability Insurance Scheme. Some inside the government felt that, in the circumstances, they couldn't do both.

But what gave the fiscal challenge an especially sharp edge was the politics. The government had successfully protected Australia from the economic devastation experienced elsewhere around the world during the 2007–2008 Global Financial Crisis, but now, Opposition Leader Tony Abbott was ritualistically declaring that the country faced a 'debt and deficit disaster'. It was one of the three-word slogans, enthusiastically amplified by some sections of the media, that was hurting the government badly, and Treasurer Wayne Swan had attempted to neutralise it by promising a speedy return to surplus.

Influential figures inside the government believed the Gonski Report was asking for too much, and the reform was unaffordable. At the same time, the Prime Minister had to keep her promise that no school would lose a dollar – or else risk antagonising the private school lobbies and the parents they represented. As described in chapter 2, Gillard ultimately buckled in August 2012, and promised every school would get a funding increase. At that point, the cost of the Gonski reforms blew out even further, intensifying the pressure it would place on the budget. Hypothetically, it would have been possible for the government to save money by cutting funding to overfunded schools (or freezing it, at least), but doing this would have been even more politically explosive than failing to deliver a surplus.

So, even as support for the Gonski recommendations was growing in the community, opposition was firming inside the Cabinet. When in July 2012 Minister Garrett presented Cabinet with his plan to translate Gonski into action, the reaction from some quarters was hostile. 'The key issue really for us became one of trying to persuade our Cabinet colleagues to come up with the necessary commitment for the funds to flow in the forward estimates', Garrett explained in an interview with us. 'I'm not one for sort of going over the entrails of Cabinet decisions – and Cabinet in confidence still means something to me – but the truth of it is that it was contested', Garrett says.[26] Gillard recalled the events in a similar way: 'Even as prime minister, I had to fight it out'.[27]

The government was trying to return the budget to surplus in straightened fiscal circumstances, and spending on Gonski was going to make an already difficult task even harder. In the abstract, there were economically defensible ways to fund the reform. Personal income tax cuts initiated by Peter Costello as treasurer during the first phase of the mining boom, and implemented by the Rudd Government, were now costing the budget over $26 billion each year – $11 billion dollars of this was flowing to the top 10 per cent of income earners.[28] Clawing back just half of the benefit enjoyed by the very wealthiest Australians alone would have been enough to pay for the Gonski reforms. Similarly, the government could have paid for Gonski by restoring indexation of fuel excise, as recommended by the Henry Tax Review, or by eliminating the capital gains tax discount, which was driving up house prices across the country.

But if there were plausible policy options, the politics was another matter. Inevitably, there would be political pain involved in paying for Gonski, whether by raising additional revenue, cutting expenditure elsewhere, or delaying the promised return to surplus. The government would have to be willing to spend political capital which, at that point in the life of the Labor Government, was in very short supply.

So ultimately at issue was how much the government believed in the reform recommended by Gonski, how much it wanted it. That, in turn, depended on the narrative the Labor Government told itself about the past, present and future of school education in Australia. There was an instinctive sympathy for needs-based funding as a policy that was in the interests of Labor's constituency, and which reflected Labor values and Labor history. But this was a $5 billion decision. Sentimental attachment would not be enough. Was the additional expenditure demanded by the Gonski review essential to improving the educational outcomes of Australian children? Did schools really need more money to improve the outcomes of the children in their care? Many members of Cabinet remained unconvinced.

'Funding is a massive distraction': resistance to Gonski mounts

In practice, Gonski was vying with an alternative narrative about how to improve Australian schools. And this one was much cheaper. At the heart of Julia Gillard's tenure as education minister had been the belief that competitive pressures in the school education market were central to improving student outcomes. The driving rationale for her signature achievement, the My School website, was that empowering parents to vote with their feet would give schools a reason to keep improving. Parents equipped with information about school performance could ask tough questions of principals who would, in turn, be forced to hold teachers to account. As Labor had announced during the 2007 election campaign, the 'publication of school performance information will form an integral part of federal Labor's plan to improve literacy and numeracy'.[29] And, as it turned out, My School would be accompanied by other initiatives designed to marketise public education, like performance pay and school autonomy.[30]

This focus reflected the prevailing belief in market-driven school reform. With the right carrots and sticks in place, so the argument went, schools would be forced to continually improve the way they operate – and use available resources more effectively. As long as Julia Gillard and members of her Cabinet believed that the discipline of the market would drive school improvement, their motivation for engaging in a big fight to deliver Gonski would be correspondingly diminished. If choice and competition was what really delivered improved student outcomes, why spend big dollars and even more political capital on Gonski?

Acting as proof positive that more money was not the solution was the widespread claim that government funding of schools had increased by almost half over the previous decade, while student outcomes had declined. The most prominent proponent of this claim was Opposition Education Spokesperson, Christopher Pyne. In September 2012, Pyne told the host of ABC's *Lateline*, Emma Alberici: 'Now, in the last 10 years, Emma, we've spent 44 per cent more on public schools and our outcomes have gone backwards. So not every argument is about more money … That's why the Coalition's focusing on the things that parents know that are important, like teacher quality.' Pyne made the claim that school funding had increased by 44 per cent over and over again, and alleged that funding was 'a massive distraction'.[31]

Pyne's repeated claims, which made it sound like there had

been a huge increase in school funding in the decade before the Gonski Report, had widespread currency among the political class. Writing in *The Australian*, Ben Jensen, head of education policy at the influential centrist think tank, the Grattan Institute, gave expression to the zeitgeist: 'Despite its strengths, the Gonski review retells the same old, and failed, story of Australian education: that the only way to fix our schools is to spend more money and to change the way it is divided between schools and students'.[32]

Public schools did not need more money, according to Christopher Pyne. 'We should be making government schools more like non-government schools', he declared in August 2012.[33] Speaking over lunch to former Labor Leader Mark Latham, now writing for the *Australian Financial Review*, Pyne argued that private schools simply did a better job of delivering what parents wanted. That's why so many parents had moved their children from public schools to the non-government sector over the course of recent decades. For Pyne, this was the market at work and it was time for public schools to get with the program; a view that received glowing approval from Latham.

Pyne did not speak for Labor. And nor did Mark Latham, who was now well on his way to One Nation via a stint on Sky News after dark. But, as Julia Gillard's time as education minister had indicated, the enthusiasm for private enterprise and the market were also a core part of Labor's outlook. The same month that Pyne and Latham did lunch, Prime Minister Gillard expressed sentiments that were not far removed from those of the Opposition Education Spokesperson. 'I've never looked at a big independent school in an established suburb and thought, "That's not fair". I look at a big independent school in an established suburb and think, "That's a great example"', Gillard told a private school conference. She had certainly travelled some distance since 2001, when she had attacked the funding of big independent schools in established suburbs.[34]

Harnessing competitive pressure and getting resourcing right didn't have to be mutually exclusive. Labor MPs, from Julia Gillard on down, believed both were part of the answer. But the political and fiscal circumstances made it tempting to choose one ahead of the other. If shifting the dial was partly about the way public schools were operating, then why go over the top to deliver a large injection of additional funding?

And then there was another argument that carried considerable weight inside Cabinet. From day one, there was strong pushback against the Gonski Report from the Treasury and Finance departments. The enmity of the econocrats went beyond a reflexive desire to keep a tight rein on the purse strings; it also involved an ideological opposition to an enhanced Commonwealth role in funding public schools. Peter Garrett recounts how there was 'a reluctance on the part of Treasury and others to want to see the Commonwealth essentially become a prime mover in education … [and] not only in terms of the provision of support for independent non-government schools such as exist at the moment'.[35]

Treasury head Martin Parkinson was especially hostile to the core of Gonski's plan. When Parkinson went on to serve as head of Prime Minister and Cabinet under Malcolm Turnbull, Turnbull floated the possibility of ending all Commonwealth Government funding to public schools. When Parkinson retired from the public service, he called for the federal government to get out of funding schools entirely, and leave it all to the states.[36] Key Cabinet ministers, influenced by Parkinson's views, were not just arguing that the government couldn't afford Gonski but that it wasn't Canberra's responsibility. As Finance Minister, Penny Wong was in charge of maintaining fiscal discipline, but Peter Garrett was surprised by the intensity of her opposition: 'Penny Wong didn't appear to care for the reform at all', he commented in his memoir.[37]

So if Julia Gillard had chosen to be candid when asked in

Brisbane in July 2012, 'What is stopping the implementation of the Gonski Report?', she might have replied as follows: 'My colleagues and I are yet to be convinced that Gonski can be afforded, that it will make a difference and that it's even our job to get more involved in funding public schools'.

Why money matters: Gonski's case for the link between resourcing and results

The first problem with the case against school funding reform was that it was based on a falsehood. Christopher Pyne had incorrectly claimed that funding had increased by 44 per cent in the same decade that student results had gone backwards. In Senate hearings with senior education officials in June 2015, Senator Penny Wright inquired as to where the figures Pyne was continuing to proclaim had come from.[38] The bureaucrats pointed to the Report on Government Services published annually by the Productivity Commission.[39] However, that report contained no 44 per cent figure at all, and what it *did* show was that between 2003/04 and 2012/13 real combined government funding per student had increased by 12.68 per cent.[40] That figure was a fraction – around a quarter – of the 44 per cent claim Christopher Pyne had been repeatedly bandying around in public.

And, as the Productivity Commission report stated, the 12 per cent increase over nine years included a series of book entry items that are important for government accounting but have no impact on the resources available to a school. For example, it included something called the 'user cost of capital', which refers to the opportunity cost incurred by governments when they use an asset in one way and not another. If, for instance, the value of the land on which a school is located increases, the opportunity cost of continuing its current use rather than selling it to developers also goes up. While that cost does need to be accounted for, it does not mean that schools have any more resources with which to educate their students. It certainly isn't recurrent income. The same went for other factors included in the Report on Government Services, such as increases in payroll tax and capital depreciation. The indefatigable education analyst Trevor Cobbold estimated that when such factors were excluded, 'the increases in real funding per student was only 5.6 per cent which is seven times less than what Pyne claim[ed]'.[41]

Even given the increases in real expenditure that had actually occurred in the 21st century (which were only a fraction of the size claimed by Christopher Pyne), Australian schools were still less well-resourced than schools in similar countries. The Gonski Report found that spending by all governments on school education in Australia was considerably below the OECD average: 3 per cent of GDP as compared to 3.5 per cent across the OECD in 2008.[42] Combined public and private expenditure in Australia was also below the average: 3.6 per cent here; 3.8 per cent on average across the OECD.

But there was a deeper problem with Pyne's attempt to summon up the past in an endeavour to obscure the link between resourcing and student outcomes. The funding increases that had occurred in the previous decade had been sector-based and needs-blind. Over the course of the Howard Government's period in office, Commonwealth funding to non-government schools more than doubled, from \$2.9 billion to \$6.5 billion.[43] The Howard Government system had delivered huge increases to the wealthiest private schools.[44] For example, Melbourne's Wesley College received an additional \$10.4 million in Commonwealth Government funding over four years, and The King's School in Sydney \$4 million more. This additional government expenditure would fund all sorts of bells and whistles, but it was unlikely to improve results in any significant way simply because of the law of diminishing returns.

It was therefore no surprise that this funding had failed to improve educational outcomes. The whole point of the Gonski Report was that to improve educational outcomes, resourcing had to be consistently and comprehensively aligned with educational need. Had Christopher Pyne not simply dismissed the Gonski Report within hours of receiving it, he might have recognised this.

The Gonski review's central achievement was to advance a rigorous rationale for educational expenditure where previously there had been no rationale at all; establishing a robust link between resourcing and results. At the very core of the report was the argument that school funding needed to be based on an explicit educational rationale that reflected both the nature of student need and agreed ambitions about desired outcomes. The purpose of Gonski's proposed resource standard was to define the funding a student needed to reach a specified level of educational achievement.

To determine the level of the resource standard, the review employed a benchmarking methodology. The basic logic underpinning the methodology was that the expenditure in schools where a reasonable proportion of students were succeeding provided the best possible indication of the necessary resourcing for all schools. So the review identified a group of reference schools where at least 80 per cent of students achieved above the national minimum standard in both reading and numeracy in 2008, 2009 and 2010.

Analysis of the funding enjoyed by the reference schools was used to derive a baseline per-student amount. And then funding loadings to meet the additional costs of specific categories of disadvantage provided the needs-based component of the resource standard. The benchmarking methodology indicated that it would require a significant additional investment to bring all Australian schools up to the level of the reference schools, where at least 80 per cent of students were achieving above-national minimum standards.

The Gonski review did not start by claiming that we should spend more money on schools and then provide a justification for that. Rather, the argument of the report, then before Cabinet, was that the resource standard represented the price of bringing all students up to a minimum standard. The case, then, that ministers had to consider was, in essence, very simple: if you want this result, this is what it will cost. The Gonski Report argued that we needed to spend billions more on our schools because that's what the evidence about the cost of educating children to a minimum standard indicated. It was true that the price tag had been inflated because the Gonski panel endorsed the continued funding of non-government schools above the resource standard. But cabinet knew all about political compromises.

While the Gonski Report's benchmarking methodology was rigorous and remains almost completely unchallenged, the technical work underlying a resource standard is extremely complex. The report was not premised on its own infallibility. On the contrary, it proposed the creation of a National Schools Resourcing body – a kind of standing Gonski review – to continuously assess new evidence about the efficient price of achieving agreed educational outcomes.

The panel envisaged that, over time, there was potential for greater ambition in terms of what the benchmark was aimed to achieve.[45] Research commissioned by the review had examined a benchmark which relied on schools where 90 per cent of students were consistently above the minimum NAPLAN standard, but only 271 schools (or 3 per cent) qualified, providing an insufficiently large sample size on which to base a resourcing standard. The proposed resourcing body could continue to investigate the cost of more ambitious targets, as well as identifying when innovation allowed schools to get the same results more efficiently. While the accuracy and the ambition of the standard would be reviewed every four years, more straightforward indexation, based on a schooling-specific basket of labour and other costs, would occur annually, to ensure the standard kept up with inflation.[46]

What the Gonski panel was offering the government, and Treasury in particular, was a funding model that told them what they could expect in return for their expenditure. This was in stark contrast to the mechanism that was then being used to fund schools, known as the Average Government School Recurrent Cost (AGSRC) measure. Gonski rightly saw the AGSRC as a 'monkey see, monkey do' approach, in which the Commonwealth simply imitated state government behaviour without really knowing why. 'In essence, AGSRC is a measure of historical expenditure levels in average government schools', the Gonski Report explained. 'As such, it is a backward-looking approach to resourcing schools, based on past levels of inputs from governments.'[47]

There was no link in the AGSRC measure between the resources going in and the results that would be expected to come out. And, even worse, the resources going in were based on a per student average, instead of reflecting individual student needs. Whenever a state government delivered additional funding to disadvantaged students in public schools, or maintained a school in a remote location, average government school expenditure would rise. The AGSRC ensured that this would, in turn, flow through into increased Commonwealth expenditure on all schools. As a result, annual increases enjoyed by private schools often far outstripped the actual growth in the costs they faced, effectively delivering funding increases each year, without any clear justification. It was the opposite of targeted needs-based funding.

'While AGSRC is based on average expenditure in government

schools, there are schools with vastly different characteristics and student cohorts across all schooling sectors and states and territories', the Gonski Report observed.[48] The solution was to make a clear distinction between two different things: a resource standard and annual indexation of that standard, and then supply each with a cogent rationale. In place of the AGSRC, the report recommended an indexation measure 'based on actual changes in the costs of schooling incurred by reference schools'.[49]

Cabinet faced a practical choice between two funding models. Under the old system, there was no persuasive rationale for either the level or distribution of resourcing, no clear relationship between inputs and output, spending was needs-blind and annual indexation often outstripped actual cost-growth. The new model, by contrast, specified the price of achieving a nominated educational result, acknowledged that the price varied for different children and created an indexation measure that accurately reflected changes in costs over time. Treasurers and finance ministers rightly want to ensure that taxpayers are getting bang for their buck. In this case, the choice was clear.

If this wasn't apparent from a reading of the Gonski Report, the sheer hypocrisy of those arguing that money didn't matter should have set the alarm bells ringing. Throughout 2012 and 2013, Christopher Pyne simultaneously claimed that money wasn't important *and* fiercely resisted the possibility of any private school losing a cent. In fact, he demanded that they had to continue to receive the same turbo-charged annual funding increases that they had been enjoying under the discredited Howard model.

In the middle of 2012, the private school lobby groups conducted modelling of Gonski's recommendations, based on 2009 and 2010 data, and found the indexation rate from the first year to the second would have been around 3 per cent.[50] That was about half what had actually occurred historically under the AGSRC measure. Head of the NSW independent schools lobby group, Geoff Newcombe, claimed that if indexation fell below the whopping 6 per cent annual increases private schools had been enjoying, the 'feasibility of the Gonski model will be struck a severe blow'.[51] It was at this point that Newcombe started asserting that Prime Minister Gillard had broken her 'no losers' promise and called for a two-year extension of the existing arrangements.

The private schools were no longer just demanding that no school lose a dollar. They were demanding a continuation of the extraordinary rates of funding growth that private schools had enjoyed over the previous decade. In pursuing this line of attack, they dropped any pretence of working within the Gonski consensus. They were now insisting on the effective maintenance of the AGSRC – the measure that Gonski had shown was not only needs-blind, but lacked any coherent justification at all.

Christopher Pyne jumped on the opportunity that had opened up. Suddenly recalling the importance of funding – for some schools, at least – he revived the case for retaining the status quo. 'More details are emerging of a new Labor Private School Hit List, with some New South Wales schools facing up to $4 million in cuts under proposed changes to the school funding system', he declared in April 2012.[52] 'Labor is planning to cut non-government school funding by stealth', he claimed the following month.[53] Funding was only a 'distraction' when it came to disadvantaged public schools, apparently.

Pyne knew money mattered. That's why he fought for it tooth and nail. His beef with the Gonski Report was that he was ideologically committed to the old sector-based, needs-blind funding system established by the Howard Government. And yet, he perversely relied on the claim that because the Howard Government funding increases to elite private schools had failed to improve outcomes, delivering additional resourcing to disadvantaged students in struggling schools was a distraction.

Like Treasury Secretary Martin Parkinson, Pyne was an ardent opponent of a Commonwealth role in funding public schools; a position that went hand-in-hand with a rejection of needs-based funding. The Gonski panel recognised that needs-based funding would not become a reality as long as resourcing of the most needy schools was left to the revenue-starved states, while the more pecunious Commonwealth looked after private schools. 'Greater [Commonwealth] support for government schools is particularly important', the report argued, 'given the need to lift the outcomes of a greater number of students, the comparatively poor state of government school infrastructure, and the higher concentrations of disadvantaged students in government schools'.[54]

This position flowed from a recognition of the basic reality facing Australian governments: state governments have big spending responsibilities, like running schools and hospitals, and only limited revenue-raising capacity, while the Commonwealth has the power to tax income but doesn't have the same obligation to provide costly basic services.[55] Until such time as income taxation powers are transferred back to state governments, Martin Parkinson's proposals effectively mean that the schools serving the poorest students, and the schools that need the most resourcing, would have to rely solely on the governments least able to support them. It was a recipe for relegating public education to second-class status. Despite that, Parkinson's position was highly influential, including inside Cabinet.

Labor and public education – competition or solidarity?

But there was a deeper problem with the position of the Gonski sceptics inside the Labor Government. The government's choice-

and-competition agenda did not offer an alternative means of school improvement. This view was premised on a misreading of the nature of competition between Australian schools. Choice and competition were not driving school improvement. Rather, they were driving the concentrations of disadvantage that were at the heart of Australia's educational decline.

If public schools became more like private schools, as Christopher Pyne advised, there was no evidence that student outcomes would improve. The public and private sectors were performing similarly given the students they enrolled, as the Gonski panel had reported.[56] Because competition between Australian schools occurred on an unlevel playing field, characterised by disparities in resourcing and responsibilities, schools' competitive strategies were focused primarily on enrolling lots of bright and engaged students who started ahead and enhanced each other's learning.

Private schools were really good at doing this. If public schools were to be more like private schools, they would follow suit. In fact, some already had. This is effectively what selective public schools were about. But attracting academically successful and socio-economically advantaged students from other schools was doing nothing to lift our educational performance overall. In fact, it was making the job even harder for the schools those students left behind, where concentrations of disadvantage intensified and negative peer effects prevailed.

In the decade preceding the Gonski review, government funding – particularly from the Commonwealth – had skewed sharply in favour of schools in the non-government sectors. This had increased the resource advantage enjoyed by many private schools which, along with their greater capacity to pick and choose their students, gave them a pronounced marketplace advantage. As a consequence, public school enrolment share had sunk to a historical low, and a third of Australian school students attended private schools. Public schools were increasingly characterised by the concentrations of disadvantage that Gonski had found were so harmful to learning. In this context, a competition initiative like My School simply added fuel to the fire.

The promise of Gonski, for all its limitations, was that it could dramatically rebalance the scales, providing an injection of resources which would enable public schools to fully address the needs of students in their care – and in the course of doing so, become more attractive to prospective enrolments, too. Needs-based funding would help create a more level playing field among three sectors currently operating on decidedly different terms.

For the most fervent believers in the Gonski reforms, the acute challenges presented by concentrated compound disadvantage at many public schools put the whole enterprise of public education in jeopardy. The risk was that public education would become, as John Howard had imagined, merely a safety net for those who couldn't afford better. For public schools to succeed, they needed to be adequately resourced and able to compete on a relatively level playing field.

And it was essential for public schools to succeed because they were open to all – irrespective of differences in wealth, income, power or possessions. As a result, they were the only schools available to most disadvantaged children, and they also conveyed lessons that could not be measured in NAPLAN tests. In offering education to children from every walk of life, public schools embodied and engendered a distinctive set of values: above all, the idea that we are all in this together.

If this was the belief of Gonski supporters outside of Parliament House, the passion for public education was not always shared by ministers inside the Labor Government. 'I had a strong conviction that we needed to have a well-resourced and expanding public

FROM THE PRINCIPAL'S DESK: COMPETITION FOR STUDENTS ON AN UNLEVEL PLAYING FIELD

How did Australia's school system look from the principal's desk? Many gave reflections for this book. They served in different schools but share a deep commitment to lifting the strugglers and were all highly regarded by their colleagues. They are now retired: principals eventually leave school ... but school doesn't always leave them.

For principals, the experience of losing high achievers to neighbouring schools while supporting a disproportionate number of strugglers can be particularly galling. Former principal Bernie Roebuck describes how nearby non-government schools 'did not carry the load of students with significant disabilities and very, very rarely students with high level behavioural needs'. Roebuck explains how this was a function of the divergent obligations and responsibilities between competing schools. 'Time and again in a rural school we accepted back into our school those students who had headed off to the boarding school/school out of town and when things went wrong or they were asked not to return to such institutions, we were expected to enrol them as part of our obligations.'

'I was directed to enrol a student who had moved into my area without any record of his previous school', recalls John Frew. 'Within days, teachers were drawing my attention to this student who finally exploded in a science class throwing his chair in the direction of the teacher and stormed out. His behaviour was so outrageous I directed the rest of the school to go into lockdown and called the police.'

Betty Harper reflects on the challenges that arose when her school gained a reputation for excelling when it came to supporting underachievers. 'We were exceptionally good at raising students' literacy, and later, numeracy growth levels, especially for our least able students with mild or moderate intellectual disability. In other words, we were the school of choice for less able students. Now this is great if you're a parent who wants the best program for your struggling daughter, but many parents openly resisted enrolment because we were perceived as the school for "dummies"; not quite academic enough. Obviously this perception leads to a slippery slope.'

Principal Peter Morgan saw the phenomenon from both sides. 'At Belmont High, we were a school of choice. The school was oversubscribed with non-local enrolments. Spaces were limited ... Wealthier families rented properties for three months to get kids in as locals. The school had the capacity to choose.' But, Morgan says, he experienced a very different dynamic in other schools he led during his career. 'At two we faced white flight of the middle class to the Catholic system', he recalls.[57]

---

education system', Peter Garrett says. 'And I was surprised to find that to some extent that wasn't shared universally in the cabinet.'[58] Garrett noticed signs of coolness towards Gonski almost as soon as he took on the portfolio. 'From early on, I wasn't confident about some of the advice the prime minister was receiving, particularly after she hired a former adviser to British prime minister Tony Blair, John McTernan, to run strategy', Garrett wrote in his memoir. 'At the beginning of the term, the suggestion was that the government simply note, rather than endorse, the Gonski Report when it was handed down and, according to McTernan, we should avoid mentioning "fairness" when discussing the new funding model.'[59]

McTernan categorically rejects Garrett's account, insisting that the only dispute between him and the education minister was over the publication of Gonski's secret modelling. But it's clear from the public record that McTernan's boss, Julia Gillard, was, at the very least, entirely agnostic when it came to public and private provision of school education. This was not surprising. Gillard had frequently declared that the public–private school debate was over.[60] From a contemporary Labor perspective, growth in enrolments at private schools represented choice, accountability and aspiration in action – precisely what My School had been intended to encourage. Because Labor largely viewed schools as operating in isolation from each other, there was little energy to level the playing field.

The government commits to Gonski (sort of ...)

As it turned out, Cabinet determined to proceed with the reforms, but in reality the result was a draw. Gillard and Garrett had won a sizeable additional investment in education, over considerable opposition inside the Cabinet room. But they had not succeeded in persuading their colleagues to commit to the additional expenditure over the four years of the budget forward estimates. Instead, the increase to the education budget would be stretched out over six years, with two-thirds of the additional funding deferred until the final two years, 2018 and 2019, in the funding quadrennium after next. This made the commitment extremely vulnerable to the vicissitudes of the electoral cycle, as would become very apparent in the not-too-distant future.

After more than a decade of handsome funding increases to

the private sector under the Howard model, new money would arrive at public schools, but only slowly and eventually. It looked less and less likely that this reform was going to make a big dent in the resourcing differentials between the school sectors any time soon.

It was a decision made in an extremely challenging budgetary context. But it also reflected the fact that when it came to school funding reform, the Rudd–Gillard Governments had never been willing to crash through. On ABC Radio National, Prime Minister Gillard would tell Fran Kelly, 'Budgets are about choices, Fran, and you show what you value through the choices you make'.[61] That is correct, but the choices the Labor Government made reflected an essential ambivalence about school funding.

It went back to the moment the funding review had been promised in 2007 – a promise to do nothing immediately, but something later. In 2008, the Rudd Government rolled over the Howard SES funding system for four more years. At the 2010 election, it was extended for a fifth year. Julia Gillard waited until the third year of government to commission a review that would go for 18 months. She would not even start negotiations with the states until nine months after receiving the Gonski Report in December 2011, so the Commonwealth found itself negotiating with the states in a federal election year. Now most of the increases in Commonwealth funding would be delayed until 2018 and 2019, beyond the forward estimates.

In a speech on 3 September 2012 at the National Press Club in Canberra, Prime Minister Gillard finally embraced the core recommendations of the Gonski Report.[62] Nine months after David Gonski and his team had delivered its comprehensive report, the Gillard Government was committing to its central animating idea: needs-based funding. But what also became apparent, if only by omission, was that key elements of the funding architecture envisaged by the Gonski review would not be implemented. The proposed National Schools Resourcing Body had fallen victim to a bureaucratic turf war. Treasury and Finance believed that an independent body, which gave expert advice on the resources schools needed to succeed, would loosen their control over the purse strings. Wayne Swan and Penny Wong argued the position of their departments, so Gonski's proposed resourcing body was a non-starter inside the government.

Also gone were the school planning authorities that Gonski recommended should operate in each jurisdiction. These bodies were intended to enable coordination between the three school sectors, especially with respect to projected student enrolments, new schools and school closures. This would help ensure that public funds were being spent efficiently and effectively in the public interest. However, the proposal had met with staunch opposition from the non-government school lobbies, particularly the independent sector. 'Any structure which operated to impede or artificially restrict the growth of the independent sector would be vigorously opposed by ISCA', the head of the Independent Schools Council, Bill Daniels, had declared upon the release of the Gonski Report. It was a battle the Gillard Government did not have the strength to fight.[63]

In place of the architecture proposed by the Gonski review, the Prime Minister set out a National Plan for School Improvement. In return for extra money, schools and school systems would have to sign up to new requirements, including school improvement plans; annual performance reviews for teachers; and more power for principals over budgets and hiring and firing staff ('unencumbered by stifling bureaucracy'). In essence, Gillard's plan complemented the My School objective of making schools, principals and teachers more accountable with a range of carrots and sticks. Even the modest respects in which the Gonski review addressed the way schools worked as a system, like the school planning authorities, were not pursued.

In November 2012, Minister Garrett introduced the Australian Education Bill to parliament. The bill gave legislative form to the announcements Prime Minister Gillard had made in September, outlining the principles of the government's version of needs-based funding and setting out the school improvement agenda that would accompany it. The essential detail concerning the precise allocation of funding to schools and school systems would depend on negotiations with the states which had only just begun. And then there was the question overshadowing everything else: would Prime Minister Gillard, and the school funding reforms she had launched, survive 2013, a federal election year?

2012: YEAR 5

Kim's mum could see problems in the local school: it just didn't have the facilities and resources of the larger schools in Rivertown. The Gonski review came with a promise that things would improve. It revealed that not everyone had equal chances in their schooling – something that Kim's mum saw in the local school but was even more obvious in the high schools in Rivertown.

Then came a shock: the Prime Minister announced that the additional funding wouldn't fully arrive until 2019. 'They have to be kidding', Maria's mum declared, 'our kids will have almost left school by then!' Kim's parents pondered what this might mean. The small town was in slow decline, two businesses and a bank branch were shuttered up and some families were thinking about life elsewhere. They began to canvass what alternatives were available for them ... and also for Kim. (*To be continued ...*)

5

A new national consensus? (2013)

> As far as school funding is concerned, Kevin Rudd and I are on a unity ticket ... There is no difference between Kevin Rudd and myself when it comes to school funding ... We will honour the agreements that Labor has entered into, we will match the offers that Labor has made, we will make sure that no school is worse off ...[1]
>
> *Tony Abbott, Leader of the Opposition, August 2013*

> We are going to keep the promise that we made. Not the promise that some people thought we made, or the promise that some people might have liked us to make.[2]
>
> *Tony Abbott, Prime Minister, December 2013*

Just days before the 2013 federal election was finally officially called, the Opposition Leader Tony Abbott announced the Coalition was on a 'unity' ticket with Labor on school funding. But almost as soon as Abbott had shaken off the shackles of the election and was safely ensconced in the Lodge, he tore up the unity ticket and threw it to the wind. Then, within the space of a week, there was yet another reversal. An immediate and overwhelming popular backlash forced Abbott and his education minister, Christopher Pyne, to scrounge around for the pieces of the severed unity ticket, clumsily sticky tape it back together, and wave it in the air as though nothing had happened.

The Coalition had now executed a triple backflip. It was a spectacular display of a newly elected government being forced to act against its own will. For Julia Gillard, who had lost the prime ministership to Kevin Rudd in June and then watched on as Labor was unceremoniously ejected from office in September, her successors' embarrassing attempts to undo one of her signature achievements must have offered no small consolation. Abbott and Pyne's humiliating backdown was, she could reflect, vindication of her stewardship of the Gonski reforms, evidence of the extent to which she had transformed the politics of school funding.

As Tom Bentley, Gillard's top education advisor throughout her time in government, wrote in late 2013, 'the furious reaction that Pyne has unleashed was entirely predictable, because the Gonski school funding reforms, which were conceived and delivered by Gillard, have been worked through, tested, legitimised and implanted in the Australian community so thoroughly over the last five years'.[3] On this account, Gillard had initiated a rigorous, comprehensive review process, persuaded the public, and won over the stakeholders, the media and key figures across the partisan divide. Even though Labor had lost government and Gillard had left the parliament, she had created a national discourse centred on the idea of needs-based funding, with widespread popular appeal and backed up by a broad-based constituency heavily invested in that principle. The overwhelming public reaction that forced the new government's ungainly reversal was conclusive evidence of that.

And yet there was an alternative interpretation of what transpired in 2013. On this view, all the political drama that accompanied the change of government did not change the fact that Prime Minister Gillard had compromised Gonski beyond recognition.

First, the government had delayed, deferred (and demurred) through the course of 2012, undermining the momentum created by the Gonski Report; then they had found themselves negotiating funding agreements in an election year when their leverage was lowest. The result was a series of special deals over the course of 2013 which meant that school funding would continue to be just as sector-based and needs-blind as before. These deals came on top of the guarantee that every school would get a funding increase. The integrity of the new funding system was fatally compromised and the delivery of additional funding to schools that needed it was delayed for years.

'The basic reason we do not have Gonski today is not because we elected the Abbott Government but because the previous government failed in the politics of its delivery', Gonski panel member Ken Boston told a Senate committee in 2014. 'There was ample time during that period, in my view, for Gonski to have been implemented satisfactorily with the support of the states', Boston said.[4]

Which interpretation is correct – Ken Boston's or Tom Bentley's? Did the political compromises pursued by the Gillard Government sink Gonski or save it? Was the commitment that no school would lose a dollar vital to the successful implementation of the report's recommendations? Or, on the contrary, did it distort them beyond recognition?

The Nat who gave a Gonski: New South Wales signs up

If the Gillard Government had not successfully secured the participation of New South Wales (on top of the ACT, South Australia and Tasmania) in its bid to reform school funding, it is highly unlikely that either the unity ticket moment or the events that followed it would have ever occurred. While it was inevitable that the Labor jurisdictions of South Australia, Tasmania and the Australian Capital Territory were ultimately going to get on board, a national initiative made up of just those three was not going to amount to much. But when New South Wales signed up for Gonski in April 2013, Prime Minister Gillard now had the largest jurisdiction in the country – led by a Coalition government – on her side. Moreover, a National Party minister in New South Wales, Adrian Piccoli, was spruiking her policy, giving it serious bipartisan credibility.

The tale of Piccoli and education policy under the O'Farrell and Baird governments is a critical element of the Gonski story, and not just because New South Wales is Australia's most populous state. The New South Wales State Government's support for Gonski established that, in as far as the proposal reforms represented a challenge to the educational status quo, it was possible for them to be embraced by conservative Australia. As a social justice Catholic representing a rural seat,[5] Piccoli could see that Gonski had the potential to be a big winner for the constituency he cared about. In his first weeks as minister, he had successfully championed an agreement with his state and federal counterparts to bridge the growing gap in the educational achievement of city and country kids.[6] He recognised that the schools which would benefit most from Gonski were disadvantaged schools in rural and regional Australia, like many in his own electorate of Murrumbidgee in south-western New South Wales.

In explaining his decision-making, Piccoli gives considerable credit to senior figures in the New South Wales Department of Education like Leslie Loble and Michelle Bruniges. 'I mean, they were showing me charts of where the schools would benefit and what percentage increase in funding', he said. 'Schools in rural and remote benefited the most, then provincial, Western Sydney and then cascading down. And when I say rural and regional, [I mean] including low-fee Catholic and independent schools.' Piccoli could see also that the Gonski Report's characterisation of existing funding arrangements as opaque, inconsistent and illogical applied to his own state. 'You know [some] schools would be part of some program and the school across the road wasn't', he commented. 'So one school got three hundred thousand extra. The school across the road got no extra money … They did a very good job of explaining to me the problems with the existing system.'[7]

While Piccoli had plenty of reason to give a Gonski, New South Wales' participation was not a sure thing. Indeed, throughout 2012, Piccoli and Premier O'Farrell occupied an ambiguous, often awkward position. On the one hand, both figures made positive overtures about the Gonski Report, a report everyone knew called for an annual injection of $5 billion into Australian schools. But at the same time, Piccoli and O'Farrell were cutting funding to their own schools.

In September 2012, the day after Prime Minister Gillard had declared her intention to implement Gonski's major recommendations at the National Press Club, Adrian Piccoli called in major education sector stakeholders for a meeting. The lobbyists arrived, anticipating that Piccoli wanted to talk to them about the Prime Minister's announcement the day before, but they were in for a nasty surprise. Piccoli provided a confidential briefing that the following week's state budget would include a $1.7 billion 'saving' in the education portfolio over four years. That $1.7 billion was about to come out of the schools represented by those in attendance. The briefing didn't stay confidential for long.

A state government focused on finding efficiencies in the education budget hardly looked like a promising partner in the Gonski project. And yet, as savings were pursued across the budget, Piccoli and Premier O'Farrell were aware that the Gonski process had the potential to change the equation. 'In that first year, it was really hard', says Piccoli.[8] 'This report was coming. It was going to recommend changing the way money was distributed to schools, but it would also come with the idea that there would be a greater contribution from the Commonwealth.' Even as Piccoli presided over budget cuts in September 2012, he recognised that New South Wales would be in a powerful position in the Gonski negotiations, one he could exploit to the state's considerable financial advantage.

Piccoli's analysis was straightforward. Politically speaking, Julia Gillard had to secure the reform. So in any negotiations about who would pay for it, the New South Wales Government would have all the bargaining power. Piccoli recalls a conversation with Barry O'Farrell one day in 2012, after they had met with educators who urged them to back the Gonski Report: 'This was during that period, that phoney war time, when the Commonwealth weren't quite sure what they were going to do', explains Piccoli. 'And one day it's "yes", and the next day it's "no" and then "We've got no money".' O'Farrell, like many, was not convinced Gillard was really committed to Gonski. After the meeting had finished, and Piccoli and O'Farrell were left alone, the Premier turned to his education minister and said, 'Adrian, I think Gonski is dead'. But Piccoli disagreed, telling O'Farrell, 'Barry, Julia Gillard needs this more than we do'. And that meant New South Wales could use its involvement to draw an even greater commitment of funds out of the Commonwealth.[9]

In the event, Piccoli turned out to be right. When negotiations with the Commonwealth began, the starting point was that Canberra would contribute one-third of the additional money in return for a two-thirds contribution from the states, as Gonski had recommended. But Piccoli and O'Farrell had all the leverage. Victoria was ambivalent, and Queensland, the Northern Territory and Western Australia were all resistant.[10] 'Julia Gillard was under the pump on everything', Piccoli recalls. 'And this was the one, this was her signature thing and the next federal election was closing in. She needed a big win. Prime Minister Gillard needed one of the big states to sign up – either Victoria or New South Wales. Victoria had played politics. It was a Liberal government. New South Wales was the one large state saying, "Yep, we're really interested". It was good policy and good politics.'

The Commonwealth upped their offer, agreeing to go dollar for dollar with New South Wales to deliver the additional Gonski money. But by the time the negotiations entered the final phase in March and April 2013, the federal election was rapidly approaching. 'It's getting closer every day, right', Piccoli says, recalling the dynamic. 'No good having this win three days after the election.' Ultimately, the Gillard Government accepted the New South Wales position that the Commonwealth would contribute two-thirds of the additional Gonski money while New South Wales contributed one-third. 'What kept me thinking "We have really got to do this"', remarks Piccoli, 'is the system wasn't particularly effective in New South Wales, the funding model. If we then added money to it, the schools that would actually get the biggest benefits were the most disadvantaged schools. And then thirdly it was actually an opportunity for us to contribute New South Wales money and then leverage two dollars of Commonwealth money for every dollar we put in. So those three things were completely compelling.'

At one level, this is an old story. 'Never get between a premier and a bucket of money', as Paul Keating once said.[11] Add to that the element of a Nat looking after his electorate, and it can all seem very familiar. Piccoli and O'Farrell played the politics to their own advantage and that of their constituents. At another level, however, this is a story about how the Gillard Government successfully used Commonwealth money to change New South Wales' behaviour.

A government that had been cutting funding to schools had now agreed to index it at 3 per cent per annum – and to allocate it on a needs basis. This simply wouldn't have happened if the Gonski sceptics inside Treasury and Cabinet had prevailed. Prime Minister Gillard was continuing in the tradition initiated by the Whitlam Government of using active Commonwealth involvement in school funding to ensure adequate resourcing for the most disadvantaged Australian children.

Moreover, the New South Wales story cannot be reduced to a cash grab. If that was all that was at stake, New South Wales would have been joined by the other conservative states and territories, especially Queensland and the Northern Territory which stood to benefit enormously from Gonski. What made New South Wales different was that Piccoli and O'Farrell resisted intense partisan political pressure from Christopher Pyne and Tony Abbott, influence which other Coalition state governments succumbed to.

Abbott and Pyne, driven by the most narrow political calculations, were willing to apply maximum pressure in an attempt to thwart a victory for their political enemy. 'When the report was dropped,' says Adrian Piccoli, 'there were plenty of Liberals and National Party people who put a lot of political pressure on Barry and me and others within the government to not sign up. To not give Julia Gillard a win. Because this was her centrepiece thing. She'd been the Minister for Education ... This touched every community, school funding. And they just didn't want to give her a win. So there was a lot of political pressure on Barry and others not to sign up'. The intensity of the pressure on Piccoli should not be underestimated. 'There were plenty of people on my side of politics who wanted me sacked', Piccoli states bluntly. 'And not least of all Tony Abbott and Peta Credlin. They in no way wanted a win for Gillard.'[12]

As a consequence, the Coalition Government in New South

Wales, along with their interstate counterparts, had to choose between partisan loyalty and the interests of the voters who had elected them. Adrian Piccoli and Barry O'Farrell chose policy over politics, all children in their state over a narrow electoral base. Piccoli was strongly motivated by what Gonski would do for country kids, something that might seem second nature for a Nat. But it was critical that Piccoli was the kind of National MP who believed in representing his whole electorate and not just the wealthy graziers who send their kids to boarding schools. 'There are some people in the National Party who would say that our constituency is the squattocracy when the reality is rural electorates are some of the poorest in the state', Piccoli reflects. 'I had party members say to me, "School funding? It doesn't matter – it's all hopeless. That's why we all have to send our kids to Riverview".'[13]

If there is any doubt that Piccoli and O'Farrell displayed leadership that required both imagination and courage, we need only compare the path they pursued with their interstate colleagues. Piccoli and O'Farrell withstood the partisan political pressure, where figures like Queensland Premier Campbell Newman and Northern Territory Chief Minister Adam Giles failed to. Many of the country's most disadvantaged and underfunded schools were in Queensland, and that state stood to benefit handsomely from the Gonski reforms, especially after Prime Minister Gillard announced the Commonwealth's commitment to invest two dollars for every additional state dollar. Public schools in Premier Newman's own electorate of Ashgrove stood to receive an additional $27 million over the subsequent six years.[14] And yet Newman and his education minister, Jean-Paul Langbroek, dismissed Gonski outright.

The Northern Territory Government, responsible for many children who experience the most acute levels of social disadvantage in the country, was similarly obstructive. In Victoria, schools stood to gain $4 billion if the government signed up. But while the Victorian Government did not close the door on Gonski, it showed nothing like the openness to constructively engage with the federal government displayed by New South Wales.[15] The Western Australian Government had a more substantial reservation, complaining that it was being penalised because that state provided more funding to its schools than other states. But even when the federal government tripled its offer to nearly a billion dollars, Western Australia still held out.[16]

In New South Wales, enlightened leadership was decisive but there was one more critical ingredient. The reality was that the Prime Minister's commitment that no school would lose a dollar also provided shelter for state governments. Without it, it is highly unlikely that Piccoli and O'Farrell could have withstood the pressure from Coalition colleagues to disown the reform. Piccoli had firsthand experience of the immense power of the non-government school lobbies to seek retribution if they perceived a policy went against their interests. After all, a year earlier he had proposed that New South Wales state government cuts be applied equally across all three sectors. And he was still scarred from the response.

Within days of Piccoli's supposedly confidential 2012 briefing, waves were being felt. Sydney Archbishop Anthony Fisher had mobilised the Catholic community, issuing a statement that was sent home with children, calling on parents to lobby their local MP. As a result, Piccoli's colleagues were being inundated by calls and emails. 'By Sunday, there were Catholic priests in Church telling people to lobby their local Liberal-National Party member because there was going to be this outrageous attack on school funding for Catholic schools', Piccoli recalls.[17] Meanwhile, Archbishop Fisher lobbied Tony Abbott, who, in turn, put in a call to Barry O'Farrell, insisting that non-government schools be excluded from the cuts.

Suddenly, there was talk of a no-confidence motion within the

Coalition party room and Minister Piccoli's job was on the line. 'On the Tuesday, we had a party meeting and it went for over an hour, just for discussion on this. And I've got to say, I thought I was going to have to resign. I would have resigned that day if I had been rolled in the party room.'[18] Ultimately, however, a compromise deal was reached, and Piccoli announced that the proposed cuts had been more than halved, for non-government schools at least. But not before Premier O'Farrell called Cardinal Pell to apprise him of the government's change of course. 'It was a good result even if there was still pain in it', Archbishop Fisher told the *Sydney Morning Herald*. 'I think our message got through.'[19] Geoff Newcombe of the independent schools lobby agreed. 'It will make governments of all persuasions realise the funding of non-government schools is extremely sensitive and not to be meddled with.'[20] 'This is how hard it is to take a few dollars off non-government schools', Adrian Piccoli reflects.[21] It was a bracing experience for a relatively new minister, and one that would not soon be forgotten.

So when it came to the Gonski reforms in 2013, Prime Minister Gillard's ironclad guarantee that no school would lose a dollar meant figures like Adrian Piccoli and Barry O'Farrell could contemplate Gonski without their heart rates going through the roof. It also ensured that those who would seek to sabotage the reform had little to work with. 'Why did Julia Gillard say no school would lose a dollar?' Piccoli asks before answering his own question: 'Because she was copping it ten times worse than I ever copped it … I think if she hadn't done that, it probably wouldn't have happened. The pressure on us not to sign up was immense enough even though non-government schools were to be no worse off. And it probably wouldn't have happened'. It is powerful testimony in favour of the view that Julia Gillard's compromises were as necessary as they were unfortunate.

On the morning of 23 April 2013, Angelo Gavrielatos, head

of the Australian Education Union, was in a meeting when his phone started ringing repeatedly. It was Peter Garrett's chief of staff, Denise Spinks. After numerous unanswered calls, Spinks texted, 'You must answer this call. I need to speak to you now.' The union chief stepped out of the meeting and phoned Spinks back to discover that Prime Minister Gillard and Premier O'Farrell were about to sign the instrument that would commit New South Wales to the Gonski reforms. 'I started crying at that point', recalls Gavrielatos. 'I didn't think we would get there. The fact that we did was a fucking huge moment.'[22] Gavrielatos, who had been fighting for school funding reform for decades, adjourned the meeting so that he and his comrades could watch history unfold.

The history of the Gonski reforms is marked by a series of moments which suggested it had the potential to transcend the political perils and policy impasses that had preceded it – this was one such moment. Gonski had reached across the partisan divide, embracing a Coalition government, a Liberal premier and a Nationals education minister – despite intensive lobbying from their conservative colleagues in the Commonwealth parliament. It was the most convincing evidence yet that the Gonski formula had the potential to transform the politics of school funding in Australia.

By this time, the 'I Give a Gonski' campaign had developed into a medium-sized social movement. The Gonski coalition not only included the parents and principals associations, but also organisations like Children with Disability Australia. A coup for the campaign was the public endorsement of Dr John Falzon, the chief executive of the Catholic social justice organisation St Vincent de Paul. In expressing his support, Falzon was candid about the fact that most of the children served by his organisation were in public schools.

Whatever it takes: Gonski becomes law

With O'Farrell's commitment in late April 2013, New South Wales was now on board. But Prime Minister Gillard still needed to persuade the other Coalition states, as well as finalise deals with the Labor jurisdictions – South Australia, Tasmania and the ACT. As if that wasn't challenging enough, Gillard and Minister Garrett still had to make Gonski into law by amending the Australian Education Bill, imbuing what was essentially a statement of principle with the detail that would give it practical effect. With a September election date already announced, the amendments would need to pass the parliament by the end of June, before the winter break. The government had the numbers in parliament. The Greens and the crossbench had indicated their support long ago. The challenge was to keep all major stakeholders in the tent as the detail of new funding arrangements was hammered out.

As Minister Garrett would later reflect in his memoir, the 'no school loses a dollar' commitment 'made the development of a nationally consistent funding model painfully difficult, given thousands of schools would have to make the transition to the new system'.[23] To deliver on the promise, the government included in the legislation a guarantee that schools already funded above their entitlement would receive annual increases of 3 per cent. The education and training wage price index – the best measure of changes in recurrent costs in schools – only increased at about 2.5 per cent annually for the rest of the decade. So Australia's most abundantly resourced schools would receive funding increases in real terms.

This meant many non-government schools would continue to be overfunded indefinitely.[24] The Abbott Government's commission of audit found that it would take more than a century for the most overfunded schools to be brought into line with their actual needs-based allocation.[25] New South Wales parliamentarian the late John Kaye estimated that it would take 202 years for Sydney's Loreto Kirribilli to have its funding reduced to the level of the Schooling Resource Standard.[26] In reality, the Gillard Government was introducing two inconsistent funding systems, effectively reproducing the discredited 'funding maintained' deals it was ostensibly replacing. In 2014, overfunding amounted to $235 million, 70 per cent of which went to schools where more than half the students came from the highest SES quarter.[27] Under the trajectory established by the Gillard Government, governments would still be spending over $100 million annually in funding schools above the Schooling Resource Standard in 2050.[28]

But the total cost of the 'no losers' commitment was much greater than this, because the Schooling Resource Standard had to grow at an even faster rate. That was the only way the overfunded schools would be brought into line with the Schooling Resource Standard. So schools already at the resource standard would receive 3.6 per cent increases each year, much higher than inflation. The result was that both overfunded schools and schools already at the resource standard would be awarded funding increases in real terms, year in, year out, indefinitely. All the money going to schools at or above the resource standard was money *not* going to underfunded schools.

And so the timetable for delivering needs-based funding to disadvantaged students blew out. At best, the Gillard Government's transition would involve a long wait for the children who needed additional help, many of whom would spend most of their subsequent years of schooling in under-resourced schools. But the trajectory was so slow and partial, it was doubtful that the transition would ever be completed. Even under the government's plan, most underfunded schools were only scheduled to receive 95 per cent of their Schooling Resource Standard entitlement by the end of the six-year transition period.

But the most egregious special deal was still to come; the private school lobbyists were just getting started. As Minister Garrett tried to steer the new funding system to safety, he was concentrating on 'not allowing the endgame runs from the bishops and others to try to weaken or water it down'. But there were pressures on the minister and the legislation coming from multiple directions. 'Of course, they were working over my colleagues in the caucus, particularly those with which they had existing relationships', he commented. 'And that's just part of the politics of education funding in Australia … Since [the 1962 Catholic schools' "strike" in] Goulburn you're always dealing with pretty aggressive lobbying on the part of the Catholic system.'[29]

When, in April 2013, Prime Minister Gillard announced the government's plan to deliver an additional $14.5 billion dollars of government funding over the subsequent six years, her statement included the allocation of additional funding to each of the school sectors. Catholic schools across the country were set to receive $1.4 billion in new funding. According to Catholic Education Office Melbourne executive director, Stephen Elder, that figure fell one billion dollars short of what the Catholic sector was entitled to. On Elder's argument, this was because funding would increase faster to public schools, which would then reduce the Catholic sector's share of taxpayer funding. The reaction was immediate, and they confronted the Prime Minister in a private meeting the day of her announcement.[30]

Later that same day, the Prime Minister provided a written assurance that the Catholic sector would continue to enjoy at least their present 16.8 per cent share of overall public funding – a guarantee later also extended to the independent sector. The backdown resulted in 'approximately $1.6 billion in additional funding to 1650 Catholic systemic schools over six years'.[31] Not bad for a day's work. When the amendments to the Australian

Education Bill were tabled in parliament in June, Jacinta Collins, Parliamentary Secretary for Education, reiterated the commitment. 'The government has assured, for example, that Catholic schools will maintain their proportion of funding', Collins stated. And 'the overall share of public funding, over time', she continued, 'is maintained for non-government schools'.[32] The 'no losers' promise had now morphed into a guaranteed private school share of the public dollar. When Collins left politics a few years later, she would be appointed Executive Director of the National Catholic Education Commission.

This assurance given to the Catholic and independent sectors was the antithesis of needs-based funding. The Gonski Report had recommended that public schools should receive three-quarters of additional funding, because that is what a needs-based formula produced. From that recommendation, however, things had now shifted to a point where there could be no change in the proportions of public funding the sectors received. It was the very epitome of a sector-based approach to funding schools, and completely unrelated to educational need.

It takes no little effort to comprehend how an ostensibly needs-based funding system could also guarantee each school sector their existing share of the funding pie. How did the government square the circle? It had to do more than provide funding increases for *overfunded* schools. The solution was to artificially increase the number of non-government schools that would be treated as *underfunded.*

Gonski had recommended that the proportion of the resource standard received by private schools would decrease from 90 per cent to 20 per cent as the socio-economic status of its student population increased. The logic behind this was that the greater parents' 'capacity to contribute', the more they would be expected to meet the costs of their child's education out of their own pockets.

Instead, two special deals meant that all Catholic schools would be entitled to close to 90 per cent of the resource standard.

The first special deal was called the system-weighted average. It gave one socio-economic status score to every Catholic school in a whole state irrespective of the students the school actually enrolled. And then there was a second deal for Catholic primary schools which enhanced the impact of the first. Even the average scores assigned to each state Catholic system meant that all its primary schools were funded as though they were highly disadvantaged.[33]

These legislative sleights of hand meant that every Catholic primary school in South Australia was entitled to over 88 per cent of the resource standard, no matter how privileged their student population – or how high their fee income. Any Catholic primary school not receiving that level of taxpayer support would be considered underfunded. By such alchemy, it was ensured that the introduction of ostensibly needs-based funding would not reduce the proportion of public funding flowing to private schools.

In this light, it's not hard to see why a figure like Ken Boston, who had worked tirelessly on the development of a rigorous and rational funding model, blamed the Gillard Government for its demise. But the Gillard Government was not playing to the purists. It was concerned solely with the art of the possible. And on this criteria, it succeeded. The amendments to the *Australian Education Act* passed the Senate on 26 June 2013. Gonski had become law. In time, and with luck, significant additional resources would flow to some of the most disadvantaged children in Australia. For the parents, teachers, unionists and politicians who had been fighting for a fairer funding system for years, if not decades, it was a historic moment.

Celebrations were soon underway in Peter Garrett's office, where the minister's staff were joined by lobbyists and senior public servants who had all shed plenty of blood, sweat and tears making

Gonski into law. But just as the party was getting started, the Prime Minister appeared on the TV screen. Voices in caucus in support of a return of Kevin Rudd to the top job had reached a crescendo that Julia Gillard could no longer ignore. She announced there would be a spill of the leadership of the Australian Labor Party the next day. Minister Garrett disappeared inside his office in a huddle with top advisors to gauge what was going on. The bureaucrats who had come to celebrate the legislative success made a quick exit, eager to ensure they were not embroiled in the politics of the moment. Suddenly the mood had soured and, once again, Labor leadership divisions were overshadowing the Gonski reforms. The day the school funding legislation passed would also turn out to be Julia Gillard's last day as prime minister.

Although Gillard had seen Gonski across the finish line, big questions remained. Would the hold-out states, especially Victoria, Queensland and Western Australia, sign on? What about the non-government school sectors? And could Gonski survive the election looming on the horizon in which Labor was almost certain to be defeated? These challenges were closely related. Every state that signed on to Gonski locked in increased funding to their schools, leaving the federal Coalition having to explain why they intended on pulling the additional funding if elected.

In May, the ACT had followed in New South Wales' footsteps and signed on to Gonski. Then, in June, the South Australian Government joined them. But getting the other jurisdictions on board was a task left to the second Rudd Government and the new education minister, Bill Shorten. In early July, they secured the support of Tasmania. But as the smallest state, with a Labor–Greens Government which had always been committed to the principles of the reform, this news did little to shift the dial in terms of the calculations of Christopher Pyne and Tony Abbott.

However, the next day, the Independent Schools Council of

Australia (ISCA) signed a memorandum of understanding with the federal government, formalising the independent sector's participation in the new school funding deal. Explaining their agreement, ISCA executive director Bill Daniels declared with satisfaction, 'the commitment from former Prime Minister Gillard that no school will be worse off compared to their 2013 Government funding has been built into the calculations of the new funding model'.[34] Pyne and Abbott had been deserted by a major ally, and worse was to come. Negotiations between education minister Bill Shorten and the Catholic sector were proceeding apace.

The sticking point between the Commonwealth and the Catholic sector was how block grants to Catholic system authorities were distributed between schools. The Commonwealth was insisting that Catholic authorities distribute government funding to Catholic schools on a needs basis (in the same manner as it required the states to). But the Catholic hierarchy demanded the right to distribute the funding as they wished.[35] On 23 July, they secured the demand, and Catholic education commissions in each jurisdiction signed a memorandum of understanding with the government. As a statement from the Sydney Archdiocese explained, 'under the agreement announced today the Catholic education sector will maintain their autonomy and ability to distribute funds to the schools they manage and run according to local need'.[36] What exactly was meant by 'local need' would be revealed in time.

It was another major blow to the integrity of the new funding model. Even after all the special deals, the Catholic systems did not even have to allocate Commonwealth funding to their schools according to a transparent needs-based criteria. But with both private school sectors behind the Labor reform, it was becoming harder and harder for Christopher Pyne and Tony Abbott to hold out against it. And signs were emerging that the Napthine

Coalition Government in Victoria was moving to reach a deal with the federal government. When the deal was finally announced, hours before the federal election was called on Sunday, 4 August, it was revealed that the Victorian Government was not required to begin indexing its funding by 3 per cent until 2016, and Victorian schools would not reach 95 per cent of the resource standard until 2022.[37] But Victoria was on board.

Abbott and Pyne's triple backflip: Gonski survives the 2013 election

On 1 August 2013, the Shadow Education Minister, Christopher Pyne, was still saying of Labor's school funding reforms, 'the truth is of course it's a great con'.[38] But the next day, just two days before Kevin Rudd called the election, the Opposition Leader, Tony Abbott, announced a complete about-face: 'As far as school funding is concerned, Kevin Rudd and I are on a unity ticket', he said. 'There is no difference between Kevin Rudd and myself when it comes to school funding... We will honour the agreements that Labor has entered into, we will match the offers that Labor has made, we will make sure that no school is worse off'.[39]

Abbott's announcement was misleading. Labor's agreements ran over six years, with most of the additional funding arriving in the final two; the Coalition was only committing to match Labor's commitments for the first four. But the Opposition Leader's backdown was no less sudden or dramatic for that. It was more than a compromise. It was a complete U-turn, and self-evidently Abbott's heart was not in it. For more than 18 months, Abbott and his Education Spokesperson, Christopher Pyne, had attempted to undermine the Gonski reforms with a campaign of constant sniping and sabotage. Now came a candid and unqualified concession of defeat, an acknowledgment that they had been unable to erase

Gonski's powerful electoral appeal, or diminish the substantial enthusiasm the reforms inspired across a wide cross-section of the community. Humiliating, deeply humiliating, but necessary, adjudged Abbott and co., despite their incredibly dominant position in the broader contest with the Labor Government.

That was the first backflip. Then, on Monday, 25 November – less than 12 weeks after being elected to government – came the second. 'Back to drawing board for Gonski', ran the headline in *The Australian*. The new education minister, Christopher Pyne, was claiming that 'Everything needs to be examined fresh because the model that Labor came up with is a shambles and quite unimplementable'.[40] The government now only intended to deliver Gonski funding for one year, not four, clearly contradicting its pre-election promise. This was going to leave thousands of schools worse off.

At the time of this backflip, the Abbott Government was still within its first 100 days in office. The dishonesty was startling in its brazenness, and the backlash was instant and overwhelming. Tony Abbott, who had so sanctimoniously lambasted the last government on the matter of promise-keeping, was embracing what he claimed to despise. Abbott had articulated his pre-election retreat in classically strident terms, unadorned by nuance or qualification, unleavened by ambiguity, and now he was practising precisely what he had preached against. The hypocrisy was rank. It was a measure of the federal Coalition's desire to break out of the schools funding straitjacket they'd been placed in.

When Abbott and Pyne attempted to abandon Gonski, they were attacked from both sides of the political divide – not just by the new Labor Opposition Leader, Bill Shorten, but also the Liberal Premier of Abbott's home state, New South Wales, Barry O'Farrell. 'Can I just make this point to the federal Education Minister', O'Farrell inquired, offering Pyne some free advice.

'When you move into government, you have got to stop behaving like an opposition'.[41] O'Farrell was accompanied by his education minister, Adrian Piccoli, in delivering frank criticism of the federal government. They would be joined, in turn, by interstate counterparts on both sides of the partisan divide. On the Friday following Abbott and Pyne's second backflip, education ministers from Tasmania, Victoria, South Australia, New South Wales and the ACT joined together to condemn the federal government. 'Here's a unity ticket for you right here', said Tasmanian education minister Nick McKim. 'A Labor minister, a Greens minister, National ministers, Liberal Party ministers, sticking up and unified behind Australian schools and behind funding certainty for Australian schools.'[42]

Not only did Christopher Pyne elicit the predictable outrage from public school communities across the country, but also criticism from non-government school lobby groups. And from the right-of-centre as well as the left. Gonski panellist and member of Liberal Party royalty, Kathryn Greiner, urged Pyne to reconvene the Gonski panel, if only for a day, for the purpose of providing the minister with a refresher on the reforms.

When Tony Abbott went on Network Ten's *Bolt Report* on the Sunday following the bombshell announcement, even his most enthusiastic media cheerleader practically pleaded with him to honour his unity ticket commitment.[43] Abbott doubled down: 'We are going to keep the promise that we made', he told Andrew Bolt. 'Not the promise that some people thought we made, or the promise that some people might have liked us to make'. But by the next day, the government conceded to political reality, announcing the restoration of the August commitment to deliver the Commonwealth share of Gonski funding over the next four years.

The new government looked impotent as well as impure. Worse than seeming cruel, it allowed the appearance that it had lost control. There was a reckless, quixotic character to Abbott and Pyne's antics, an awareness that they likely wouldn't get away with it but were determined to try anyway.[44] Their actions would come at significant political cost. Newspoll analysis the following fortnight showed the Coalition's primary vote had dropped three points and, for the first time, the Abbott Government trailed Labor in two-party preferred terms.[45] It never recovered.

Making the policy and the politics rhyme?

The Coalition Government's attempt at a swift decapitation of Gonski had failed, only confirming the enduring vitality of the reforms. It is a cliché of Australian politics that when the government changes, so too does the country. But, in this case, Tony Abbott and Christopher Pyne found the country had already changed and the new government would have to adapt. The newly elected Prime Minister and education minister were constrained to govern contrary to their own ardently held beliefs. It was powerful evidence of how deeply embedded the idea of needs-based funding had become in the school funding debate, along with the emergence of a broad-based Coalition deeply attached to its implementation. This, Julia Gillard could plausibly muse to herself, was the art of reformist politics.

The practical upshot of Gillard's triumph was that, eventually, fresh divisions would be sent to the front lines of Australian education: teachers, school psychologists, speech pathologists, youth workers, student mentors, occupational therapists, community liaison officers and others. The most disadvantaged children in our community would benefit from a substantial national investment, helping to unleash their full potential. Or so it was possible to believe.

But had Julia Gillard prevailed where many others had tried and failed? Or had she simply conceded defeat in advance? The Abbott Government's acrobatics on school funding only underscored the question. Abbott's pre-election claim that there was no difference between the parties when it came to schools funding was deceptive, but it was only possible because Labor had delayed the delivery of the real additional money for so long. Abbott could commit to Labor's program over the entire course of the forward estimates without really committing to it, and he took advantage of an opportunity that had been left wide open for him. Thus the *Sturm und Drang* could play out in November and December of 2013, the Abbott Government could be compelled to back down and still, there was no guarantee that needs-based funding would ever arrive. That would depend on what occurred in 2018 and 2019 – still political light years away.

Moreover, even when fully implemented, this was not a needs-based funding model. It was the opposite. It guaranteed the Catholic and independent sectors the same proportion of public funding as before. And like what had gone before, the new funding model was not even a single coherent system: special deals meant overfunded schools would remain overfunded. Even the minimum objective of applying the same rules to all schools had not been achieved.

Compounding the compromises, the Gillard and Rudd governments had not implemented the critical elements of the schools funding architecture recommended by Gonski. There was no National Schools Resourcing Body to ensure vital decisions about the size of the funding pie, and how it was sliced up was informed by independent expert judgments about educational need. There were no school planning authorities to bring coordination and clarity to the functioning of the different school sectors in each state and territory.

It was possible that Gillard advisor Tom Bentley and Gonski panellist Ken Boston were both right. The political compromises were truly necessary; but the policy that was left after all the deals had been done would fail to solve the problems facing the nation's schools – and the students they served. Maybe it was impossible to successfully reform Australia's school system within the constraints of the Karmel paradigm, the framework of assumptions that had defined school funding debates since the 1970s. Blood, sweat and tears had gone into the creation of the Gillard Government's National Plan for School Improvement. But what was all this sweet work worth? Had anything really changed? Would the reforms that had passed the parliament really change the lives of the disadvantaged children they were intended to help?

2013: YEAR 6, GETTING READY FOR HIGH SCHOOL

The year 2013 was a big year for Australia, and Year 6 was a big decision time for Kim's and Maria's families as they prepared for high school in Rivertown the following year. At first sight, it seemed they had some choice: Rivertown had a public, a Catholic and an Anglican high school.

Having enjoyed her primary school, Maria wanted to stay with most of her friends in the public high school. The school had a solid reputation. Her folks were relieved – they were a Catholic family, but the Catholic school fees would have been out of their reach, especially as her dad had lost his farm job. Declining numbers in the local town also meant that Maria's mum now had to commute to a new job in Rivertown.

The transition to Year 7 meant bigger decisions for Kim's family. The shop wasn't doing well, so they sold up and prepared to move to Rivertown to join a larger family business. Schooling also became more complicated. Kim's parents had toured the public high school, but it looked worn and lacking in resources. If media reports were any guide, that wasn't likely to change anytime soon. They realised that they could afford to send Kim to the new Anglican school on the edge of Rivertown. (*To be continued ...*)

6

A mixed-up kid (2014–16)

> In 2016, 35 per cent of Australia's private schools received more public funding than the typical similar public school, up from 5 per cent in 2009.[1]
>
> *'Counting the cost of the education revolution', ABC News, 22 November 2018*

In early 2011, the Gonski panel travelled to Innisfail, just a little south of Cairns, where they visited a small public primary school. At Innisfail State School, more than two-thirds of students came from the poorest quarter of Australian families. Almost as many were Indigenous. On that day in 2011, the school community had no way of knowing what the expert panel would ultimately recommend, let alone what the Australian Government would do with their report. But it had reason to hope that help was on the way. And yet by 2017, after four years of so-called Gonski funding, the school was worse off than ever. It had lost over $1000 per student in funding, even before adjusting for inflation.[2] It certainly hadn't shed its disadvantaged student population in the intervening period. In 2017, three-quarters of the kids at the school were from Australia's poorest families. This was the kind of school Gonski was meant to help.

When the Gonski panel had visited Geelong Grammar the same year, non-government sector lobbyists were still fiercely resisting the possibility that any private school could face a funding freeze. In the 97th percentile of Australian schools in terms of socio-educational advantage and in receipt of over $16 000 per student from fees and other private sources, the prestigious private school could well have feared what the review might entail. But as it turned out, it had no need to. Taxpayer funding, in fact, grew by $1000 per student in the first four years of the Gonski era. Far from being frozen, it increased by 23 per cent.[3]

In Alice Springs, the Gonski panel had visited Bradshaw Primary School. In the third percentile of Australian schools, it was at the opposite end of the socio-economic ladder from Geelong Grammar. But between 2013 and 2017, Bradshaw's combined government funding was cut by $668 per student, even more in real terms. It turned out the 'no losers' guarantee didn't apply in Alice Springs or Innisfail. And the 'needs-based' funding model was delivering increases to the schools that needed them least. The exclusive independent school the panel visited in Bendigo, Girton Grammar, enjoyed a 23 per cent increase in government funding between 2013 and 2017. By that year, the school was receiving around $10 000 per student from taxpayers, in addition to fees averaging around $13 000.[4]

The needs-blind, rather than needs-based, character of the new funding system was also in evidence at the Catholic school the panel visited in Bendigo, Catherine McAuley College. In 2013, it received around $1000 more per student in combined state and federal government funding than at Bendigo South East College, the public school also visited by the Gonski panel. By 2017, the Catholic school had expanded its advantage in total taxpayer funding to $2000 per student.[5]

In Perth, the Gonski panel had visited Holy Cross College, a combined primary and secondary college in the suburb of Ellenbrook. Remarkably, in 2013, each student at Holy Cross received $1500 more in taxpayer funding than students at the nearby public high school, Ellenbrook Secondary College, even though the public school had more disadvantaged students. So the school facing the greater challenges, and which was legally prohibited from charging fees, received less taxpayer funding than the better-off school community that could raise substantial revenue from its parent community. This was exactly the kind of illogical and anomalous funding arrangement the Gonski Report was intended to fix. And yet, four years after the introduction of the new funding formula, the situation had got even worse. By 2017, Holy Cross' advantage in taxpayer funding had grown by over 10 per cent; by the following year, it received around $2500 more in public funding per student than Ellenbrook Secondary, despite continuing to enrol fewer disadvantaged students.[6]

The profiles of the schools visited by the Gonski panel in 2011 were not isolated examples. They represented national trends. In 2018, the ABC published a detailed report on what My School data revealed about public funding of our schools called 'Counting the cost of the education revolution'. 'In 2016', the report found, '35 per cent of Australia's private schools received more public funding than the typical similar public school, up from 5 per cent in 2009'.[7] This meant that over a third of private schools received more public funding than at least half of all public schools serving similar students and of comparable size and location. As far as funding was concerned, 'private school' had become a misnomer.

The ABC analysis focused only on public funding. Once fees were included as well, the two non-government sectors had a considerable advantage over public schools in net recurrent income per student. By 2017, public schools operated with a little over $14 000 per student on average; Catholic schools had over $500 more per student; while independent schools enjoyed a $6000 advantage in total income per student.[8] An historic transformation had occurred. Once underfunded, Catholic schools now enjoyed resource advantages over public schools – even before accounting for their more privileged student profiles. The public system, the sector with the most educational need, was the least well resourced, and this situation was being fuelled by decisions made by Australian governments.

In aggregate, between 2013 and 2017, school income from all sources, adjusted for inflation, grew by $1250 per student in independent schools, $1000 in Catholic schools, but only $200 on average in public schools.[9] How could it be that the introduction of a supposedly needs-based school funding system was delivering more additional resourcing to the children who needed it least, and increasing resource disparities between Australian schools? On the one hand, Commonwealth Government funding increases overwhelmingly favoured non-government schools – schools like Geelong Grammar, Girton Grammar, Catherine McAuley and Holy Cross College. And at the same time as this was happening, state governments cut funding to public schools like Innisfail State School and Bradshaw Primary.

No strings attached: the Abbott Government allows the states to cut school funding

Even though most attention was focused on the Commonwealth Government, what really mattered for public schools in the first years of the new funding system was what state and territory governments did. To understand why, we need to recall a key feature of the school funding arrangements that existed at the time of the Gonski review. Under the Howard Government, the proportion of Commonwealth school funding that went to public schools had shrunk to just 36 per cent.[10] Despite educating two-thirds of Australia's school students, public schools received little more than one-third of Australian Government funding. This proportion increased slightly under the Rudd and Gillard Governments but was still at a historically very low level – 40 per cent – when the new Gonski funding arrangements were introduced.[11]

That was the status quo, and then the Gillard Government legislation delivered Commonwealth funding increases primarily through annual indexation of existing spending. Of the total of $61 billion in proposed extra expenditure, around $45 billion would be delivered through indexation. The remaining $15 billion envelope would be top-up money to bring schools that continued to be underfunded up to their entitlement. But around $10 billion of that was not due to arrive until 2018 or, more likely, 2019.[12] So in the first years of the new system, additional Commonwealth funding was delivered overwhelmingly through indexation. Indexation, by its nature, amplifies the existing state of affairs, primarily benefitting the schools already receiving significant funding from the national government. And those schools were overwhelmingly in the non-government sectors. Public schools continued to be predominantly funded by state and territory governments.

With mixed success, Julia Gillard and Peter Garrett had pursued bilateral agreements requiring all jurisdictions to at least maintain their existing funding effort in real terms. And Gillard had used the carrot of additional Commonwealth money to effectively purchase an additional investment by the states. While in late 2013 the Abbott Government had been forced by a widespread public backlash to adhere to its commitment to deliver four years of Gonski funding, it simultaneously released the states which had not signed up to the Labor Government's national reform agreement from any requirement to maintain their own education budgets. At the same time, it signalled that it would make no effort to enforce the agreements that the previous government had succeeded in negotiating.

Justifying this position in November 2013, the new education minister, Christopher Pyne, declared: 'we said before the election we would have a no strings attached school funding model in time. The Commonwealth would put the money that it wanted to put in. And whether the states and territories put the money they wanted to put in would be a matter for them'.[13] Days later, Prime Minister Abbott was asked, 'In the deals that you've done is there any requirement that the states don't reduce their funding as you increase yours? In other words, cost shifting?' Abbott replied, 'We would certainly regard it as very poor form for the states to reduce their funding because they're getting extra funding from the Commonwealth. But what we don't want is to micromanage the states'.[14] It was clear that the Commonwealth had no intention of applying any serious sanction on governments that did just what the question anticipated, and substituted additional Commonwealth funding for reduced state expenditure.

Cash-strapped states were practically being invited to shift the cost of running public schools to the Commonwealth, leaving students no better off than they had been before. Confirmation that the states were off the hook came with the May budget. On ABC's *Lateline*, Emma Alberici remarked to Minister Pyne that 'the funding model under Gonski required states to guarantee not to cut school funding in return for that federal money that was allocated by Labor. Will you therefore not be enforcing that part of the agreement?' 'Correct', was Minister Pyne's reply.[15]

Pyne drew, rhetorically at least, on the Liberal Party's traditional commitment to states' rights. 'Madam Speaker,' Pyne told the parliament in December 2013, 'we said that we would dismantle the command and control features from Canberra, and we will'.[16] And yet Christopher Pyne had no qualms about commissioning a review to alter the contents of the National Curriculum, the document that prescribed what was actually taught in schools. The ostensible devotion to respecting state sovereignty was no doubt genuine at some level, but it was also very convenient. In reality, Pyne was opposed to needs-based funding, and was driven by his allegiance to non-government schools, as had been amply illustrated in his simultaneous insistence that no private school could lose a dollar in funding *and* that funding of public schools was a distraction. Pyne's argument against what he called the 'command and control' features of agreements that required the states to maintain their funding effort can only be understood in this light.[17]

To adopt a 'no strings attached' approach and to say, as Pyne did, that what the states did was a matter for them alone, was to completely jeopardise the whole project of coordinating government effort to ensure a needs-based allocation of taxpayer resources to support individual students. Moreover, given vertical fiscal imbalance, it was to show an indifference as to whether public schools, overwhelmingly funded by state governments, would ever receive resourcing adequate to the scale of the education challenge they faced. In reality, Pyne's public statements were a series of convenient rationalisations for a sabotage job. Unable to get away with breaking the pre-election promise to fund the first four years of Gonski, there were no longer any budget savings to be made. But Pyne could still wreck a signature initiative of his political opponents.

The sabotage job worked, and the inevitable resulted. This is how Innisfail State School, the small primary school south of Cairns mostly attended by Indigenous kids from very poor families, lost around $1000 per student in funding. Between 2013 and 2017, the Commonwealth contribution to Innisfail rose by 18.7 per cent, or $800 per student,[18] but it came, in Christopher Pyne's words, with 'no strings attached', and the Queensland Government, free to do what it liked, cut funding to the school by over $2000 per student. The 'no school loses a dollar' promise didn't count in Innisfail, apparently. At Bradshaw Primary in Alice Springs, the dynamic was the same as at Innisfail. Bradshaw received a very substantial boost in Commonwealth funding – over $3000 per student, in fact – reflecting a high degree of educational disadvantage among its students. But the Northern Territory Government cut funding to the school by even more, leaving the school in receipt of over $600 per student less in government funding in 2017.[19]

Between 2013 and 2017, all states and territories, except for Victoria and Tasmania, cut funding to public schools in real terms.[20] The Commonwealth no longer had any intention of compelling them to maintain their pre-existing funding effort. As a result, any funding increases to public schools from the Commonwealth were largely negated, sometimes completely. For public schools, the story repeated itself around the country. The Australian Government might deliver substantial percentage growth, but the impact would be largely or entirely erased by state government cuts. Some public schools were more fortunate and came out on top in real terms, but usually only slightly.

This was politics of the worst kind – destructive, petty and heedless of the consequences for some of the most innocent and vulnerable members of our community. Christopher Pyne and Tony Abbott stand condemned. For all that, state and territory governments bear a large share of the responsibility for the failure to effectively transition to a funding system based on need.

The conduct of some state governments was unsurprising. In Queensland, blind partisanship had caused Premier Campbell Newman to reject an offer of billions of additional dollars for Queensland state schools. When the new Abbott Government delivered the additional Commonwealth dollars anyway, but with no strings attached, it was little surprise that the Newman Government took the opportunity to cut their own funding to public schools.

Between 2013 and 2017, the Northern Territory Government cut funding of public schools by $4500 per student.[21] The Giles Government in the Northern Territory, meanwhile, was a rolling debacle of resignations, desertions and scandals. Amid the chaos, it failed to sustain a coherent position on school education, one of the core functions of the territory government. 'The federal government handed an extra $272.5 million to the NT to spend on government schools for 2014 to 2017, despite Giles' refusal to sign on to the Gonski agreement', wrote Jarvis Ryan, the president of the Northern Territory branch of the Australian Education Union. 'Not only has the Giles Government pocketed a big chunk of the windfall', Ryan observed in 2016, 'it's reduced its own contribution to public schools'. 'The cuts compound an already dire situation for remote schools', Ryan explained. 'A major review of Indigenous education in the NT, completed two years ago by education consultant Bruce Wilson, found that many Indigenous children were worse off than at the time of the last comprehensive study in 1999. The declining education budget has also meant staff cuts and, in an alarming development, the Indigenous workforce has been hit disproportionately. Unfortunately, by drastically cutting the resources going to public schools, the Giles Government has squandered the opportunity that Gonski presented.'[22]

In Western Australia, budget cuts to public schools amounted to around $700 per student, in real terms, between 2013 and 2017.[23] The Productivity Commission's Report on Government Services revealed that student–teacher ratios jumped after cuts delivered in the 2013/14 budget, leaving the state's primary schools with the largest class sizes in the country.[24] The 2016 budget indicated that spending was increasing at a slower rate than growth in student numbers and, by 2017, the Barnett Government had cut the state's education budget by hundreds of millions of dollars.[25]

But if spending cuts in the states that had refused to sign on to Gonski in the first place were unsurprising enough, the really disappointing trend in this period was the real decline in spending on public schools by states that had signed up: New South Wales, South Australia and the ACT. Despite all the drama and noble statements, the New South Wales Government actually cut real funding to public schools in the first four years of the Gonski period, by around $200 per student or 2.4 per cent.[26] This came on top of an earlier cut of $400 per student between 2009 and 2013. While reducing overall spending on public schools, New South Wales did introduce a needs-based funding formula called the Resource Allocation Model (RAM). The effect of this was that changes in state government funding favoured disadvantaged schools with an ICSEA score below 1000 (a 10.6 per cent increase in nominal terms, on average) compared to schools with an ICSEA over 1000 (a 5.1 per cent increase).

These states did what states generally do, given the chance: they shifted costs to the Commonwealth. The children in the schools they owned and operated gained nothing from this exercise; in fact, often they lost out. Public schools were disproportionately affected by state and territory funding cuts because they are reliant for most of their funding – around 85 per cent – from that source. And while state governments cut funding to public schools, they generally maintained real funding to schools in the non-government sectors.[27] On average across the country, state and territory governments cut real funding to public schools by $233, but increased it by $24 per student in Catholic schools and $62 in independent schools.[28]

As it transpired, the fabled 'no school loses a dollar' principle only applied to independent and Catholic schools. Where public schools were funded above the schooling resource standard, particularly in Western Australia and the ACT – jurisdictions which had historically resourced their schools above the national average – funding was cut with little fuss or fanfare. In Perth, the Gonski panel had visited Shenton College, a secondary public school whose students came from very privileged backgrounds on average, similar in social background to many of the exclusive private schools the panellists had visited on the east coast. In 2014, Shenton College received $12 508 per student in combined government funding, a shade above the schooling resource standard base per student amount of $12 193. With very few disadvantaged students – just 7 per cent – from below-average backgrounds, the school was entitled to little additional funding through disadvantage loadings. And so, over the successive years, its funding from both levels of government was reduced. By 2017, it received $12 202 in taxpayer funding per student.[29] Schools funded above the resource standard could and indeed did have their funding cut – but only if they were public schools.

Manna from Canberra: funding of private schools keeps growing and growing

Because increases of Commonwealth funding were primarily delivered through indexation of existing spending which already heavily favoured independent and Catholic schools, and because special deals accentuated that favouritism, taxpayer funding to non-government schools continued to grow handsomely – and outstrip increases to public schools. The indexation rate varied between 4.7 per cent for schools under their schooling resource standard entitlement, 3.6 per cent for schools at their entitlement, or 3 per cent for schools already above it. But what was more important was the initial amount being indexed. Three per cent of a large amount is always going to add up to a whole lot more than 4.7 per cent of not much. Non-government schools, which received around three-quarters of their public funding from the Commonwealth government, were positioned to prosper.

This could be seen in the three Bendigo schools visited by the Gonski panel, one independent, one Catholic and one public. The public school's funding from the Australian Government increased by $600 to approximately $2100 per student.[30] But at the independent Girton Grammar, Commonwealth funding increased by over $1700 per student to an allocation of around $8300 per student by 2017. And at the Catholic school, Catherine McAuley College, an increase of almost $2000 over the period brought Commonwealth funding up to almost $10 000 per student. The public school, Bendigo South East Secondary College, actually enjoyed the greatest increase in percentage terms. But the non-government schools were starting from substantially higher levels of Commonwealth funding, which meant that their resourcing grew by a much larger amount.

The Bendigo story represents an exaggerated version of the national trend. Australian Government funding to public schools increased at a faster rate: more public schools were funded below the schooling resource standard so were indexed at 4.7 per cent, as well as also receiving some additional top-up money. But because public schools started from much lower levels of Commonwealth funding, the higher percentage increases produced lower amounts than at non-government schools. Australian Government funding increased by around $750 per student in private schools, but less than $500 per student in public schools.[31]

The Gonski Report had recommended that indexation be employed for the conventional purpose of preserving the real value of funding. If this recommendation had been adhered to, additional funding could have been delivered to under-resourced schools on an equal basis, or priority could have even been given to the most needy and disadvantaged schools. Instead, the Gillard Government's utilisation of indexation to deliver funding increases had the perverse effect of amplifying and exacerbating the imbalances and inequities of the status quo. It also meant that even when Abbott and Pyne were forced to deliver the first four years of Commonwealth funding, they could do so knowing it would overwhelmingly benefit the non-government schools to which they felt an overriding allegiance.

The use of indexation to deliver real funding increases was significantly responsible for the much greater growth in Commonwealth funding to non-government schools than to public schools. And the problem was then compounded by the special deals associated with the 'no losers' promise. Wealthy non-government schools that already received taxpayer funding above the resource standard continued to receive funding increases. In 2014, taxpayer funding to Loreto Kirribilli amounted to a whopping 283 per cent of its actual entitlement under the schooling resource standard.[32] And yet Commonwealth funding was not reduced or even frozen. Over the first four years of so-called Gonski funding, Commonwealth funding at the Sydney school grew by 14 per cent or over $750 per student.[33] With net income per student of over $29 000 in 2017, Loreto enjoyed almost three times the income of comparable public schools. This is what the concession that every school would enjoy funding increases actually meant in practice. It was profoundly wasteful, and it was completely contrary to a needs-based system.

One way of ensuring that no school lost a dollar was by guaranteeing 3 per cent indexation even for schools that were over-funded under the new formula. But another way was to manipulate the formula to maximise the number of non-government schools that were technically funded under the entitlement defined by the schooling resource standard. This was achieved by the special deals hashed out in 2013, such as the system-weighted average and the manipulation of the 'capacity to contribute' curve.

At Geelong Grammar, where almost three in every four kids

were from the most privileged Australian families, net recurrent income was around $21 000 per student in 2014. Of this, $4500 came from the taxpayer. But this was assessed as only 87.5 per cent of its funding entitlement.[34] Thus Australian Government funding to one of the country's most exclusive private schools – deemed to be underfunded – increased by 25 per cent or almost $1000 per student in the first four years of the Gonski era.

In Bendigo, Commonwealth funding to Girton Grammar increased by around three times as much as at the nearby public school, Bendigo South East. As discussed above, that was partly because the indexation of Girton's funding was off a much higher base. But it was also because Girton Grammar was 'underfunded' and so eligible for the maximum rate of indexation of 4.7 per cent plus top-up money. In 2014, Girton received around $12 000 per student from fees and other private sources – about equivalent to the schooling resource standard for secondary schools – and then, on top of that, it received taxpayer funding of nearly $8000 per student. Despite serving a highly privileged student population, it was assessed as receiving only 80 per cent of its entitlement under the schooling resource standard.[35] And so Australian Government funding grew by 26 per cent over the subsequent four years.

Block funding of system authorities

The needs-based character of school funding was further undermined because block grants were provided to non-government system authorities which could then dispense them as they pleased. There was no assurance that systems would apportion it to individual schools on a needs basis. In immediate terms, this was the product of the deal Bill Shorten made with the Catholic sector in 2013, but ultimately it was because the Gonski review had not seriously tackled the topic.

Gonski recommended that system and sector authorities should continue to exercise discretion when allocating public funding among their schools. This was despite the fact that the Australian National Audit Office had found that systemic non-government schools received 'less Federal funding through general recurrent grants per student from their school systems than if they were directly funded under the SES arrangements in the same way as non-systemic private schools'.[36]

The Gonski Report acknowledged that 'block funding of systems does raise issues about the transparency of funding allocation by systems'.[37] However, while encouraging increased transparency, the report's ultimate recommendation was that the Commonwealth Government should refrain from calculating each school's individual entitlement, let alone delivering it directly. 'Given the primary responsibility of government and non-government system authorities for the funding and operation of their schools, Australian Government funding for all systems should be assessed and calculated at the system rather than the school level.'[38]

Ken Boston, for one, regrets that the panel did not recommend stronger oversight over government and non-government systems, which could have ensured that each individual school received a genuinely needs-based funding entitlement. Within discussions among the expert panel, Boston argued for provisions to ensure that 'a disadvantaged school in one part of the country, be it public, Catholic, Independent or Lutheran, should receive the same funding as a similarly disadvantaged school in another part of the country, regardless of its system. My view', Boston says, 'was that the needs-based funding entitlement for each school should be public information on the My School website'. However, the panel as a whole was not persuaded by Boston's argument. 'Such issues were seen as too complex, and as matters to leave to implementation',

Boston reflects. 'Given the manner in which subsequent Labor and LNP Governments have dealt with this issue, that was a mistake. I should have stood my ground and argued that that was absolutely fundamental.'[39]

A more unlevel playing field

In an analysis of 2017 My School data, Chris Bonnor compared government funding of Australian schools that had student populations close to the national socio-economic average.[40] Taking schools with a score between 950 and 1000 on the Index of Community Socio-Educational Advantage (for which the national average is 1000), Bonnor found that the median Catholic school received 7 per cent more taxpayer funding than the median public school, while the median independent school received 3 per cent more.[41] For Australian schools with a broadly average-looking student profile, whether nominally public or private, by 2017 there was really very little difference in terms of the taxpayer funding they received. Regardless of whether these schools were in the Catholic, independent or public systems, they were more or less fully public funded. The difference in terms of resourcing was that the non-government sector schools could charge fees on top of the public funding they received, and so they enjoyed a distinct advantage when it came to total resourcing, from both public and private sources.

Between 2011 and 2017, private school fees increased by over 30 per cent on average – more than 4.5 per cent annually.[42] Private school principals and lobbyists often point to rising costs, but these increases equated to an average annual hike more than twice the rate of inflation. Just in the first four years of the new funding system, from 2013 to 2017, independent school fees grew by over $400 in real terms, while Catholic fees rose by more than $200 on average over the same period.[43] At Loreto Kirribilli average fees jumped by more than $4000 to $19000 between 2013 and 2017, notwithstanding the generous growth in taxpayer funding the school enjoyed in those years. At Catherine McAuley College in Bendigo fees jumped from $3600 to $4600 in four years, while it received more taxpayer funding than ever. At Our Lady of the Sacred Heart in Alice Springs fees averaged $2700 in 2011 but had risen to $3900 in 2017 – a 41 per cent increase.[44] Increased public funding was not putting downward pressure on fees. It was not enhancing choice or improving affordability. And, as discussed in chapter 3, this was not an accident. The express intention of government policy, endorsed by the Gonski review, was to provide public funding in a way that did not hinder the capacity of private schools to raise income from private sources.

The consequence was that the forces driving disadvantaged children into comprehensive public schools were working unabated, exacerbating the problem of negative peer effects. In Alice Springs, between 2011 and 2017, fees at Our Lady of the Sacred Heart Catholic College increased by 41 per cent, even though Commonwealth Government funding grew by more than half over the same period. But the growing fees made the school less accessible than ever, and the proportion of kids from the most disadvantaged quarter of the population fell to 14 per cent.[45] That compared to 57 per cent from the same group at the nearby Centralian Middle School.

In December 2016, the results of Australian students in the first round of PISA since the new funding system began were released. In just three years, mean scores in all three learning domains tested (reading, maths and science) had declined significantly. Australian 15-year-olds were now averaging 25 points less in the reading test than they did in 2000, and 30 points below the first maths tests in 2003 – equivalent to almost a full year of learning.[46] The decline was disastrous, but it represented the continuation of a long-term trend, one that was already apparent in the Gonski Report produced five years earlier. But the continued deterioration in student achievement should not have surprised. Nothing had changed in terms of the underlying dynamics which were harming student learning – in fact, they had only got worse.

FIGURE 3

Australian achievement in PISA since 2000

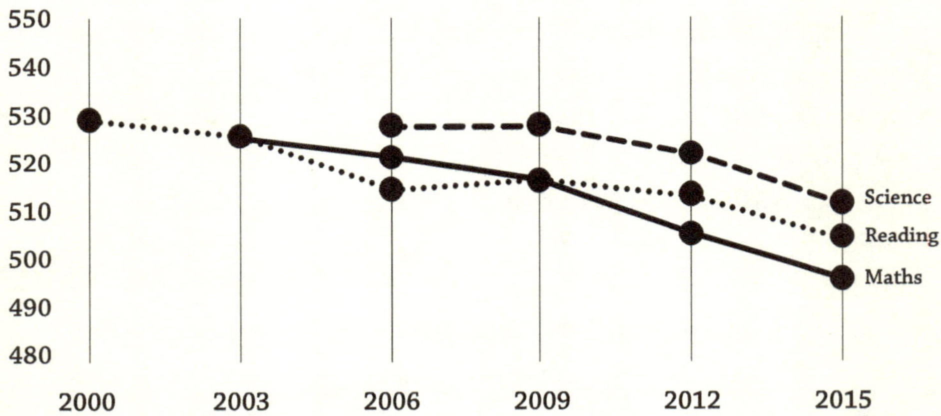

SOURCE Sue Thomson, Lisa De Bortoli, Catherine Underwood, PISA 2015: A first look at Australia's results, ACER (2016). <www.acer.org/au/discover/article/pisa-2015-australian-students-achievement>.

FROM THE PRINCIPAL'S DESK: WHAT HAPPENED WHERE ADDITIONAL FUNDING ARRIVED?

Gonski was all about getting the right resourcing where it was needed most. Too often the funding didn't arrive. And the consequences were often extremely concerning. 'We do not have a school-based counsellor, so teachers end up providing informal counselling', one teacher explained. 'The school is rife with undiagnosed cognitive and physical impairments – FASD, PTSD, ADHD, hearing disorders – so teachers impute diagnoses in the hope of accessing further support. We are not trained in these areas, nor do I believe we should be. This is the work of social workers, psychologists, nurses, pathologists and parents.' A teacher at a school with a high number of students with a language background other than English explains, 'We need a helping hand in every class with disadvantaged students to spend more one-on-one time and provide ongoing mentoring to students around the basics of operating in a classroom environment'.

But when additional resourcing did arrive, how did schools use it to advance the welfare and learning of students in their care? We get an insight from our principals' panel. 'The placement of a highly trained and skilled instructional leader in the school was inspired', one principal, Peter Morgan, recalls. 'Using our Gonski money we were able to release teachers to work with the instructional leader weekly to learn, do, reflect and refine their work. Teachers and the school felt empowered. The data shifted. It worked through to Year 3 NAPLAN results where [the school] was at or above state average.'

Another principal, Andrew Newman, describes losing around 20 per cent of his Year 11 cohort each year, many of whom did not gain employment. To turn things around, the school invested in a sophisticated program of customised professional learning and whole school improvement programs. 'Considerable funding was focused on students and staff selected for the program', Newman says. 'As the program grew, students were more motivated and connected with their own education and classrooms were much more settled and focused.'

Having the resources to provide individual attention to students made a world of difference, explains principal Bernie Roebuck. 'Having the financial capacity to have some "special classes" with small numbers – not specifically for just poorly behaved kids but to meet the needs of many different types of students, including very able kids. We had a lot of success in special education because there were small numbers of students involved and some excellent resources to support them.' For Roebuck, the key was 'having high-quality teachers and high-quality executive staff who are fully committed to meeting the needs of a wide range of students. That means high level recruitment and retention, and high level ongoing training and support'.[47]

Signs of hope: the schools which started to receive more money

The aggregate picture was very dismal indeed. However, as always, there was immense variation from one school to another. And all the hard work by the Gonski reformers and activists could be seen to be making a positive difference in some contexts. Even though they didn't represent the general trend, some schools serving disadvantaged children in particular places and jurisdictions did start to experience increases in real funding. Their initiatives demonstrated how additional resourcing could make a profound difference in the lives of Australian schoolchildren.

Darlington School is a primary school located in Adelaide's southern suburbs, where three-quarters of students came from below-average socio-economic backgrounds. One in five students was Indigenous, and half came from non-English-speaking backgrounds. To target additional funding effectively, Darlington identified children who would potentially benefit from intensive, short-term intervention to support the development of their numeracy and literacy. Throughout 2015, Darlington used additional funding to employ a teacher to work closely with very small groups of two to four children. It further used the additional resourcing to give staff dedicated time to closely track the learning of these students, to develop appropriate teaching strategies, and to ensure continuity between the intervention program and general classroom learning. The results of these measures were positive. The school reported that every 'intervention student' achieved above expected targets, with some achieving 12 months of learning in just over one term of support.[48] The most recent NAPLAN results show that the school continues to improve.[49]

Like Darlington, two public schools in Queensland offered further examples of how increased funding was used effectively. Eagleby South State School employed extra teacher aides for the early years of schooling. Their NAPLAN results improved and continue to compare favourably with other schools enrolling similar students. Minimbah State School, meanwhile, made good use of achievement data to drive its improvements and increased its resourcing of support teachers. In more recent years the school has caught up with schools enrolling similar students.[50]

Two schools in New South Wales told a similar story. Barrack Heights Primary is a small school just south of Wollongong. Its enrolment included significant numbers of Indigenous students and children with a language background other than English. The school also supported significant numbers of autistic students. Like many disadvantaged schools, Barrack Heights used its funding to improve student engagement, particularly through programs for those with identified disabilities. The school especially welcomed the flexibility that came with the funding. The other school, Wadalba Community School, is a large and growing K–12 school on the New South Wales Central Coast. It has targeted vulnerable students in the early secondary years, while also creating innovative programs to encourage students interested in later tertiary study. In reality, outcomes such as NAPLAN fall well short of measuring the range of achievements in such schools, but in both cases the schools have increasingly performed at, rather than below, the level of schools enrolling similar students.

Too often in the past, additional funding came in the form of one-off grants and lacked the continuity and flexibility needed to create success over the longer term. The Gonski review especially recognised the value of flexibility in targeting disadvantage. St John's Park High School in south-west Sydney demonstrated the value of applying funding to meet a variety of needs. It was able to invest in speech and occupational therapy, revamp learning spaces and integrate student learning with real-world experiences.[51] The effects of these measures have been obvious: the school has seen rising HSC results and its more recent NAPLAN results have continued to improve.

All these schools have demonstrated a success derived from many factors: expertise, leadership, initiative and commitment. But the common ingredient in these stories has also been the potential difference made by additional funding. A final example is presented by Mount Austin High School, mentioned previously in chapter 3. Unlike in many other schools, between 2012 and 2016, Mount Austin's public funding increased by almost a third – well-timed because its enrolment became increasingly disadvantaged over the same period.[52] Something happened around that time: the school's NAPLAN results started to improve to the point where it was above schools with similar students. This would have been unlikely to have happened without the additional funding support.

Even though Gonski had been distorted and delayed, and the Gonski Report's prescriptions had not tackled the deepest problems, more money *was* flowing to *some* schools serving some of the most disadvantaged children in our community. Maybe, in time, it would help turn around the story of decline that had beset Australian education. The arrival of a new prime minister in the form of Malcolm Turnbull in September 2015 did not, at first, appear promising as far as Australia's schools were concerned. But that was about to change.

2014–16: THE JUNIOR HIGH SCHOOL YEARS

From day one at high school, Kim and Maria found themselves in very different places. Kim had to make new friends in her new school, but so did most others in Year 7. They were now in the big school, and the architecture and resources of Kim's new Anglican school were certainly in a different league.

Maria's start was different. It was a well-regarded public school, which, like her primary school, enrolled a variety of students. The teachers were great, but there weren't many 'Kims' in her class. The teachers were stretched to devote enough time to each student, and seemed to spend more time dealing with distractions. They worked hard to meet student needs, but sometimes this would morph into lower expectations. Over time, this impacted on the school's reputation, and some of Maria's friends drifted off to other schools. Her mum wasn't too surprised; the town's two private schools seemed to be doing very well out of 'Gonski' funding. Something wasn't quite adding up.

Kids certainly didn't leave Kim's school; indeed there was apparently a waiting list to get in. There weren't many 'Marias' in Kim's classes. The well-funded Anglican school had a variety of subjects and after-school programs, and her family could afford the fees. Kim's public school teacher mum had her own regrets, and she kept her 'I Give a Gonski' sticker firmly attached to the rear window of her car. But she wondered if 'Gonski' would really make any difference. (*To be continued ...*)

7

Gonski's Second Coming (2017–21)

When we were at school, we used to joke about our respective destinies; David [Gonski] asked me to appoint him chief justice when I became prime minister. But among the many grandiose visions we had for ourselves, they didn't include David becoming a secular saint and political icon of the education unions and the left of the Labor Party.[1]

Malcolm Turnbull, Prime Minister of Australia (2015–18), 2020

The Federal Government has locked in a model where every private school will get fully funded by 2023, whereas very few government schools will ever get fully funded. By 2030, we're going to be having this same argument and it's all predictable from now.[2]

Peter Goss, Program Director of School Education at the Grattan Institute, 2020

Birmingham's bombshell

A quarter of an hour into ABC TV's *Q&A* program on the last Monday of September 2016, host Tony Jones called on a question from Pam Kent, the president of the South Australian Primary Principals Association. Kent addressed her question to Senator

Simon Birmingham, the man who had replaced Christopher Pyne in the education portfolio. With the kind of steady demeanour that let you know you were in the principal's office now, Kent eyeballed Birmingham as she spoke. 'How can you justify allocating generous amounts to wealthy schools when impoverished and disadvantaged students attending their local public school need so much more support?' she asked.[3]

Birmingham's appearance on the ABC's flagship talk show, broadcast from Adelaide that night, came just days after he had hosted a meeting of his state and territory counterparts. The headlines generated by that gathering had focused on funding, and a question on the topic on *Q&A* was inevitable. But his answer certainly wasn't.

At first, Birmingham's response to Kent sounded like it would be straight out of the politician's playbook: the government was growing funding, to record levels even – and it must be remembered that states and territories have primary responsibility for education. But then the redoubtable Jones intervened: 'Okay', he said, 'you've made that point. I'm going to bring you to the question now'.

Referring to the guarantee that no school will lose a dollar of funding, Jones asked, 'Should that change?' At this point, Birmingham adopted an unforeseen candour. 'That's not a promise I have ever made', he remarked, 'and I've been very cautious not to do so'. Jones sought confirmation he had heard correctly: 'You have not made the promise that no school will be worse off?' 'Correct', came Birmingham's full-throated reply.

Jones leant in, sniffing the heady scent of tomorrow's headline. 'If you are not making the promise', he said, 'does that mean you are saying some schools could be worse off?' 'That is possible', Birmingham confirmed. 'Are the wealthier private schools over-funded?' Jones persisted. 'There are some that fit that bill', Birmingham replied. 'Yes. There are.'

Birmingham's mild manner and measured tones could not disguise the fact that he had just dropped a bombshell on national TV. Jones said he must have a hit list, evoking the controversies that dogged Labor's election policy in 2004 and the Hawke Government education minister, Susan Ryan, 20 years before that – the argument that Julia Gillard had so ardently avoided. Now, a Liberal politician had said the unsayable, exploding bipartisan orthodoxy, transforming government policy and launching an assault on his party's base in one fell swoop.

Simon Birmingham had just touched the high-voltage third rail of Australian politics. He hadn't been electrocuted – at least, not yet – but what on earth was he doing wandering across the tracks like this?

For 12 months, the Turnbull Government had wrestled unconvincingly with the Abbott legacy, and the failure to firmly establish its own identity had been exemplified by the floundering in the education portfolio. In March 2016, Prime Minister Turnbull had publicly countenanced the possibility of the Commonwealth completely ceasing to fund public schools, entirely abandoning responsibility for two-thirds of Australian school children to revenue-starved state and territory governments, and turning the clock back to the pre-Whitlam period.[4] The optics, then, were of a government doubling down on the path forged by its predecessors.

Turnbull's thought bubble quickly burst under a welter of criticism, but it had left every impression that the change of prime minister had done little to change the Coalition's stance on schools funding. This impression was only barely modified when the government delivered its pre-election budget in May 2016. Tony Abbott and Christopher Pyne had decided there would be no further increases in school funding, apart from annual indexation against the Consumer Price Index (CPI), once the 'unity ticket' commitment expired in 2018. As Turnbull would note in his memoir, that was 'less than the annual increase in teachers' salaries alone'.[5] So, in practice, Pyne and Abbott's plan meant that school resourcing would start going backwards again. The 2016 budget changed this, aligning indexation with actual cost growth in schools, allowing Turnbull to go to the polls, inoculated against the charge that he planned to cut real spending.

However, as the July election approached, it remained clear that only one of the major parties gave a Gonski. Labor had promised that two-thirds of the additional Gonski funding would arrive in 2018 and 2019. The Turnbull Government, meanwhile, was promising no real increase in spending at all.

The 'I Give a Gonski' campaign was determined to make sure voters knew about the difference when they went to the polls. The Australian Education Union (AEU) employed campaign organisers in marginal seats throughout the country to run phone banks, street stalls and community events, and make sure polling booths were plastered with Gonski signs and staffed with Gonski supporters.

'It actually polled – schools funding, not even just education; schools funding polled as one of the top three issues that people say they took to the election in 2016', says AEU president Correna Haythorpe, relying on polling data the union commissioned throughout the election campaign.[6] For the many voters who cared about needs-based school funding, the chasm separating the policy offerings of the government and the Opposition presented a stark choice.

And the teachers' union believed they achieved a sound return on their investment, with the swing against the government in the seats they targeted exceeding the general trend.

As much as Birmingham's statements on *Q&A* three months later came as a shock, they could be explained in large part by simple electoral politics. Malcolm Turnbull knew that the government had allowed itself to be framed as not giving a Gonski. 'Abbott's cuts in the 2014 budget had broken a signature promise', Turnbull reflected. 'It simply added to the political catastrophe of that budget.'[7] But the reality was that at the 2016 election, the Turnbull Government had done little to disentangle itself from the impression that the Coalition couldn't be trusted on Gonski. 'Malcolm Turnbull and Simon Birmingham knew they had to neutralise it', says Correna Haythorpe. 'Because their polling was telling them exactly what our polling was telling us, and that is that parents understood it, parents thought it was important.'[8]

When Turnbull had ascended to the prime ministership in September 2015, the ever-incisive gadfly of Australian education, Dean Ashenden, had asked whether the new Prime Minister could give a Gonski. 'Why go to the next election, less than a year away, with the electorally popular Gonski in Labor's hands?' he asked.[9] But now, in the wake of the loss of 14 seats and near electoral death, the Turnbull Government had cause to revisit that question. Having scraped back into government, was the Coalition going to continue to give Labor a free kick on schools funding?

The case for a course correction went beyond the issue of schools funding itself to broader questions about the meaning of the Turnbull prime ministership. When Turnbull had his turn on *Q&A* during the 2016 election campaign, the disillusionment among voters was palpable. Those who had welcomed the ouster of Tony Abbott were now asking what the point was.

'Can you convince me to trust you', one audience member asked, 'when you've already been swayed on climate change, Safe Schools [for LGBTIQ people], Gonski and marriage equality by the ultra-conservative wing of your own government?' Another question was even more blunt: 'Six months ago, you convinced the Liberal Party to make you Prime Minister on the premise that you were not Tony Abbott. In two weeks, will you keep the job on the premise that you are not Malcolm Turnbull either?'[10]

In his prescient analysis a year earlier, Ashenden had pointed out that Gonski offered Turnbull a golden opportunity to distinguish his government from Tony Abbott's. 'Among the many areas in which the Abbott administration was gratuitously adversarial, and blatantly deceitful', Ashenden wrote, 'was schools funding ... What better way for the new minister to distance himself from his predecessor, or for the new government to demonstrate that it is not the old one in drag, than to reverse the ill-judged and petty decision to dump Gonski?'[11]

Above anything else, Malcolm Turnbull knew he had to definitively establish that he was in charge. His failure to deliver on a moderate, liberal policy agenda and inability to stamp his authority on issues like energy policy and marriage equality had created the impression he was not really running the show. 'Nothing is more damaging than the appearance of impotence', Turnbull would later reflect – a theme that featured when the Prime Minister appraised the government's fortunes with John Howard, while watching the Cronulla Sharks prevail over Melbourne Storm in the 2016 rugby league Grand Final.[12]

Turnbull and Birmingham had not seized the moment before the election, but Gonski still presented them with a unique opportunity to demonstrate that they were in control and that theirs really was a government of the sensible centre. The existing funding quadrennium was due to expire at the end of 2017, so a new school funding agreement would be needed for 2018. For a government still rebounding from electoral catastrophe, it was a chance for a do-over.

The electoral imperatives were sharpened by legislative realities, as Minister Birmingham explained to Cabinet.[13] If the government left unaltered the legislation put in place by Labor, it could claw back about $6 billion in projected funding growth using administrative decisions. But almost all of that would come from public schools – a politically explosive proposition for which they would pay an even higher electoral price than they had already. Any new laws would require the vote of a significant section of the Senate crossbench, whose numbers had ballooned to 20 after July's full Senate election. To get legislation through this motley crew of Greens, centrists, social conservatives, deficit hawks and ethno-nationalists, the government would need to put on the table a proposal with genuinely broad-based appeal.

Simon Birmingham's departure from orthodoxy in his appearance on *Q&A* was open to a perception of recklessness. But in fact, by signalling that the government intended to execute an about-face on school funding, he was surgically removing an electoral thorn from the Turnbull Government's side while simultaneously launching a major effort to establish that the moderates were in charge.

The admission that schools above the resource standard should lose some of their funding was the cut-through moment that garnered the headlines, but it also gave Birmingham much-needed credibility as he executed a broader policy U-turn. Birmingham was telling the Australian people that the government now gave a Gonski, when for the last five years his Coalition colleagues had been saying (and doing) exactly the opposite. What better way to establish his bona fides than a move as audacious as acknowledging some schools should lose funding? Simply saying it out loud demonstrated a willingness to put principle ahead of politics.

In the lead-up to the meeting with state education ministers days earlier, Birmingham had released figures drawing attention to huge variations in Commonwealth government funding across the country. Government schools in Tasmania were attracting 40 per cent more funding than comparable schools in Western Australia, while one Victorian Catholic school received more than double the funding of a similar Catholic school in New South Wales.[14]

The Coalition supported the core principles of needs-based funding, Birmingham told the *Q&A* audience, but the previous Labor government had traduced those principles with a series of special deals. It was time, Birmingham declared, to revisit the recommendations of the Gonski Report to deliver funding on a fair and consistent basis.

The resurrection of Gonski

One observer watching Birmingham's manoeuvres with acute interest was Peter Goss, the head of education policy at the Melbourne think tank, the Grattan Institute. The week before Birmingham's bombshell on *Q&A*, Goss had penned an opinion piece in the *Australian Financial Review* in which he set out a plan to revive the Gonski process. Goss believed it was possible to generate new momentum around school funding reform by reframing the case for needs-based funding in a manner that could transcend entrenched partisan divisions.[15] Encouraged by the public signals that the government was contemplating a root and branch policy overhaul, Goss set about turning his op-ed into a robust, fully-fledged policy proposal, and two months later, the Grattan Institute published *Circuit Breaker, a new compact on school funding*.[16]

The Grattan Institute's proposed compact started from a simple observation: inflation and wage growth were at historically low levels and set to remain so for the foreseeable future. That meant that the annual indexation rates that had been locked into law in 2013 were too high. The schooling resource standard was being increased by 3.6 per cent every year, but teachers' wages, the main cost driver in schools, were growing at only 2.5 per cent. General inflation was even less than that. Even overfunded schools, which were benefiting from 3 per cent indexation, were enjoying funding increases in real terms.

So, the first step in Goss' argument was a straightforward one: the government could reduce projected expenditure in a way that was consistent with the principles of needs-based funding, making savings that were also sellable. 'The 2013 Education Act', Goss pointed out, 'legislates the indexation and so commits the Commonwealth to spending an estimated $7 billion above wages growth over four years'.[17] The Gonski Report had argued that the one and only purpose of indexation should be to preserve the real value of funding. Now Goss was saying the same thing. Thus the Grattan argument spoke to the Coalition's fiscal conservatism, but also recalled the Gonski Report's aspiration to buttress educational expenditure with a robust rationale.

The second step in the Grattan plan addressed the Turnbull Government's political problem: the need to deliver on its centrist promise. What if the billions of dollars saved by aligning indexation rates with actual cost growth were then redirected to the under-funded schools that were not receiving their entitlement according to the resource standard? 'Our current economic circumstances', Goss wrote, 'have created an unprecedented opportunity to fix school funding without blowing the budget'.[18] The Turnbull Government could deliver the core of Gonski's plan without spending anything more than had already been budgeted for under current legislation.

Additionally, Goss argued that a rational approach required that overfunded schools lose funding, just as Simon Birmingham had intimated. 'Former prime minister Julia Gillard's promise', he argued, 'designed to counter claims that Labor had a hit list of private schools, can no longer be justified'.[19] This would mean cuts where the overfunding was extreme, and a funding freeze for schools where resourcing only moderately exceeded their entitlement, reprising an idea that dated as far back as 1973 and the Karmel report.

Goss and his Grattan Institute colleague Julie Sonnemann were pitching a budget-neutral path to needs-based funding. For Goss, this was an elegant policy solution, but he also believed it was good politics. 'The idea of indexation and reducing that', Goss told us, 'freed up an enormous amount of money'. He went on, 'And in designing the model, there was an opportunity to say this could be a cost-saver or you could do a whole lot more, but I very explicitly said you could use the same amount of money you were already planning on spending, and get a whole lot more from it. And that was an offer to Birmingham and Turnbull to co-opt the bipartisan aspiration using the conservative framing of not spending more money'.[20]

Before publishing *Circuit Breaker*, Goss briefed key figures inside the government. Senior bureaucrats were dismissive – spurring Goss to get wonkier and wonkier in an effort to address their objections – but Simon Birmingham's office was harder to read. Goss had cultivated a strong working relationship with the minister's chief advisor, Scott Prasser. Prasser had held the same post in Christopher Pyne's office, and indicated the government retained its determination not to encroach on the autonomy of state governments. At the same time, Prasser evinced an openness to Goss' argument. 'There was a real interest in listening, but there was no sharing of what was to come', says Goss. 'They wanted to do something that was worthwhile for education and listened but didn't give very much in return.'[21]

Little was being revealed to Goss, but behind the scenes the government was coalescing around the concept he was championing in public. At the core of deliberations in the minister's and Prime Minister's offices was his idea of reducing indexation and redeploying the savings to underfunded schools. Under the government's emerging plan, indexation would be determined by a composite measure of teachers' wages and CPI, an accurate indicator of actual cost-growth in schools.[22] The 'no school loses a dollar' mantra would be dispensed with and overfunded schools would be brought back to the resource standard in a timely fashion, while the special sector-based deals wrangled out of the Gillard and second Rudd governments would be terminated. The dividends would then be reinvested in underfunded schools.

For Prime Minister Turnbull, there was an overarching political logic to the policy being devised in the strictest confidence among his inner circle. 'I became increasingly convinced that if we were going to break out of this "You don't give a Gonski" paradigm we found ourselves framed in', he wrote in his memoir, 'we'd have to craft a new deal, true to David's original vision, and show our good faith by investing more in it'.[23] And Turnbull saw an opportunity to take the plan one step further.

Shortly after becoming minister, Simon Birmingham had reached out to David Gonski, consulting with him as the minister's thinking about school funding evolved.[24] But Gonski and Turnbull had been friends for decades, ever since they were on the same schoolboy debating team at Sydney Grammar. Now Turnbull believed he could lean on his old friend to provide the final piece of the puzzle: a new review on how schools and systems should spend the billions of dollars the nation was investing in them.

This second Gonski review was one of many unimplemented recommendations left over from the first. Launching it now would enhance the case that the Coalition Government was helping to restore Gonski's original vision, a program that had been diluted and distorted by Labor. Moreover, the new review would directly respond to the argument, prominent among conservatives, that schools didn't need any more money, they just needed to spend it more effectively. Who better to adjudicate on the most efficient and effective ways to improve educational outcomes than the irreproachable David Gonski?

And so Turnbull put the idea to his old school friend. David Gonski immediately recognised that his association with the government's new policy, although formally limited to the conduct of a new review, would inevitably be read as an endorsement of the whole package. And so, as Malcolm Turnbull relates, before agreeing, Gonski demanded a price: '"Malcolm," David replied, "as you know I love you dearly. But" – I could sense this was going to be expensive – "if you want to get people behind a new approach that delivers the better results we all want, you'll have to put more money on the table"'.[25]

The two businessmen and lifelong friends made a deal. In addition to the billions saved by correcting indexation, the government would invest an additional $2.2 billion in schools over the next four years, and more after that. In this way, the plan would bring all schools up to at least 95 per cent of their funding entitlement over the next decade. Gonski agreed to conduct the new review, and, tacitly at least, bless the government's new policy with his considerable personal prestige.

On Tuesday 2 May 2017, journalists waited for Prime Minister Turnbull and Education Minister Simon Birmingham in the Commonwealth Parliament Offices in Sydney, speculating about who the third podium was for. The press conference that was about to unfold would include some momentous announcements, not least a commitment to grow Commonwealth spending on education from $17 billion to $30 billion a year over the ensuing decade. But the policy detail would be overshadowed by the identity of the third man. As the media pack drew a sharp intake of breath, in walked David Gonski, the businessman and philanthropist who had come to personify the policy of needs-based school funding.

In the blink of an eye, Malcolm Turnbull had just stolen Labor's policy, storming the political centre and taking it by force. Nobody could mistake this for an Abbott Government announcement –

or doubt who was in charge. Turnbull credibly presented his new policy as an evidence-based, non-partisan approach to achieving the long-term national interest, a far cry from his uncompromisingly tribal predecessor. Just when it seemed that the Gonski edifice, half-built, was turning into a testimony to unrealised ambitions and that many Australian schools would continue to be grossly underfunded, the Turnbull Government was announcing it believed in needs-based funding, and it had a practical plan to implement it. The government had resurrected Gonski, and the man himself had made an appearance in the flesh.

The political commentators were naturally dazzled by the audacity of Turnbull's move and cooed along with the Prime Minister that he had forced Labor and the teachers' unions to tear up their 'I Give a Gonski' corflutes and send their bright green t-shirts to the Museum of Australian Democracy. Labor and the teachers' unions had made David Gonski the voice of education, and now Gonski himself was backing the conservative government's plan. It was clearly a deft political manoeuvre, cutting through the knots the Coalition had tied themselves in and immediately neutralising Labor's electoral advantage on the issue.

Still wowed by his own agility, Malcolm Turnbull would reminisce about his school days with Gonski, marvelling at the irony of it all. 'When we were at school', Turnbull recalled, 'we used to joke about our respective destinies; David asked me to appoint him chief justice when I became prime minister. But among the many grandiose visions we had for ourselves, they didn't include David becoming a secular saint and political icon of the education unions and the left of the Labor Party.'[26]

But there was another irony Turnbull did not note. The similarities between the new policy he had just announced and the one which the Mark Latham-led Labor Party had taken to the 2004 election were much more striking than the differences. The

Coalition now supported needs-based funding, based on a schooling resource standard, requiring the injection of billions of dollars into the public schools that most young Australians from disadvantaged backgrounds attended. The Coalition was even proposing cuts to overfunded high-fee non-government schools. What had once been derided as a 'hit list' was now a sign of political virtue; what had previously been decried as class warfare had become the basis of a new national consensus; and the policy that had occasioned the reunion of these two Sydney Grammar old boys had once been championed by Mark Latham of Green Valley.

As much as Turnbull might have gloated about his clever tactical victory, 2 May 2017 also marked a resounding strategic defeat. Thus it is fitting to contemplate what Julia Gillard thought and felt as she viewed the events of that day. Gillard, as inscrutable as ever, declined to be interviewed for this book, so we can only speculate as to how she interpreted this moment. But it is possible to piece together a plausible picture.

In 2004, Gillard, then a shadow minister herself, had had a front row seat when Mark Latham took a schools funding policy that had been carefully crafted in Jenny Macklin's office and disastrously mismanaged the politics of selling it. Gillard had seen how John Howard and Cardinal Pell, along with much of the Murdoch media, had exploited Latham's missteps, reducing the policy to a 'hit list'. And when Labor finally got into government, she had set about ensuring that her party would not make the same mistake twice.

As minister, Gillard had hastened slowly, focusing first on building relationships, cultivating trust and establishing the transparency and accountability mechanisms which would allow informed, rational debate to occur. She had commissioned a review led by widely respected experts. And Gillard had compromised – even when compromise was very unpleasant – in order to keep everyone in the tent and give the review a chance to generate a new consensus. There were wild cats to herd, diametrically opposed forces to keep apart and protagonists that played hard, sometimes dirty.

Gillard persevered and kept her eyes on the prize. She stroked egos, mollified erstwhile opponents and placated the powerful players. It wasn't fun, and didn't necessarily make her look clever but, she could reflect, this is what had to be done to achieve real long-lasting change. Yes, the legislation that had passed on her last day in office would only take effect over six long years and contained some unseemly compromises. The deals with state and territory governments were imperfect and incomplete. But the Gonski process had irrevocably changed the way Australians talked and thought about school funding. Because of her government, when voters turned their minds to school funding they now instinctively asked whether it was needs-based.

This fundamentally constrained the actions of political leaders long after Gillard had left the political stage. This had been evident when Tony Abbott and Christopher Pyne promised their 'unity ticket' before the 2013 election; even more so when they were forced to honour it. But Turnbull's move made it clear just how fundamental and long-lasting the shift was: the idea of sector-blind, needs-based funding now occupied the centre of Australian politics. Any politician who ignored that would do so at their own peril – as Turnbull learnt the hard way at the 2016 election. That day in May 2017, Turnbull captured the political centre but Gillard had redefined what the centre was. Now four years out of office, Gillard could plausibly view the unfolding events as the ultimate vindication of her stewardship of school funding policy.

This is certainly how senior Labor figures like Tanya Plibersek, member of Gillard's Cabinet and Shadow Minister for Education since 2016, think about the long journey of school funding reform.

Looking back on the period from the vantage point of 2020, Plibersek reflected: 'The biggest achievement so far, I think, is that we are now in a world where sector-blind needs-based funding is something that everybody says they are doing and wants to do and should be done … That explicit goal of sector-blind needs-based funding is something that most people signed up to, at least in name. And I think actually that is a very big change.'[27]

Assessing Gonski 2.0

But in May 2017, as the Labor Opposition absorbed the Turnbull Government's surprise announcement, and debate unfolded inside the offices of Plibersek and Bill Shorten about how to respond, there was little appetite for supporting the Coalition's version of Gonski, or celebrating a long-term policy win. In determining upon a policy of steadfast opposition to Gonski 2.0, there were a number of overriding considerations for Labor, most obviously the desire to maintain a political advantage in a key election battleground. Even if Turnbull's surprise announcement had permanently taken the sting out of the issue, it remained a natural Labor strength where votes could still be won.

But while political considerations were primary, Labor also believed that there were a range of deeply problematic elements in the funding model the government was proposing. This was a view shared by the Australian Education Union. Thus the two major progenitors of the first iteration of Gonski rejected its belated embrace by their political opponents. To many, it seemed like opposition for opposition's sake, motivated exclusively by small-minded political considerations.

In media coverage, the rejectionists struggled to cut through, and their critique was reduced to the soundbite that Gonski 2.0 was really a $22 billion dollar funding cut.[28] This wasn't true.

Under the Coalition plan, the Commonwealth would spend $242 billion over ten years compared to $264 billion under Labor's plan. But the government was going to increase funding compared to current levels, albeit at a slower rate than Labor had promised.[29]

Meanwhile, the AEU was being criticised from within its own ranks. In June 2017, former AEU federal president, Diane Foggo, spoke out in support of the government, telling the ABC's *7.30*, 'it provides an amazing opportunity for the future of public education in this country, and I just couldn't let this go by without saying something'.[30] Momentarily, the Western Australian branch of the Australian Education Union appeared to waver too, before being corralled back into line.[31] Federal president Correna Haythorpe describes it as one of the worst periods in her life.[32]

Despite the opprobrium, both the Opposition and the Australian Education Union presented substantial objections to what Turnbull and Birmingham had announced. The first problem was that the journey to needs-based funding was excruciatingly slow. Most of the funding growth was delayed until beyond the forward estimates, and the Commonwealth would not deliver its full share of the schooling resource standard until 2027.

Meredith Peace, the president of the Victorian Branch of the Australian Education Union, spelt out the implications in concrete terms: 'A student in Year 4 today will have left school by the time this funding is delivered'.[33] Instead of the nearly $4 billion of additional funding that was originally scheduled to arrive over the next two years, the Turnbull Government was only committing to an extra $2 billion over the next four years.

Gonski true believers had seen it all before. The Year 4 student of 2017 wasn't even in preschool when David Gonski presented his report to the Gillard Government in November 2011. Now, just at the point when the big bucks were supposed to arrive, delivery had been deferred yet again. As the preschool parents of 2012 had discovered to their chagrin, commitments beyond the forward estimates have an especially nebulous quality. Unfolding events had offered a striking illustration that a week is a long time in the politics of school funding. Prime Minister Turnbull was asking Australians to believe in a ten-year timeline.

The critics of Gonski 2.0 also decried the division of labour between the Commonwealth and the states. Most (though not all) disadvantaged young Australians attended public schools. Under Turnbull and Birmingham's plan, the Commonwealth would provide 80 per cent of the schooling resource standard to non-government schools, but just 20 per cent of the funding entitlement to public schools.

In his memoir, Malcolm Turnbull decries 'the loopiness of the Labor attack', insisting that they 'ignored the fact that the 20 per cent was a significant increase on the federal government's support for those public schools – which are, after all, the responsibility of the states and territories'.[34] In 2017, the Commonwealth provided an average 17 per cent of the schooling resource standard to public schools across the nation.

Labor and the AEU responded to this point in two ways. Firstly, Turnbull's plan increased the Commonwealth share of funding in some jurisdictions but reduced it in others, namely Tasmania and the Northern Territory – jurisdictions with a lot of disadvantaged children and limited revenue-raising capacity.

Under the Gillard Government plan, the Commonwealth share was projected to grow above 20 per cent in other jurisdictions as well. Now Gonski 2.0 was capping that growth. Julia Gillard had committed to an increased Commonwealth role in funding public schools, because she recognised the realities of vertical fiscal imbalance. Now the Turnbull Government was announcing that Canberra intended to shrink from the task.

Tanya Plibersek singles out David Gonski for criticism

on this score. 'The arrangement that Turnbull came to was that public schools will never get more than 20 per cent funding from the Commonwealth', she told us. 'And I think allowing that to happen when Gonski had originally made the point that the Commonwealth Government should bear a larger responsibility for fair funding for public schools was exactly the wrong thing to do. It was exactly the wrong policy, and it was exactly wrong for him to allow his name to be associated with something that went completely contrary to what his original report had called for in terms of fair funding.'[35]

Compounding this issue, Turnbull and Birmingham's plan left it up to the states and territories as to whether they would actually deliver the remaining 80 per cent of the funding entitlement of public schools, which the overwhelming majority of disadvantaged Australian school children attended. Because Gonski 2.0 released the states from the funding agreements that defined Gillard's National Plan for School Improvement, it would be up to states and territories whether they would deliver increased investment. Trevor Cobbold warned about what would happen if they didn't. 'If there is no increase in the state/territory funding share', he wrote, 'public schools in NSW will be funded at 91 per cent of their SRS in 2027, only 86 per cent in Victoria, 93 per cent in Queensland, 92 per cent in South Australia, 96 per cent in Tasmania and only 87 per cent in the Northern Territory'.[36]

Julia Gillard had not just delivered more Commonwealth dollars to the kids facing the highest hurdles; she had used the injection of Commonwealth funds to elicit funding increases from the states and territories. This worked most obviously in New South Wales, in large part due to the leadership of Barry O'Farrell and Adrian Piccoli. It manifestly failed in the Northern Territory, Western Australia and Queensland, where Christopher Pyne succeeded in persuading his conservative counterparts not to cooperate. But in 2013, the Gonski reforms included a plausible story about how governments would work together to deliver needs-based funding. Turnbull and Birmingham's announcement jettisoned both the agreements and the concept of an agreed approach.

States and territories had not even been consulted on the proposed division of labour. So just as there was no guarantee that they would deliver 80 per cent of the schooling resource standard to public school students, it was unclear that they would constrain funding of non-government schools to the 20 per cent share stipulated by the Commonwealth. In fact, in all jurisdictions except the Northern Territory, non-government schools were already funded at or above 20 per cent.[37] In a number of states, so-called nexus agreements guaranteed the non-government sectors an agreed percentage of public school funding, ensuring they would be funded over the schooling resource standard.

Because Gonski 2.0 legislated Commonwealth increases to private schools on top of generous state funding, critics claimed, it would actually increase the number of overfunded independent schools. Cobbold, for instance, calculated that 'the proportion over-funded will almost double from 17 per cent to 32 per cent. By 2027, a total of 531, or 66 per cent of all independent schools and systems, will be over-funded and some by very large amounts ... 289 will be newly over-funded as a result of increased Commonwealth Government funding [under Gonski 2.0]'.[38]

And then there was a question of trust: could the Coalition really be trusted to deliver genuinely needs-based funding over the long term? Was this Prime Minister, who one year previously had been arguing that the Australian Government should cease funding public schools altogether, leader of a party that had opposed Gonski for years, whose predecessor had publicly professed an emotional commitment to non-government schooling, really going to substantially shift resources to the public sector? Labor wasn't buying the government's Road-to-Damascus act, and senior opposition figures were deeply frustrated that the government's U-turn had been so widely accepted.

For Labor, what Australian schools needed was a change in government. This was what Peter Goss had in effect been told when he had briefed the Labor Opposition on his *Circuit Breaker* proposal in late 2016, and had received a polite 'thanks, but no thanks' in response. Goss was not only more willing to trust the sincere intentions of Malcolm Turnbull and Simon Birmingham, he saw the moment as a unique opportunity to consolidate an enduring consensus around needs-based funding. With Gonski 2.0 legislated, Goss told us, 'the foundations of Gonski funding would be so deeply embedded in that bipartisan sense that we might just be able to get it to a point where people would stop questioning "if". And then start questioning "how" and "how fast"'.[39]

Goss was also unpersuaded by some of the criticisms. 'One of the problems with the Labor model was the incentives to states which cry poor', Goss observed. 'I did feel that Commonwealth consistency was a good thing … Otherwise federal policy rewards states like Victoria, which had been parsimonious, and punishes states like Western Australia, which had been generous with their funding.'[40] Yes, the Commonwealth was acting unilaterally but it was also being fair and consistent. 'It means students with similar educational needs will receive similar amounts of funding from the Commonwealth, regardless of where they live', Goss told the Senate inquiry into the legislation.[41] And, as Turnbull argued, it was increasing the overall share of funding that public schools received from the Commonwealth.

However, Goss agreed with some of the criticisms made by Labor and the education union. A decade-long transition was too long, he acknowledged. 'The bulk of expenditure is beyond the budget forward estimates, which creates two big problems: the risk that the bulk of funding will not eventuate, and that very underfunded schools have to wait too long to get their target funding'.[42] His own plan had envisaged the goal being reached by 2023 – four years earlier than Turnbull and Birmingham were proposing. And the critics were right that proposed legislation lacked a robust mechanism to ensure states and territories did their fair share to deliver needs-based funding. 'The original legislation that was introduced by Birmingham and Turnbull let the states off the hook', Goss remarked. 'And just said, "In a sense, do what you can. We're going to do our thing. You do what you can."'[43]

Goss agreed there were problems with what had been announced on 2 May 2017. The difference for Goss was that he believed the deficiencies in the initial legislation warranted amendment rather than outright opposition. Unlike those who wanted to sink Gonski 2.0 altogether, Goss was convinced that the core idea – correcting indexation and using the savings to deliver needs-based funding faster – was worth fighting for. So he developed a series of propositions about what would improve the legislation which he took to the Senate crossbench. 'I said to the crossbench', he recalled to us, '"You will need to have something to take back to your electorate. These are the things you should make the price of a deal"'.[44] Goss proposed they push for a faster transition, incentives to ensure states would deliver on their part of the bargain, and a National Schools Resourcing Board that would provide independent expert advice on the schooling resource standard and its major constituent parts, as envisaged in the original Gonski review.

Turning Gonski 2.0 into law

Simon Birmingham was responsible for navigating the government's legislation through the Senate. With Labor opposed, the position of the Greens was critical. If the nine Greens senators voted in support of the Gonski 2.0 legislation, Birmingham would need to persuade only one more member of the crossbench.

Greens education spokesperson Sarah Hanson-Young was on board from the beginning. 'The current system is inherently broken and will only get worse over time. We have a once-in-a-generation opportunity to fix the flaws in the funding model. The truth is, if we don't fix the model, the gap between rich and poor schools will get bigger', she said.[45] This didn't go down well with sections of her own party and she was forced to execute a partial retreat, clarifying that the Greens would reserve their position until hearing evidence from the Senate inquiry into the legislation. Unless Simon Birmingham could bring the Greens back on board, he would have to persuade most of the remaining crossbench senators.

Peter Goss lobbied this group energetically, advocating that they move his proposed amendments and then support the legislation. The Centre Alliance listened carefully and led by Rebecca Sharkie were early backers. Jacqui Lambie was also open to persuasion, as was One Nation.

At the same time, Goss was in communication with Scott Prasser to ensure the amendments he was proposing were palatable from the government's perspective. 'I was able to test with Birmingham's office, "If I were to make this sort of a suggestion, broadly how would you feel about that?" And get an indication of was I going to propose anything that was likely to be seen as an absolute red line? No, nothing I proposed came back as an absolute red line.'[46]

As Goss advocated, the Senate crossbench made three major amendments to the government's legislation. The transition period was brought forward from 2027 to 2023, meaning the Commonwealth would now start delivering its full share of the Schooling Resource Standard in six years' time instead of ten.[47] The second major amendment introduced a clawback mechanism which gave states a strong incentive to do their bit. After the Commonwealth provided its 20 and 80 per cent shares to government and non-government schools respectively, states would be expected to provide the remainder of the funding to get all schools to at least 95 per cent of their resource standard entitlement. If a state didn't deliver their share, the Commonwealth would reserve the right to decrease its funding to that jurisdiction by an equivalent amount.

'Here's where the political logic was', says Goss. 'One, if a state doesn't value education or thinks education is so cheap, fine – we'll agree with you. But, two, the state would then have to take that to the next election and be told, "Hang on, you're underfunding by 1 per cent, let's call it $100 million dollars. You have just left $100 million dollars' worth of federal funding on the table".'[48]

The clawback mechanism was an attempt to reconcile two competing imperatives. On the one hand, Goss saw the force in what the AEU had told him: if the Commonwealth simply acted unilaterally, the states would not increase investment, and public schools would remain under the resource standard. On the other, he accepted the position put to him by Simon Birmingham's advisor, Scott Prasser, that state sovereignty ought to be respected. An incentives-based approach provided the states with some freedom without allowing them to walk away from their responsibilities completely.

The third major amendment to the legislation established a National Schools Resourcing Board, an independent body to provide expert advice on the resource standard. 'For me, this is one of the huge steps forward, right?' says Goss. 'How funds get allocated within systems – we now have an independent group of standing that can look at that.'[49]

With the amendments secured, the Senate voted in favour of the government's legislation and it was returned to the House of Representatives where, in the early hours of 23 June, the *Australian Education Amendment Act 2017* was voted into law. For Malcolm Turnbull and Simon Birmingham, it was a stunning political victory; for Labor and the Australian Education Union, a bitter defeat. But this was only a debate about which party had the best Gonski. Everybody gave some kind of Gonski now. And so, in this moment, it was possible to believe that needs-based funding was a policy reality, built on the solid political foundations of bipartisan consensus. If this was true, the reform project that had begun when Julia Gillard announced a review in April 2010 had effected an epochal transformation of the politics of school funding in Australia.

Revenge of the discontents: Labor and the Catholics join forces

Gonski 2.0 had become law, but the law's critics did not rest. In abolishing Labor's special deals, Turnbull and Birmingham had antagonised some of the most powerful interests in the school education sector. The plan they had announced in May 2017 removed the so-called system weighted average and bow curve, two special arrangements carved out in the chaos of 2013 which meant that even Catholic schools with very affluent students were treated as average, thus entitling them to almost the same government funding as public schools.

The Catholic lobbyists did not stand by and let a conservative government undo the deals that they had hammered out with the previous Labor Government without putting up a serious fight.

Using allies inside the Turnbull Government, and exploiting the residual desire of the Abbott forces to undermine Turnbull in any way they could, the Catholics fiercely resisted Turnbull and Birmingham's moves. The immediate result was an amendment to the legislation that delayed any changes with respect to the special arrangements for one year.[50] The fight had been put off to another day.

In the meantime, the government agreed to a review of the methodology for determining the socio-economic status of non-government schools. One of the key bones of contention for the Catholic sector was that they believed the area-based measurement of socio-economic status – used for determining the percentage of the resource standard that non-government schools were eligible for – was understating the level of disadvantage in some Catholic schools. One of the first tasks of the new National Schools Resourcing Board would be to undertake the review.

The tense relations between the Turnbull Government and the Catholic sector were compounded by a further issue. Non-government school systems, particularly the Catholic education offices in each state, received block grants which they divided up and distributed to their schools as they saw fit. While there was a nod to doing so in accordance with the principles of needs-based funding, there was little accountability around how public monies were actually spent. In May, Turnbull and Birmingham signalled that they intended to require greater transparency around how the funds were allocated to individual schools, while still providing systems with complete discretion, as the Gonski review had recommended.

Catholic opposition was immediately conveyed directly to Prime Minister Turnbull by the Archbishop of Sydney, Anthony Fisher. In a lengthy phone conversation with Fisher, just six days after the press conference that launched Gonski 2.0, Malcolm

Turnbull, who believed that the Catholic Church cross-subsidised its most poor and needy schools, was shocked to learn that the reverse was the case. In the call, Fisher frankly admitted to him that, in fact, the Church was overfunding schools in affluent areas, and underfunding disadvantaged children – a distribution designed to maximise enrolments in the face of competitive pressure from free public schools and better resourced independent schools.

Turnbull was further taken aback to hear the Archbishop objecting to the government proposal that discrepancies between needs-based and actual funding allocations be publicly reported. If people could see that the Church was channelling public funding intended for disadvantaged schools to more privileged communities, they wouldn't tolerate it, the Archbishop complained. 'The conversations and written exchanges with Fisher were some of the most unedifying and disappointing I'd ever undertaken with a Church leader', Turnbull would later relate.[51] If the Archbishop's pragmatism is striking, Turnbull's naivety is also noteworthy. Almost a decade earlier, the Australian National Audit Office had publicly reported that block grants were not being distributed by the Catholic system as intended.[52]

The one-year extension of Labor's special deals and the review into the SES methodology had temporarily appeased the Catholics. But this was a ceasefire not a resolution, and the Catholics continued to campaign hard against Turnbull, Birmingham and their reforms. 'We faced continued resistance from the Catholic school system in Victoria', Malcolm Turnbull remarked, 'where a particularly vicious campaign was waged by their chief executive, Stephen Elder, who tried to mobilise Catholic school parents in Liberal seats to protest and, when the time came, vote against us'.[53]

Meanwhile, Labor had consistently opposed the government's efforts to take funding off overfunded schools. The moment Simon Birmingham first suggested that the 'no losers' shibboleth should be reviewed, Tanya Plibersek looked to score political points. 'If he thinks that some schools are over funded, the obvious question is, "which ones?" Does he have a secret hit list?' she responded in September 2016.[54] 'Which kids will be robbed by this Minister who seems incapable of being upfront about his secret plans for school funding?' Plibersek asked. As the Opposition Leader, Shorten demanded Malcolm Turnbull reassure non-government schools they were not about to get 'hit in the back of the head with a funding cut'.[55] Labor seemed to be stumbling over itself to reenact the trauma of 2004, with the roles reversed this time.

Shorten, who boasted about a special relationship with the Catholic sector, saw an opportunity to strike. The greatest hostility to Gonski 2.0 came from Catholic authorities in Shorten's home state of Victoria and, in the wake of the passage of the legislation, he held a series of private meetings with the Catholic leadership. Those meetings soon bore fruit.

In March 2018, in a letter addressed to the Australian Catholic Bishops Conference, Shorten promised that Catholic schools would be $250 million better off in the first two years of a Labor government, and gain billions over the decade.[56] 'When it comes to school funding', Shorten declared in the letter, 'my party stands shoulder to shoulder with the church'.[57]

The public positioning behind the Catholic lobby paid immediate political dividends for Labor in the Batman by-election in Melbourne's inner north – a contest in which Labor was pitted against the Greens. In the days leading up to voting day in March 2018, the Victorian Catholic Education Office paid for 30 000 robocalls, endorsing Labor and portraying the Greens as a threat to the affordability and very existence of Catholic schools in the electorate. That Saturday night, as it became clear Labor had won a resounding victory, Shorten was on the phone to Stephen Elder, the head of the Catholic Education Office in Victoria, thanking him for his organisation's backing, and singling out their support as a key ingredient in Labor's win.[58]

While the Batman by-election was a skirmish with a minor party, there was now a prospect that Elder and his colleagues would endeavour to do a Batman on the Liberal Party at the 2019 election. 'The Batman example may just be a foretaste of the next federal election, when a national campaign could be run from every Catholic school in every electorate', commented *The Australian*'s Dennis Shanahan, offering a reliable insight into how the by-election result was being received by the right.[59]

The growing pressure forced an uncharacteristic misstep on the part of Simon Birmingham, who publicly complained that the Shorten–Elder deal showed that Victorian Catholics could be 'bought by a few pieces of silver'.[60] The public gripe amplified the growing antagonism with a major stakeholder, and served only to undermine Birmingham's own position. By July, *The Australian* was referring to the 'government's bungled education funding policy' and 'the Coalition's targeting of the [Catholic] faith', in putatively straight reporting.[61] Birmingham was increasingly seen as a liability in the education portfolio, and schools funding had become grist for Liberal insiders seeking to undermine Turnbull's leadership.

When the winds finally shifted against Turnbull, Dan Tehan was put into the portfolio to mend the relationship with the non-government sectors, especially the Catholics. And Simon Birmingham's scalp paid direct dividends. In the first month of the Morrison Government, Tehan and the Prime Minister announced an additional $4.6 billion dollars over ten years for non-government schools, badged as a Choice and Affordability package.

The Morrison era: Gonski delayed until 2030

In 2018 the review of the SES methodology conducted by the new National Schools Resourcing Board recommended a transition to a Direct Measure of Income (DMI). The review found that the area-based measure of SES unfairly benefited some schools, while disadvantaging others. Generally speaking, the independent sector came out ahead as a result of the inaccuracies of that measure, and it tended to disadvantage Catholic schools. The review was able to discern the anomalies because the government had developed the capacity to link census data, income tax data and student residential addresses. And it recommended that this new capacity be employed to develop the DMI, based on the actual circumstances of families enrolled in non-government schools rather than area-based averages.

And so $3.2 billion dollars of the Choice and Affordability package was presented as funding the implementation of the new direct measure. However, the announcement of the $3.2 billion figure preceded the measure's development. The reality was that this figure was a settlement, negotiated after a long and fierce campaign which had culminated in a Commonwealth minister being shifted sideways out of the portfolio.

The second component of the package was an extra $1.2 billion ostensibly to promote choice and affordability. It was a slush fund. The government had removed old special deals – the system-weighted average and bow curve – and replaced them with a new one. 'After the coup in August 2018', Malcolm Turnbull commented ruefully, 'Scott Morrison agreed to give the Catholics and independent schools … an additional $1.6 billion over 10 years, without any particular rationale, other than as a way of buying some peace'.[62] Most of the additional money went to the Catholic systems. But there was also $170 million earmarked to fund a guarantee that all independent schools would receive at least 3 per cent funding growth.[63]

The battle of 2017, a valiant effort to apply a single funding formula equally to all schools, was over. The 'no losers' guarantee had yet again triumphed. As in 2004 and 1984, it had been challenged and the challengers came off second best. It was now more deeply embedded in the twisted architecture of schools funding in Australia than ever. Labor was not bashful about taking credit for the new special deals. 'We've stood with the Catholic and independent schools from day one', said Tanya Plibersek, 'arguing that the billions cut from their sectors should be restored'.[64] Bill Shorten was more blunt. 'We've won the money for the Catholic sector', he crowed.[65] In support of special deals with the non-government sectors, Shorten and Plibersek had positioned Labor in a *de facto* alliance with the right of the Liberal Party.

As far as reversing and dismantling the 2017 push to purify the Gonski reforms, worse was to come. Over the course of late 2018 and early 2019, the Morrison Government made a series of bilateral agreements with each state and territory government that would be incorporated into a new National Schools Reform Agreement. The first stage of the rollback was to push back the timeline to get public schools to 95 per cent of the schooling resource standard, reversing the 2023 deadline that the Senate had inserted in the 2017 legislation.

Now states would not have to bring public school funding up to at least 75 per cent of the SRS, on top of the Commonwealth's 20 per cent contribution, until 2027.[66] In Queensland, it was even worse: schools would have to wait until 2032. And in the Northern Territory, there was no timeline at all. The roadmap to needs-based funding had already been long and slow; now the final destination looked more like a mirage.

As well as delaying delivery of needs-based funding once again, the new deals thoroughly diluted state obligations. Special caveats in the bilateral agreements, first exposed by Save Our Schools' convenor, Trevor Cobbold, allowed a range of state government expenditures on items that were not part of school recurrent income, to nevertheless be included, up to 4 per cent of the resource standard.[67]

The special deals allowed state governments to include capital depreciation in their recurrent expenditure on public schools. They were also allowed to include the cost of providing public transport. In New South Wales, the government could count the cost of its education standards authority. In Western Australia and the Northern Territory, the budget for preschool education was thrown in as well. All these items had been excluded from the definition of recurrent income developed by the Australian Curriculum, Assessment and Reporting Authority (ACARA).[68] States other than New South Wales could also include the cost of curriculum, assessment and teacher registration boards over and above the 4 per cent of the schooling resource standard.

Because states were now allowed to include these additional expenditures, they would effectively have to reach only 71 per cent of the schooling resource standard, at most, by 2027 or beyond. The Morrison Government agreements, presided over by the new minister, Dan Tehan, would mean public schools would have to wait nearly a decade to get to only 91 per cent of their needs-based funding allocation. As the *Sydney Morning Herald* more recently reported, 'state governments will pocket more than $11 billion from 2019 until 2023 due to a change to the deal that allowed them to count costs towards their public school funding obligations that had previously been considered ineligible'.[69]

In contrast, all non-government schools are guaranteed to be funded at 100 per cent of the SRS by 2023.[70] In some jurisdictions, the average non-government school is already funded above the resource standard. And this overfunding is set to continue. While the Commonwealth will fund 80 per cent of the resource standard for all private schools by 2023, the New South Wales, Queensland, South Australian and Western Australian governments will deliver over 20 per cent.[71] State governments cannot claim expenditure items not included in the SRS for private schools as they can for public schools. Commonwealth overfunding of schools, above the 80 per cent share, is currently scheduled to continue to 2029. In Western Australia and the ACT, the only two jurisdictions that overfund their public schools, funding will be reduced to 80 per cent of the SRS by 2022 and 2023 respectively.

The meaning of 2017

In the heady days of May and June 2017, Malcolm Turnbull's push to capture Gonski for the Coalition had appeared to demonstrate how much the previous Labor Government had transformed debate over schools funding. For a moment it had seemed that a new discourse had asserted itself, presenting a case so cogent, with an appeal so broad, that the dynamics driving schools funding policy had been irreversibly changed. In hindsight, this appearance seems illusory. Any change in the discourse has not been enough to fundamentally change material reality, and even the way we talk about schools funding has not changed all that much. As the familiar old forces reasserted themselves, 'needs-based funding' was defined by a series of special deals in the name of sectoral interests. Gonski has not so much changed the discourse as been changed by it.

The Turnbull Government's reform has delivered real benefits that should not be dismissed, above all a commitment of billions of dollars some of which is enhancing the education of needy Australian schoolchildren. The National Schools Resourcing Board is a critically important addition to the architecture of schools funding. But the progress there proceeds at a glacial pace while we, in many respects, are going backwards.

In the days before the 2019 federal election, Peter Goss wrote an article entitled 'Lopsided funding gives more to private schools that need it least', appraising the course of schools funding over the preceding decade.[72] 'Australia has increased the real resources available to schools by more than $2 billion in a decade, but we spent the extra money on the schools that needed it least', Goss explained. 'New Grattan Institute analysis shows that, once wage growth is taken into account, private schools got more than 80 per cent of the extra funding, even though they educate fewer than 20 per cent of Australia's most disadvantaged students.'

If Goss had been writing in the days leading up to the 2007 election his analysis would have been equally applicable, even if the figures were not exactly the same. The whole needs-based funding intervention appeared to have changed remarkably little. 'Private schools got big funding boosts despite increasingly educating the haves, while public schools increasingly taught the have-nots', Goss lamented. And he reported that he had independently confirmed the ABC's finding that nearly one in three private schools received more taxpayer funding than the typical public school of similar size and student background.

Most revealing of all, however, was Goss' conclusion that the present trajectory suggested we would be in for more of the same in the years to come. When he was interviewed a year later, in June 2020, shortly before leaving the Grattan Institute, Goss was even more downcast.[73] 'The sad reality for Australia is that funding was unequally distributed a decade ago', he said. 'While funding increases in the next decade will be tilted a little bit in the right direction, it's not nearly enough to make up the gap. The federal government has locked in a model where every private school will get fully funded by 2023, whereas very few government schools will ever get fully funded. By 2030 we're going to be having this same argument and it's all predictable from now.'

Those who had argued that a Coalition government could never be trusted to deliver needs-based funding could jeer that they had been proved correct. But if Labor figures were to pursue that line of argument, they would also have to acknowledge that their cynicism was self-fulfilling; that Labor had joined in the assault on the core principles of needs-based funding that Goss had courageously tried to elevate. Labor's behaviour had definitively demonstrated that the undermining of needs-based funding was a bipartisan endeavour.

And so the high hopes of 2017 had ultimately only confirmed Gonski's capacity to disappoint. Rather than the denouement of a transformative reform journey, Gonski 2.0 had proved to be a sequel with all the weaknesses and limitations of the original. Having only offered a benign amelioration of the fundamental problems that had beset Australian education for over half a century, Gonski 2.0 had not resolved them.

2017: DECISION TIME, AGAIN

The transition from Year 10 to senior school was another big decision time for Kim and Maria. Kim, especially, was looking forward to senior school. Her school even brought in university lecturers to give them more insight into study and career options. Kim wanted to do legal studies and had already completed work experience in a local law firm.

Maria's school, meanwhile, was finding it hard to attract the teachers needed to offer more subjects, or even to attract proper maths teachers. There seemed little to entice her to stay at school, but she knew that the odds of finding a good job later would improve if she stayed on for two more years.

Both sets of parents were cynical about reports on what the media called Gonski 2.0. 'We knew we were dudded the first time around', Maria's dad mused. It didn't take Kim's mum too long to get the picture: 'They say that the public schools won't catch up for years to come. Will yet another generation of kids miss out?' (*To be continued …*)

8

The Gonski we got

> Socioeconomically disadvantaged students have been and are still disproportionately represented in the 'tail of underachievement' in Australian schools. If the aim of education is to improve opportunities for all students, not just maintain the social status quo, then this is not working.[1]
>
> *Sue Thomson, Deputy CEO (Research), Australian Council for Educational Research, 2021*

This book began with David Gonski's account of his 2010 visit to two quite different schools: a public and a nearby Catholic primary school in western Sydney. One was noticeably facing a bigger struggle than the other. The differences between the two left Gonski with both an impression and a mission. The story of these two schools captures, in microcosm, much of what this chapter reveals about Australia's schools.

This chapter is about what happened next – not that day or even that year, but over the ten years that followed Gonski's visit to those two western Sydney schools. It reveals critical features of the second unlevel playing field, and how widening social and educational gaps between schools are shaping our education present and future. It unfolds the consequences of a review that was poorly conceived and fell far too short, with its best recommendations sidestepped or ignored, and the flow of funding distorted by the business-as-usual special deals which followed.

Visiting those schools – Villawood North Public School and Sacred Heart School – in 2010, David Gonski witnessed the real distance between them. It reaffirmed his commitment to bringing schools closer together in the opportunities they provided and in the achievements of their students. A decade later, something has certainly changed, but not in the way he had hoped. The two schools are now much further apart. While they are both in a low SES area, 66 per cent of Villawood North Public School's enrolment now falls into the most disadvantaged quarter, up from 46 per cent in 2011. Just 30 per cent of the Catholic school's enrolment falls into this quarter.[2]

Given such a change, it could be expected that the funding differences between the schools would reflect the relative needs of each school's enrolment. But that hasn't happened.[3] For the following seven years, government per-student funding alone to the Catholic school exceeded government funding to the poorer public school.[4] Today, the less needy school still has a resource advantage when fee income is added to its public funding. In its configuration and implementation, the review that carried his name had failed one of these two schools visited by David Gonski.

Even more important are the implications of this for student achievement. Using NAPLAN as a guide, the Catholic school doesn't seem to be going backwards, but neither is it going forward. Its Year 5 reading and numeracy scores have remained largely unchanged, as has the school's position compared with schools enrolling similar students. By contrast, the increasingly disadvantaged public school's reading and numeracy scores have fallen. While many things impact on school achievement, the school's increasing concentration of disadvantaged children, along with declining results, points to the hold that peer effects have on learning outcomes. The achievement gaps between the two schools have widened. Is the Villawood story also Australia's story?

Student achievement: Where are we now?

For over a decade, Australians have been told that, based on international and local measures, student achievement is in long-term decline. A number of data sources confirm this trend. The most influential reports come from, or are based on, the Programme for International Student Assessment (PISA) periodic global measures of the performance of students in reading, mathematical and scientific literacy. What is the extent of our deterioration, and do a variety of measures tell a similar story?

The most recent (2018) PISA data doesn't provide much comfort. According to the Australian Council for Educational Research (ACER), Australia's average achievement in reading, maths and science has experienced a pattern of long-term decline. The decline is such that the average achievement of an Australian 15-year-old in 2018 is almost one year of schooling behind in reading compared to an Australian 15-year-old in 2000, more than one full year behind in maths compared to 2003, and almost one full year behind in science compared to 2006.[5]

This decline, especially in maths and science, has mostly increased since 2009, during the 'post-Gonski' years. Australia's performance has dropped relative to other countries as well. ACER also provides additional information about the performance of key groups of students. As in previous cycles of PISA, the difference in achievement between students in the highest and the lowest SES quarters is equivalent to around three years of schooling. Non-Indigenous students continue to outperform their Indigenous peers by the equivalent of more than two years of schooling. Average performance in maths and science has uniformly declined across all school sectors. As ACER's Sue Thomson reiterates, the biggest gaps in student achievement are created by socio-economic background.[6] In the light of what Gonski found and made a priority to address, Thomson's comment at the head of this chapter stands out. All our efforts to reduce the impact of social disadvantage on student outcomes have amounted to very little.

What do NAPLAN scores tell us about changes in student achievement? The Australian Curriculum, Assessment and Reporting Authority (ACARA) reports annually on these. The resulting media stories are sometimes laced with the language of sporting competition, pitching state against state and telling about records achieved or broken.

The more nuanced accounts suggest some changes, over time, by school ICSEA, location and sector. My School shows, for example, that Year 3 reading scores in more advantaged schools (over ICSEA 1000) are relatively high and have increased since 2011, but the much lower scores in the schools under ICSEA 1000 have remained largely unchanged.[7] Other NAPLAN results show mixed trends, but contrasts between locations seem consistent. There is a noticeable gap separating the city and outer regional schools in Year 3 reading, a gap that has further increased over time.

For students and parents, measures at the other end of schooling are more familiar, so what do Year 12 results reveal? This is indicated by a study which looked at the New South Wales Higher School Certificate (HSC), the Victorian Certificate of Education (VCE) and the Queensland Overall Position (OP) rank.[8] These different measures in three separate states tell much the same story. In New South Wales in 2017, around 20 per cent of HSC students in the highest ICSEA schools were Distinguished Achievers (that is, they achieved a result in the highest band in a subject), but in the lowest ICSEA schools, just 1 per cent achieved at this level. Similar contrasts, this time in VCE study scores of 40 or over, have been evident in Victoria. In Queensland, 85 per cent of the highest overall achievers come from schools above ICSEA 1000, just 15 per cent came from the schools below.

School location reveals another dimension. Seventy-five per

cent of New South Wales secondary students attend major city schools, yet they usually scoop 90 per cent of the Distinguished Achiever awards. The 20 per cent attending inner regional schools collect 9 per cent and the 5 per cent of students attending outer regional schools account for just 1 per cent of the awards.

As static measures, these results are concerning, but perhaps not surprising. It is *changes over time* which reveal the bigger story. In New South Wales, the highest ICSEA schools have increased their numbers and proportion of Distinguished Achievers since 2005–06. There were similar contrasting changes over time, increasing the gaps between higher and lower ICSEA schools across Victoria and Queensland. In all three states, there was also a widening gap between cities and regional areas, the regions being left with a reduced presence of high-scoring students.

These trends have been accompanied by an almost identical change in the distribution of higher SES students in all three states. Schools in the highest ICSEA bands have, on average, seen an increasing concentration of high SES students. The lowest ICSEA schools in all three states have an increasing concentration of low SES students. Schools like to boast about their results, some deservedly. But overall data about shifting enrolments suggests that advantaged schools are importing much of their success, while disadvantaged schools are losing many of their achievers. Overall, Australia has little reason to boast.

Are the lower SES schools to blame? Some might argue that, despite such trends, there are measures which, if successfully implemented in all schools, can still improve overall student outcomes. This was the driving logic behind the second Gonski review in 2017, the Review to Achieve Educational Excellence in Australian Schools.[9] This review was professionally conducted and well received. But given the deficiencies of the first Gonski review, and its incomplete implementation, this second Gonski review remains yet another collection of good ideas waiting for meaningful structural reform of the overall school system. We need to deal with the issues raised by the first Gonski Report before we can fully act on the second.

In the meantime, school-level reforms are often limited by assumptions about what creates student success, and even by what success looks like. Australia's education minister recently stated that the quality of teaching is the most important in-school factor influencing student achievement.[10] Labor's Tanya Plibersek similarly announced in 2020 that 'the most important ingredient in any recipe for success is the teacher'.[11] Back in 2007, Julie Bishop had a more nuanced version: she told us that 'after parents, teachers are the single most important factor in a child's educational outcomes'.[12]

Teachers are always critically important, but the wider impacts on achievement have been apparent for some time. The Gonski review clearly cited research confirming that the socio-economic status of a school affects the performance of individuals within that school, irrespective of their own socio-economic status.[13] The implications of such findings are that efforts to improve overall student achievement should not be confined to the classroom and school. Addressing one set of impacts, to the exclusion of others, is a path to failure.

School funding: the needy are still waiting

Australia continues to face overall student achievement decline, accompanied by growing achievement gaps between the advantaged and disadvantaged. The Gonski review found that we needed a school funding model that reflected the different needs of students so that resources could be directed to high priority areas.

WHEN SCHOOL SECTOR MAY NOT MATTER

Media reports and conversations about schools frequently point to higher levels of achievement in non-government schools. But as Sue Thomson reported in relation to PISA in 2009, 'the average performance differences between sectors disappear once student and average school level socioeconomic background is accounted for'.[14] What do other sources show?

The combined Year 3 and Year 5 NAPLAN reading average results in 2018 ranged from 488 in independent schools, down to 477 in Catholic schools, and further down to 454 in public schools. It seems like a good reason to tote out a private school cheer squad. But what happens when schools in different sectors enrol students from similar backgrounds? In schools around the middle ICSEA values (1000 to 1049), the average Year 3/Year 5 reading score in 2018 was 470.2 for independent schools, 469.9 for Catholic schools and 470.9 for government schools – almost identical. The story is the same for schools in the 950 to 999 ICSEA range.[15]

What about Year 12 results? If Victoria is any guide, the story is still the same. The average per-school percentage of VCE high scores in 2016 and 2017 was 12.9 per cent for independent schools, 6.9 per cent for Catholic schools and 4.2 per cent for government schools. But for a reasonably 'similar ICSEA' group (1000 to 1100) it changed to 5.7 per cent for independent, 5.8 per cent for Catholic and 5.2 per cent for government.[16] When you compare 'apples with apples,' they all taste much the same.

We still do. Poor levels of achievement were especially noticeable in specific groups of students. They still are; indeed, even more so.

The review, somewhat heroically, explained how Australia's schools were funded. As we know, it declared that public funding arrangements need to reflect the nature of the educational challenges faced by a system or school.

This isn't happening to the extent needed. Achieving greater equity, it said, was critical; the most successful school systems 'are those where students achieve to the best of their ability, without their background or the school they attend impacting on their outcomes'.[17] We weren't there in 2011; we still aren't there today. As far as needs-based funding goes, all we have is a greater commitment to the rhetoric.

Australia's chance for post-Gonski success rested on increasing our investment in school education, and making sure that the biggest increases went to those in greatest need. We completed the first task successfully. In 2011 combined government recurrent funding per student averaged $10 244. By 2019 it had grown to $13 751, an increase of 34 per cent – although much smaller when accounting for inflation.[18]

But what about the second task? The Gonski review had no doubt about where additional resources should go. The largest increase should go to government schools, not because they were government schools, but because they were simply the schools with the greatest concentration of disadvantage. It seemed quite clear at the time. It's what made Angelo Gavrielatos want to kiss David Gonski. The average ICSEA value for government schools at the time of the review was 977, as against 1039 for Catholic schools and 1064 for independent schools. Recommending that the biggest funding increases should go to government schools was a no-brainer.

But it didn't happen. Since 2011, increases in government

funding have favoured non-government schools. In rounded figures, between 2011 and 2019 combined government recurrent funding per student rose by 30 per cent to government schools, 44 per cent for Catholic schools and 50 per cent for independent schools.[19] As Trevor Cobbold has calculated, the actual increases, after allowing for inflation, have been much lower.[20] When these increases are compared with the needs of each sector, it is as if the people measuring school advantage, and the people providing the money, live on different planets.

The schools which did manage to receive additional funding provide an insight into the difference it made. The successes of schools mentioned in chapter 6 have continued. Darlington School in Adelaide has shown continuing improvement, including in its NAPLAN results. In more recent years, both Eagleby South State School and Minimbah State School in Queensland have caught up with schools enrolling similar students. Barrack Heights Primary and Wadalba Community School have increasingly performed level with, rather than below, schools enrolling similar students. St John's Park High School in southwest Sydney has seen rising HSC results, and its more recent NAPLAN results have continued to improve. Mount Austin High School, the most disadvantaged high school in Wagga Wagga, has improved to the point where the school has been above, and sometimes well above, schools with similar students.[21] It would have been less likely to happen without the additional funding support. Their successes can inevitably be attributed to a range of factors, but money does matter.

Too often, funding was misdirected in terms of overall need, and it also varied in illogical ways between the states and territories. In 2016, nine schools in the ACT were receiving, on average, 30 per cent more in public funding than the two similar ICSEA primary schools in Queanbeyan on the NSW side. Schools on either side of the Murray River, and on either side of the NSW–Queensland border, revealed very different funding stories.[22] Such oddities are a legacy of the separate deals done with the states by Labor in 2013, and the Coalition's relaxing of any funding obligations on the part of the states in the following year.

Given that funding hasn't sufficiently gone to the most needy schools, it is hardly surprising that in Australia there seem to be few direct links between increased funding to schools and overall student achievement, something which invites simplistic conclusions. More nuanced commentary and analysis point not only to the need to direct the funding to where it makes the most difference, but also the need to consistently improve teaching, resourcing and classroom practice, while seriously evaluating the claimed benefits of other reforms.[23] More research has been conducted overseas than in Australia and it consistently shows the gains achieved by better funding. A recent analysis of major studies of the relationship between funding and outcomes provides evidence enough that increased funding makes such a difference, with the impacts of funding being much larger for low income than for high income students.[24]

The 'money doesn't matter' claims haven't gone away, not least because those making such claims aren't pushed to go beyond generalisations. Christopher Pyne turned them into theatre in 2013, and Alan Tudge recycled them again in 2021.[25] The bigger problem, as we outline further in this chapter, is that our investment in schools is not accompanied by the structural reforms needed to make the money work. And it won't work as long as we continue to aggregate disadvantaged students in struggling schools. We are left with worsening problems which are a legacy of the review that pointed to the critical impact of inequity created by peer effects, without offering any solutions.

Fee vs free + government funding = a shambles

Chapter 1 described a set of circumstances which we call the Karmel paradigm. It included assumptions about what mattered and what didn't in the realm of school funding. A big assumption was that a system of competing 'free' (public) and 'fee' (private) schools was quite sustainable. In the book, we have explored how much of the Karmel paradigm emerged, largely unchanged, from the Gonski review.

'Fee versus free' is certainly still with us, and it has continued to create a hierarchy of schools unrelated to teaching and learning quality. If anything, the hierarchy has tightened, with students, those critical peers, more markedly distributed between schools on the basis of SES. If we rank the schools visited by Gonski panellists in order of their school fee income, independent schools fall in the top third of the list, followed by Catholic schools mainly around the middle and government schools in the bottom third. Then if we rank the same schools in order of the SES of their enrolments, the rankings are quite similar. There are exceptions, but clearly fees are the main mechanism in Australia by which, regardless of intention, students are allocated to schools on the basis of their social status and family income.

Levels of total resourcing mark out the differences between schools. For a long time, school fees were needed to bring up the total resourcing of some private schools, Catholic schools especially, to the funding level of public schools. That certainly worked, and even sector averages show them relatively close in 2009.[26] After that, the total resourcing of both private school sectors came to exceed that of public schools.

The outcome is well illustrated by the schools visited by the Gonski panel, with Girton Grammar in Bendigo at the top of the local hierarchy. Chapter 6 showed the variable impact of Commonwealth funding on Bendigo's schools, but what does more recent data tell about funding from all sources? In 2019, the total per-student funding for Girton Grammar was $23 700 per student. The total income figure for one of the nearby public schools, Bendigo South East College (ICSEA 1020), was almost $10 000 less. With an ICSEA of 1131, Girton Grammar serves a decidedly more privileged enrolment than the public school (ICSEA 1020). Figures for other Bendigo schools raise a host of questions. Total resourcing at Catherine McAuley College, with a higher ICSEA than the public school, was $17 700 per student: $3500 more than the public school. And the non-government school continued to receive two thousand dollars more per student in *government* funding. Bendigo South East College and Bendigo's Marist College enrol similar students, but governments alone fund each student at the Catholic school almost $2500 more. When fee income is added, those students are almost $5500 ahead. Eaglehawk Secondary College (ICSEA 929) enrols the city's lowest SES students, but it is totally funded at levels below most local private schools.[27]

Despite increases in public funding, school fees have continued their upward trajectory, making nonsense of various assurances and predictions going back years. Across Australia, between 2011 and 2018, My School reveals average fee increases of up to 45 per cent for independent and Catholic schools above ICSEA 1000. Geelong Grammar managed 38 per cent; David Gonski's old school, Sydney Grammar, 43 per cent; and Ilim College, a new independent school in Melbourne, 73 per cent.[28] It seems that the schools took a cue from the free pass given by the Gonski review. As indicated in chapter 3, the review did not address the role of fees in limiting access to non-government schools. School fees emerged untouched out of the review, and just kept rising.

The substantial public funding, combined with fee rises, has now created a host of unresolved matters which were off-limits, unknown or of little apparent interest to the Gonski panel. One is the growing mismatch between the increasing public funding of non-government schools and the extent of their obligations to the public from whom the funding is derived. The Gonski review briefly alluded to accountabilities which should accompany public funding, somewhat euphemistically referring to the responsibility of all funded schools to find a new school for students 'unable to remain within a school'.[29] But in common with the Karmel review, it didn't go any further into how the obligations of all funded schools should reflect the extent of their public funding.

By not addressing all the wider issues created by school fees and public funding, the Gonski review was partly deficient, and has certainly become dated. It paid no regard to the role that school fees played as an enrolment discriminator, substantially determining who went to which schools, with implications for others created by each school's changing mix of achievers and strugglers, with an ultimate impact on overall student achievement. This was despite the evidence in submissions to the review, pointing to the role of fees in aggregating better-off students at one end of the school SES ladder, and strugglers towards the other end. It was also apparent in the schools and the suburbs the panel visited. The same review that gave a high profile to achieving fairness and equity left untouched the forces which would continue to undermine it.

Joining the dots: What's happening to our schools?

In the decade following the Gonski review, it seems that Australia's framework of schools has resumed business as usual. There has been little, if any, improvement in student achievement and in the allocation of resources to schools. The assumptions of the earlier Karmel paradigm around fee versus free, with all that this implies, have remained unchallenged. Competition and choice has further shifted student enrolments, changing the face and character of schools, and equity has deteriorated in measurable ways. Chapter 3 highlighted the impact of families and peers on student achievement. Few expected that after another decade, this would increase.

1. Competition, choice and enrolment

For generations of parents, schools and school choice seem to rank alongside house prices as ready topics for conversation around the barbecue. But it can hardly create an inclusive conversation, because, even as Gonski indicated, not everyone can choose schools. In reality, it is largely predetermined by location, family income, support from grandparents and the availability of various concessions, bursaries and scholarships.

Those seeking choice within the public systems often have to buy a house close to a desired school. Selective and specialist schools in any system offer choice, but obviously not to everyone, everywhere. And on the flipside, many schools can, actively or passively, choose who they enrol. In addition to charging fees, non-government schools can apply restrictive enrolment criteria, as well as offering enticement for some students to enrol and also to 'disenrol' – school principals at the chalkface work daily with unequal rules. Tom Coll, former principal of one of Goulburn's public high schools, was very familiar with this scene. He pointed to the regular trickle of students from the local Catholic college: 'they didn't actually expel them, they had other terms they would use like "no longer welcome" and other euphemisms. They didn't have to go through the same rigmarole as public schools would'.[30] That's the uneven playing field in action: choice of schools, Australian style, is certainly exercised at both the supply side (schools) and the demand side (families).

It inevitably works for some, far more than others. In the process, it creates a scramble for both real and assumed advantage, with a lot of casualties among those without the resources to choose. How does this scramble play out across Australia? The changing numbers and size of schools provide a clue. There are more school students than ever before, but only 60 per cent of our schools are growing. The other 40 per cent are static or shrinking.

There is an essential caveat that should be stated about schools gaining or losing enrolments. It may reflect and can certainly impact on how a school might be regarded – yet may have very little to do with innate school quality. Ilim College, a Melbourne independent school visited by the Gonski panel, has seen a dramatic growth in enrolments. But along with this growth has come a reducing share of the most disadvantaged students. Many of these students have sought enrolment at the nearby Hume Central Secondary College. It isn't always a voluntary movement; Ilim College has a demerit point system which can lead to a student being expelled, and they can be required to leave if they are behind on fees.

Hume Central certainly finds that relations with nearby government schools can also become strained over enrolments, with at least one not too far away frequently harvesting the top students. Hume Central has grown in size, but with a significantly *less* advantaged enrolment. This inevitably creates local contrasts between schools – something which doesn't go unnoticed by those doing the choosing. To maintain its attraction to a range of students, as well as compete with other government schools, Hume Central has a select-entry accelerated learning program for students in Years 7–9. It also runs a range of other programs which have measurably improved student outcomes. Trends in NAPLAN scores compare favourably with those of students at Ilim College. Hume Central's median VCE score is in the mid-20s, up from 17 in 2013.[31] Any claim that one school is 'better' than the other is not indicated in academic results.

Growth or decline matters for schools. Larger schools are able to foster student achievement through greater choice, diversity and depth in curriculum, and in the range of cultural and sporting programs. Students in larger schools are more likely to find others with shared interests and aspirations. Smaller schools may develop closer contacts with, and quality relationships among, students and families, but having a more restricted curriculum can impact on student experience, achievement and future enrolments. There can be much at stake when a school grows or shrinks. The growers have been, on average, the higher SES schools, specifically those above ICSEA 1000. In contrast, *lower* SES schools (those below ICSEA 1000) have seen little growth – just 2 per cent in the case of public schools, with enrolments in lower ICSEA Catholic schools falling. Low SES independent schools are growing, but they are much fewer in number.

Demographic changes also impact on school enrolments, in part due to an ongoing, if complex, decline of rural towns.[32] Schools in Australia's major cities have grown, while growth in schools outside the major cities is far more subdued. The overall pattern, including in the bush, is high enrolment growth in schools up the school social ladder and much less, even negative, growth in the rest. As we'll see, this potentially leaves the strugglers in smaller schools with declining enrolments. In more than one sense, they are in a class of their own.

This is also reflected in the changing average size of schools. Since 2010, higher SES schools have grown, on average, by around 12 per cent. Lower SES schools have been growing at just half that rate. The fact that these patterns are noticeable over a relatively short time is striking. With local variations, this has played out in the schools mentioned in earlier chapters. All the government high schools in Wagga Wagga lie below ICSEA 1000 and all have seen little growth. All five of the private schools with secondary enrolments are above ICSEA 1000, and all have grown.

Ilim College in Melbourne has doubled in size, while the much lower ICSEA Hume Central is largely unchanged. There can be exceptions to the trends by sector; for instance, the little Majella Catholic Primary School in suburban Perth, visited by Gonski panellists, is still very small, while the nearby higher ICSEA East Hamilton Primary has grown.

There isn't any mystery about why this is happening. Just before the Gonski review was established, an OECD report spelt it out.[33] Schools form a local hierarchy in most communities, partly based on characteristics of the student population. In Australia, anyone can easily see this ranking by looking up the ICSEA values of their local schools on the My School website. Schools with students from advantaged backgrounds rank highest, and families with the resources to choose favour these schools, often independent of objective measures of education quality.

In effect, this has meant that the socio-educational differences between schools have become substantial drivers of enrolment shift, which itself fuels further changes to the character of schools. It is easy to see how these drivers, including location, school resources, enrolment profile, enrolment selectivity and sector image, have impacted on the schools visited by the Gonski reviewers. The different 'fortunes' of the schools David Gonski visited – Sacred Heart School and Villawood North Public School – can be partly attributed to the continuing impact of fees, student SES and sector image. Two very low SES schools visited by the Gonski panel in Queensland, one public and the other Catholic, illustrate the persistent impact of disadvantage. Both schools had substantially seen their enrolment skew further towards the disadvantaged end.

Schools that have an increasingly advantaged enrolment find it easy to tell a story about quality teaching and sustained student success. Such is the case, for instance, with Adelaide High School. The school describes itself as 'a high demand school [where] there are more students seeking enrolment than can be accommodated'.[34] Even in 2012, the school was reportedly receiving about 300 expressions of interest from outside the school's enrolment zone.[35] By 2019, almost half of the students in Adelaide's public high schools, especially higher ICSEA schools, lived outside their school's zone.[36] The figure for Adelaide High School is around

---

DOLLARS MATTER

The unequal capacity of Australian schools to attract preferred students is more pronounced than ever, and cannot be separated from resourcing levels and what money can buy. Here are some capital and recurrent expenditure figures which have emerged in recent years:

- In **capital investment**, half of the $22 billion spent on capital projects in Australian schools between 2013 and 2017 was spent in just 10 per cent of schools. Australia's four richest schools spent more on new facilities and renovations than the poorest 1800 schools combined.[37]
- My School data shows that average **capital expenditure per student** in Catholic schools was 53 per cent higher in 2018 than it was in 2012. In independent schools, it was 37 per cent higher. And in government schools it was 2 per cent lower.[38]
- It also shows that in 2018, average net recurring **income per student** (NRIPS) in Catholic schools was 38 per cent higher in 2018 than in 2012. In independent schools, it was 32 per cent higher. And in government schools, it was 25 per cent higher.

---

60 per cent, with students seeking entry into special programs in music and sport. These may be quality programs and it might be a good school, but its growth as a relatively high SES public school isn't unusual.

Clearly some schools are more able than others to make sure their features and characteristics fall on the desirable side of the ledger. Less fortunate schools wear the features that are assigned to them by systems, geography, demography, or are imposed on them by other schools. There are always examples of how good school leadership and quality teaching will help a school reach above its assigned status, but for every such example there are many more, with good leaders and teachers, where the mounting odds against success win the day.

2. The changing face of schools

How do we know that better-resourced families are avoiding low SES schools and moving, commuting or paying fees to get their children into higher SES schools? One clue might be found in the schools they leave behind: Australia's lower SES schools have a very high concentration of disadvantaged students, sometimes higher than the communities in which they are located.[39] The OECD countries where disadvantaged students are the most segregated from others are Hungary and Mexico, but Australia is not far behind, being one of nine countries where over half of all disadvantaged students attend disadvantaged schools.[40] The result in Australia is evident in the sector distribution of students: just a quarter of government secondary school students are from high-income ($8000 or more each week) families – compared with 46 per cent in Catholic and 54 per cent in independent schools.[41]

There have always been differences, sometimes considerable, between the social make-up of school enrolments, in part reflecting the communities in which they are located, or the families they choose to serve. But critically, and as My School data indicates, this segregation is increasing over time. My School shows the distribution of each school's enrolment across four socio-educational advantage (SEA) quarters, from Q1 (the most disadvantaged) to Q4 (the most advantaged). A decade ago Geelong Grammar had around 8 per cent in Q1, and Innisfail State School in Queensland had 61 per cent in Q1. In 2020 Geelong Grammar had just 2 per cent of its enrolment in the lowest quarter, while Innisfail's Q1 share had shot up to 78 per cent. The advantaged school and the disadvantaged school have become even more advantaged and disadvantaged respectively.

Does this reflect Australia-wide trends? The most disadvantaged students now form an average of 49 per cent of the enrolments in schools below ICSEA 1000. This is shown on figure 4. This graph also shows a fall in the proportion of the most advantaged students in these lower SES schools. This profoundly impacts on public schools, which make up 90 per cent of the schools below ICSEA 1000.

Significantly, these trends can be observed within, as well as between, sectors. This is especially so in New South Wales where the distribution of students by family advantage has been impacted by the state's ever-increasing number of selective schools. Recent analysis shows the impact of selective schools on any comprehensive school within reach. Even partially selective schools impact on nearby schools.[42] They draw in high-achieving and aspirant students, leaving other schools with a measurable decline in high-end achievements. Meanwhile, the NSW Government has displayed a breathtaking double standard, with yet another selective school proposed in 2021,[43] while clamping down on out-of-area enrolments in comprehensive schools. In short, this public system has demonstrated that it is part of the problem, marginalising many of its own students and communities.

FIGURE 4

Australian schools: distribution of students by ICSEA quarter

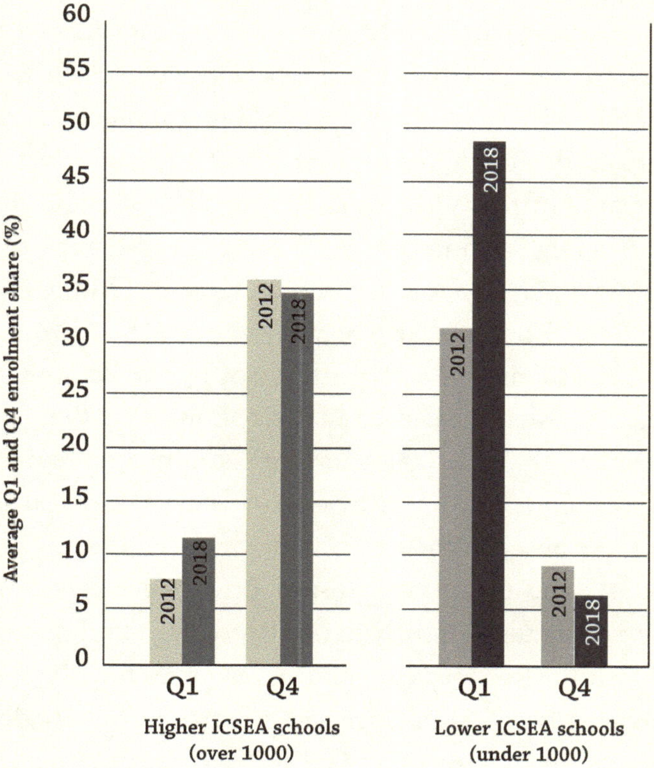

SOURCE My School 2012 and 2018.

It is also the case that high-demand schools in any sector can exercise some control over their enrolments and impact on other schools. Australia-wide data shows that the biggest school enrolment growth is happening in public schools above ICSEA 1040, essentially those with a significant number of advantaged students.

At the disadvantaged end, the marginalisation of some students can be illustrated by a close look at where First Nations students go to school. They are particularly prominent in disadvantaged schools. As we saw in chapter 3, they make up a large share of the enrolment in the public schools in Alice Springs, but are much less likely to be found in the town's non-government schools – yet another local outcome of fee versus free. Higher SES schools, in general, are not enrolling an increasing share of the Indigenous student population. Where schools and school sectors are in competition, the higher SES schools have actually *reduced* their proportion of Indigenous students, while two-thirds of lower SES schools have increased their share.[44] Closer analysis shows that the proportion of Indigenous students at many schools is not representative of the local demography. Lower SES schools have disproportionately more Indigenous enrolments, higher SES schools in all sectors have (with some exceptions) disproportionately fewer. In effect, this group of students, mostly in need, too often find themselves in schools with the least capacity and/or resources to help them.

Across Australia, an increasing portion of disadvantaged students tend to be found in the schools which enrol those without money, mobility or choice. These are the schools marginalised by the fee-chargers or by the selective, obliged to enrol anyone and everyone and wearing an image assigned to them by others, including by other schools. They can be reasonably well-funded, but are still easily outspent by others. These are the schools where kids still face the odds thrown up by disadvantaged families and peers, the ones most at risk, in the schools doing the most important work. And when insufficient and poorly directed funding doesn't make the difference everyone expects, it is apparently their fault.

And these are the schools most impacted whenever something threatens the capacity of schools to deliver; for example, during the COVID-19 pandemic,[45] or in times of serious teacher shortage.[46]

At such times, the structural inequities thwart efforts to support those at most risk. The pandemic quickly threw up a multitude of problems for schools, teachers and parents, and its longer-term impacts are still being researched. The first release of 2021 NAPLAN results was accompanied by sighs of relief that average results were apparently not affected by COVID-19.[47] But most reports caution that school closures, lockdowns and unequal access to online learning were impacting on some families far more than others. Even early in the pandemic, the Grattan Institute warned that the achievement gap between disadvantaged and advantaged students was widening at triple the rate in remote schooling.[48] More recent research from other countries confirmed this conclusion[49] and a United States study confirmed that negative impacts of the pandemic were widening pre-existing disparities between groups of students.[50]

But even more regular problems facing schools have this effect. Teacher shortages aren't new, but always seem to impact on some schools and communities far more than others. A print media report in mid-2021 mapped out the unfilled teacher vacancies across New South Wales. It graphically showed that the most disadvantaged schools had the highest vacancies.[51] Victoria offered financial incentives for teachers to relocate to hard-to-staff rural schools, but with little apparent success.[52] Given the existing disparities between schools and communities, is returning to 'normal' after such crises the best we can do?

Effectively, since 2011, Australia has continued to re-create divisions in our school system. It is more complex than rich and poor, public and private, 'good' and 'bad'; it is a hierarchical system with layers of interrelated features and challenges. There is a location hierarchy in descending ICSEA order: major city schools followed by inner regional schools, then outer regional, remote and very remote. There is a school sector hierarchy, as we've seen, explained by ICSEA. The Wagga Wagga schools enrolling secondary students, in ICSEA order, are: an Anglican school, three Catholic schools, one Christian school and three public schools. In Bendigo, there are two independent schools, followed by one Catholic, then four government schools. The hierarchy is much the same in every large community in Australia. In both private and public sectors, there are even hierarchies within hierarchies.

It would be easy to dismiss such hierarchies as long established, and even inevitable when some families and communities are wealthier and more advantaged than others. But we have *increased* the scale and reach of the resulting divides in our education system. Despite all the evidence a decade ago, outlined in chapter 3, we have sidestepped the continuing implications of concentrating disadvantage in the struggling schools. We have glossed over the ways in which hierarchical school structures have impacted on student outcomes, and even on the people who devote their lives to those in their care. We have embedded underachievement in schooling structures that don't deliver, with unhappy outcomes that go well beyond test scores.

THE VIEW FROM THE CHALKFACE: THE IMPACT OF CONCENTRATED DISADVANTAGE ON EDUCATORS

The unlevel playing field creates schools that can be incredibly challenging work environments, and where it is hard to attract teachers and keep them. 'I believed I had enough scars, bruises and calluses to survive most contexts', one educator reflects. 'However, the ongoing incidents had a profound effect on my mental and physical health. The main "symptom" was the inability to sleep.'

'It is a significant challenge to remain motivated to provide quality learning experiences for disadvantaged classes when much of your time is spent on behaviour management', one teacher says. 'I think most humans, teacher or not, need to feel some level of satisfaction from tangible results in their work. This can often be hard to find in teaching', says another. 'Low and varied attendance is really really demoralising', another teacher agrees. 'It's hard to have a sequence of lessons when each day a different set of students shows up. Sometimes I will only have three students out of about 16 come to class. It's a really hard environment to establish a culture of learning, and you can often start to feel more like a babysitter.'

'It is saddening to know our students will graduate with a fraction of the academic knowledge when compared to their peers in more advantaged settings', comments another educator. 'The work is stressful on a day-to-day basis, but I am more demoralised by the sense that things are getting worse over time and that our higher-ups are unconcerned.'

Bernie Roebuck was a long-time principal in a very comprehensive rural high school. 'I lost staff who just could not come to terms with some of the challenges difficult students presented. Some were excellent teachers who just reached the "end of their tether", and I found that at times devastating.'

John Frew was principal at Holsworthy High in Sydney. 'In the final years of my service, I witnessed a doubling of the proportion of students with a diagnosed disability. Our school had been seen as a preferable option when attracting teachers but the residualisation of comprehensive schools such as mine made it a less attractive option.'[53]

3. The slippery slope of inequity ...

Given that the Gonski review was tasked with improving equity, is there a way to measure changes in the equity of our school system? In its member countries, the OECD has found varying relationships between family/school SES and student achievement. These show up in equity gradients, or slopes, which indicate the strength of the link between SES and achievement. In other words, these gradients show the extent of the grip that peers and parents, ahead of schools, have on student outcomes. As Gonski reported, Australia's equity gradient was steeper than for many similar countries.[54]

Has this changed over recent years? One way to find out is to test the relationship between a measure of student achievement and a measure of family background. Within Australia, My School's measure of student achievement (NAPLAN) and its measure of family advantage (ICSEA) can show what has happened since 2011. How strong is the link between the two measures and is it changing? Remember, this isn't primarily about school quality – it is about the impact of ICSEA (or more broadly, SES) on student achievement.

Earlier research, published by the Centre for Policy Development, showed signs of a steepening equity slope.[55] Analysis of more recent My School data indicates a further steepening of equity gradients for NAPLAN reading in Years 3, 5, and especially 7 and 9. Steepening gradients also show up for numeracy in most years. Schools in outer regional Australia have seen a greater worsening of equity than the Australian average. And our pattern of inequity doesn't discriminate by sector: data for both government and non-government sectors reveals steepening equity gradients for both.

What have been the trends in writing and numeracy in the schools visited by the Gonski panel? Writing and numeracy are areas where the school, ahead of the family, should be expected to make a significant impact. On average, in writing, the 'Gonski schools' have unfortunately shown an increasing link between ICSEA and NAPLAN in Years 5 and 9. In numeracy, this is evident in Years 3, 5 and 9. Effectively, the trends that the Gonski review set out to slow or reverse have been worsening in the schools visited by the panel. The schools might be working hard to improve results for each student, but the increasing impact appears to be coming from who they sit next to.

4. ... shows that peers and parents rule

This chapter has illustrated that, in the post-Gonski years, student achievement has at best drifted, while the funding has fallen short of supporting the most needy students. Critics say we need to keep putting pressure on schools to lift outcomes, but that will fall short unless something else changes. That 'something else' is our slippery equity slope, telling us about the disproportionate impact of student peers and family background on student achievement. The Gonski review identified the problem, but both the review itself and its implementation didn't generate a solution.

The post-Gonski decade has confirmed that various elements, in combination, have acted as a dead weight on improving equity and achievement. The Karmel paradigm, with all its assumptions about how fee-charging and free schools might function, set the scene. The legacy continues, evident in serious funding flaws, widening financial, educational and social gaps between schools, a laissez-faire approach to school choice, a worsening equity problem and deteriorating levels of achievement. In ways well illustrated in chapter 3, the peers and parents of school students have joined forces, tightening their grip on student achievement. For students sitting in classrooms, success or failure is increasingly determined by the home they leave each morning, and by who else walks into their school each day.

The research evidence for this just continues to mount. Only a few years ago, the OECD again identified an impact of average school SES on student achievement in Australia.[56] Research has continued to show that attending a school with a higher proportion of students from educationally disadvantaged families can have a negative effect on educational achievement.[57] School segregation continues: a 2018 report shows that Australia now has the equal fourth most segregated school system of the 36 countries in the OECD.[58] We continue to bond 'like with like'. The social segregation of Australia's schools has increased markedly over the past 40 years.[59]

At the policy level, Murdoch University's Laura Perry states the dilemma. School funding, she says, is based on an inherent contradiction that reduces its effectiveness. On the one hand, we have an overall funding policy that promotes unequal resourcing between schools via a large fee-paying school sector, creating stratification and equity issues:

> We then try to mitigate those negative consequences of our funding policy with a different funding policy (redistribution via needs-based funding). The two prongs are working against each other, which is not only educationally ineffective but also fiscally inefficient. Needs-based funding is necessary, but it can only do so much. It's much more effective if we don't have schools with high concentrations of poverty and disadvantage. [It] will not be much more than a band-aid if it's not accompanied by greater structural reform in the way we fund and organise schools. Needs-based funding redistributes some funding from schools with lower needs to those with greater needs, but it will do little to reduce school segregation. And so the result of our efforts to reduce underachievement will be modest at best.[60]

In effect, increasing and compounding disadvantage gets in the way of school improvement, reducing the impact of better resourcing. We have to reduce the impact of peers and parents, and, through structural reform, increase the impact of schools on student achievement.

Conclusion

If the Gonski review was supposed to strongly support the strugglers and hence increase overall student outcomes, we've clearly failed. The problems and tensions that preceded Gonski easily survived the review. Some funding rolled out, politicians had more photo opportunities, we all 'gave a Gonski' and possibly most Australians know more about fairness and equity. But the funding didn't go where it was needed, and, in isolation, funding was never going to be the sole solution. While acknowledging that Gonski has been implemented only very partially, it is time to recognise that the Gonski Report wasn't all we thought it was. The Gonski prescriptions endorsed the continuance of the unlevel playing field, in which schools were resourced and regulated inconsistently and illogically.

In failing to address the fundamental drivers of growing concentrations of social disadvantage in our schools, its prospects of improving educational opportunity were limited from the start. Optimists argue that the great achievement has been to change the way we talk about equity and school funding, but even then Gonski has failed to focus the conversation on the ultimate causes of declining educational achievement. At the end of this book we point to opportunities to address our most pressing problems. But to get to the end we have to come to grips with what went wrong, and how to make it right. That is what chapter 9 is all about.

2018–19: SENIOR HIGH SCHOOL YEARS

Maria had mixed feelings as she settled into Year 11. Her circle of friends changed once again, some had been lured by bursaries to other schools, and others had left school altogether. Meanwhile, for Kim, school and life were looking up. In Year 11 she joined a school excursion to Japan; it was a fabulous social experience and certainly helped her language studies. Kim's parents had come to accept the reality of rising fees and the other costs. 'We do pay a lot', her dad said, 'we have to get some advantage out of it all'.

Then to Year 12 and the end of their school years. Maria struggled to complete her HSC. Looking back years later, she felt she had wasted her senior secondary years. She and her friends didn't really see the point of school. And many of them left school early or fell by the wayside.

Kim's ATAR was in the high 90s and would get her into any university law course. She and Maria would meet up from time to time, but didn't talk much about school. Deep down, they felt that the differences between their schools had impacted on their friendship. Both knew they had taken very different pathways, in different company. (*To be continued …*)

9

Gonski, a post-mortem

> [It] represented a major political settlement [and achieved] a temporary rapport between the public and private sectors of schooling … but in the end, the very settlement itself became undermined by the conflicts it had tried to suppress and by its own failure to resolve them or to provide a framework for doing so … [It] did not develop an understanding of the dynamics of the dual system of schooling that operates in Australia. It contained no analysis of the social role of public schooling and of private schooling in its various forms, and no overt analysis of the relations between the sectors … [It] failed to go to the roots of inequalities in schooling, and … can be shown to have exacerbated inequalities in education.[1]
>
> *Simon Marginson, 'Re-assessing Karmel: Results of the 1973 Education Settlement', March 1984*

Professor Simon Marginson's searing assessment of the Karmel report was delivered almost four decades ago, and yet it is eerily applicable to the Gonski review and the reforms that followed in its wake. Gonski's funding formula was designed to suppress the disagreements and divisions that had given rise to the review in the first place, but the demands of some for resource advantages, subsidised by all, were left unaddressed and unchallenged. In the end, the promise of needs-based funding was devoured by the asterisk and small print that had accompanied it. The Gonski endeavour, like Karmel, failed to get to the roots of our most fundamental educational problems because it did not comprehensively examine the consequences of Australia's dual system of publicly funded schools. It left intact the unlevel playing field on which our schools operate, and even exacerbated the existing incongruities and injustices.

Why was the unlevel playing field left unaltered and unquestioned? Why were brave and sustainable policy solutions always out of reach, unpopular or not even on the agenda? Why did even timid policy solutions end up becoming politically impossible? Why were demonstrably wrong alternatives so often preferred? Why, as a community, have we failed to put the right policy prescriptions in place?

So far, this book has told the story of how the private school lobbies fought tooth and nail to make sure the playing field remained unlevel, and succeeded. In 2010, Minister Gillard declared that no schools would face cuts. But this was not enough. The private school lobbies demanded that the government rule out a funding freeze as well. First they succeeded in having the Howard funding arrangements extended for a year. Then they ensured that existing funding to private schools became its own self-serving rationale, effectively frightening the Gonski review away from examining or articulating the purpose of public funding of private schools.

When the Gonski review proposed that private schools should, at least, be funded consistently, the lobby groups and their allies went after Prime Minister Gillard again. The Prime Minister finally conceded the issue: all schools would have existing funding maintained in real terms, no matter how overfunded they were already. But the private school lobbies did not just secure the preferential treatment of overfunded schools. In 2013, they hashed out a series of special deals which meant that even abundantly resourced private schools were technically categorised as underfunded.

It was once possible to argue, as Ken Boston did, that this extraordinary series of concessions had only been extracted from a government that lacked the courage, determination and unity to effect real change. But within a few years, the saga of Gonski 2.0 would demonstrate the problem was more profound and enduring. Malcolm Turnbull and Simon Birmingham attempted to end the special deals and reduce spending on overfunded schools. At first, it seemed they had succeeded. But in time, the private school lobbies worked with their allies in the Liberal Party and the Shorten Labor Opposition to stave off the cuts, restore the deals and get rid of the politicians who had offended them.

Why did the private school lobby groups prove to be so powerful? In part, it's because in any contest over school funding, they begin with some distinct advantages. They represent some very wealthy people and when a stoush goes public, they are guaranteed to have significant sections of the Murdoch media on their side. They have deep connections and almost unlimited access to our politicians. A letter home from a principal or a sermon delivered from a pulpit is likely to receive the kind of respectful hearing a politician cannot rely on, no matter the merits of their argument. In 2017, it was a critical reason why the Shorten Labor Opposition went in to bat for the private schools sector against Gonski 2.0. And Labor was rewarded handsomely when the Catholic lobby made thousands of robocalls, and principals sent letters home to parents, on their behalf.[2]

While private school principals, representatives and church figures can act freely and vigorously to present their case to parents and parishioners, state governments – the organisations that run public schools – are much more circumspect. Public servants are prohibited from publicly engaging in political argument. Even an education minister sympathetic to the cause of public education still has to appeal to swinging voters; they do not wish to alienate a large section of voters by associating too closely with either side of such a divisive debate. So, compared to the bishops and bureaucrats who run private schools, they are generally much less vocal in making the case for the public system.

This effectively leaves the teachers' unions as the only large organisations publicly prosecuting the case for public education. Powerful bodies that they are, they clearly played a highly influential role in the Gonski years, both through public campaigning and private lobbying. But they do not have the access to parents that a principal has, nor do they have the same extensive network of connections that the churches enjoy. They are certainly not able to exert influence across the political spectrum in the way their opponents can. And, for unions, budgets for public campaigning on school funding have to compete with the core business of any industrial organisation: negotiating the wages and conditions of their members. This all means that the school funding wars have an asymmetrical character.

But there is a deeper answer for the success of the private school lobbies: the 'no school loses a dollar' strategy and the coalition that coalesced around it. If the 'no school loses a dollar' strategy had been prosecuted only on behalf of wealthy schools and parents it probably wouldn't have worked. On their own, these proponents of the unlevel playing field would have formed a much smaller constituency than actually existed. Isolated and alone, they would have been forced to explicitly defend the indefensible position that the state should assist them in providing their children with a better resourced education than other children.

But the private school lobbies also represented a quite different group of schools, schools that were not particularly well resourced and where the parents weren't all that well off. These schools had a strong case for more public support, not less. And so, a powerful broad front was created: a fee-paying coalition between those who want a school with advantages in resources and those who choose because they want a school which reflects conscientiously held beliefs – a coalition between the religious and the rich.

The 'no losers' strategy meant that any proposed reduction of funding to even the most privileged member would provoke the opposition of the whole coalition. And so the question of funding to under-resourced non-government schools, serving disadvantaged student populations, was effectively conflated with schools that enjoyed resource advantages over others, including the resource of a preferred cohort and all the benefits that brings. The private school lobbies were able to wrap the demands of the rich within the shroud of legitimacy offered by the religious. And that gave the proponents of the unlevel playing field much greater power than they otherwise would have had.

In successfully insisting that no school lost a dollar, the private school lobbies ensured that the status quo became its own justification. The purpose of public funding of private schools was never explicitly articulated, and there certainly wasn't a rigorous examination of whether stated policy goals were being realised. Thus the private school lobbies successfully policed the borders of the Karmel paradigm and, in doing so, shielded the unlevel playing field from serious scrutiny.

Because the purposes of public funding of private schools was left unexamined, a rationale for the unlevel playing field, though unsubstantiated, was allowed to endure, convincing policy makers it served the public interest, and preserving the powerful coalition of fee-paying parents. In essence, that (unexamined) rationale was threefold: that funding private schools saves governments money overall; state aid increases choice; and choice and competition improve results overall. All the elements of this rationale are challenged by closer scrutiny.

Back to Goulburn: does public funding save the public purse?

Goulburn, in the New South Wales Southern Highlands, is bypassed by the Hume Highway, but as chapter 1 illustrated, it hasn't been missed by historians. In symbolic terms, Goulburn triggered the public funding of Catholic schools. Ever since the Goulburn strike of 1962, the persistent belief underpinning debates about school funding has been that public funding of non-government schools produces net savings for governments. On this argument, the fees paid by parents effectively equates to the amount saved by governments. Accordingly, each private school student represents a public saving. Hence such schools create a benefit for all, including governments.

Did additional enrolments in private schools automatically create savings for the public purse in 2011? Even though it was a vitally important question, it was not seriously examined by the Gonski review, as we saw in chapters 2 and 3. Over the last decade, as throughout the last half-century, the 'Goulburn argument' has been regarded as so incontrovertible that it does not have to be justified. Safe inside the sphere of consensus, it has been taken for granted by the most influential policy players and remained largely unchallenged in mainstream debate. It turns out, the argument for taxpayer savings was highly doubtful, even a decade ago. But because it was never rigorously scrutinised, it continued to help sustain the case for the unlevel playing field.

If the Gonski panel, intimately familiar with the seminal role of Goulburn in the history of school funding in Australia, had returned there in 2011, they would have been alerted to the danger of making this assumption. While the Gonski panel was trying to sort out school funding, each student at Goulburn's Trinity Catholic College was annually funded by governments at more than $10 800 per student. Each student at the similar-sized, but

Table 2
Government recurrent funding per student by sector and ICSEA band.

ICSEA range	Sector	Median government funding	% of $ to government schools
		2011	
ICSEA 950–999	Government	11017	(100%)
	Catholic	10383	94.2%
	Independent	9445	85.7%
ICSEA 1000–1049	Government	10323	(100%)
	Catholic	9044	87.6%
	Independent	8705	84.3%
ICSEA 1050–1099	Government	9704	(100%)
	Catholic	8105	83.5%
	Independent	7909	81.5%

SOURCE My School, 2011

lower SES Mulwaree High School was funded at $11200 – a difference of just $370.[3]

At numerous non-government schools that the expert panel *did* visit, the taxpayer funding was *higher* than at nearby public schools, as we have seen. These examples illustrate that across the country, while there was variation from case to case, taxpayer funding of private schools was drawing close to parity with public schools. Evidence to this effect was submitted directly to the Gonski review. In their presentation to the third meeting of the Gonski panel, Lyndsay Connors and Jim McMorrow explained that even at that point governments fully funded the teaching workforce in 95 per cent of schools, across all three sectors.[4]

In 2011, at the time of the Gonski review, two-thirds of private schools were publicly funded at between 81.5 per cent and 94.2 per cent of the funding going to similar ICSEA public schools.[5] Table 2 presents a comparison of the median funding of schools enrolling comparable student groups across the sectors.

This comparison of the public funding of similar schools across sectors is only the starting point for a rigorous analysis of the supposed budget savings created by public subsidies. An additional step is to factor in economies of scale. Growing enrolments in a non-government school often make *per-student* costs more expensive in the public schools that students turn away from. And often the marginal cost of enrolling an additional student at a public school is, well, marginal.

Between 1996 and 2006, 200 000 students moved to non-government schools. Connors and McMorrow calculated that had these students remained in public schools, it would have cost governments about $2 billion more than they actually spent. But the increase in spending on non-government schools over that period amounted to $3 billion. The cost to governments for schooling over that decade, had all those children remained in the public sector, would actually have been $1 billion *less* than it turned out to be.[6]

It is true that *state* governments saved money when a student moved to a private school – and they still do – because they cover a much larger share of the costs of educating students in the public schools they own and operate. For the same reason, the Commonwealth makes a big saving whenever a student leaves a private school and moves into the state system. But in terms of the *overall burden on the taxpayer*, it is dubious as to whether there was any saving at all in 2011. If it was doubtful then, as we will see in chapter 10, it is even more doubtful now. While our elaborate system of taxpayer subsidies to private schools might not have been saving the taxpayer any money, the Goulburn argument nonetheless still served a purpose: it continued to provide an indispensable, if largely tacit, rationale for the unlevel playing field. In Goulburn in 1962, the stark issue was one of just keeping a small Catholic school open. But by the time of Gonski, taxpayer funding was viewed as playing an essential role in making private schools more attractive – and thus increasing the supposed savings for governments. Governments had to keep providing more public support to already well-resourced private schools to help them to continue to attract students away from the burdensome public system. Thus the case for private advantage was presented as a matter of public interest.

The Gonski Report fleetingly acknowledged that where parents already pay very high fees, their preference for private education is unlikely to be affected by the withdrawal of taxpayer support. So, they recognised that taxpayer savings did not just happen automatically. But there was no effort to go beyond that to identify when and under what conditions public subsidies supposedly produced a net saving, or align funding policy with the ostensible objective. So wealthy schools and parents continued to enjoy the protection of the Goulburn argument.

There was a deeper question that was never asked. If taxpayer subsidies create budget savings, is this a good way for governments to save money? The concentrations of disadvantage generated by competition between free and fee-charging schools is a major driver of educational underperformance. So even if there was a fiscal saving, the benefit was almost certainly outweighed by the associated educational and economic costs. A full accounting would have required an analysis of the impact of the dual system on educational, employment, health and welfare outcomes.

While submissions to the review, and the schools the Gonski panellists saw with their own eyes, evidenced the reality of growing socio-economic segregation, the panel did not go beyond noting it. In Ken Boston's words:

> The [Gonski] panel as a whole supported redistribution of funding as the key to school improvement, but we really didn't dig into the longer term and more profound impact that fee and non-fee has had on the quality of Australian education … [A]nd to that extent, we didn't get to the heart of the long-term compounding of advantage and disadvantage which existed back in Karmel's day, and has now become much worse. Our terms of reference, I think, would have allowed us to do that, but there would never have been agreement in the panel.[7]

In the Gonski review, and the debate that ensued, the arguments that have dominated our thinking about school funding since Goulburn were simply assumed. The words Simon Marginson wrote in 1984 about the Karmel report apply only too well in the present. The Gonski review 'did not develop an understanding of the dynamics of the dual system of schooling that operates in Australia', and it contained 'no overt analysis of the relations between the sectors'.[8] If anything, the Gonski review agonised even less about such matters than Karmel had. If the Gonski review had developed the kind of analysis suggested by Marginson, it might have shed light on the real nature of competition among Australian schools. Far from improving overall quality by driving innovation, it was largely responsible for the segregation of students into schools with markedly differing socio-economic compositions. It was thus a major driver of the problems that the Gonski Report was ultimately unable to solve.

The illusion of choice

By keeping the purpose of funding private schools unexamined, not only did the fee-paying coalition shield the Goulburn argument from scrutiny, but there was also no examination of whether increasing public funding to private schools was actually reducing fees and expanding choice. In reality, the unlevel playing field was actually limiting choice, practically excluding the poor religious, and others, from non-government schools. But because this reality remained unscrutinised, the proponents of the unlevel playing field were able to continue exploiting the argument for school choice to their advantage.

When, at the beginning of this century, the Howard Government announced it would dramatically expand taxpayer funding of private schools, Fergus Thomson, the head of the Independent Schools Council, claimed that the new policy was about to change the socio-economic profile of non-government schools. *The Australian* reported that private schools were going to 'cut their fees to attract less wealthy families, which would then give them more government funding'. 'Many are poised to move very quickly on this', Thomson said.[9] Education Minister David Kemp similarly prophesied his policy would 'push down the pressure on school fees, making all schools much more accessible',[10] and 'the new arrangements will particularly extend choice to low income families'.[11] Warming to this theme in parliament, Kemp proclaimed, 'choice in schooling is now a reality for working-class Australian families'.[12]

The reality was that David Kemp and John Howard had perpetrated a hoax on the poor religious, pretending their new policy would make religious schools more affordable, when the impact, arguably the whole purpose, was the opposite. In the very same press release in which Kemp claimed his policy would make private schools affordable for low-income families, he also indicated that it would enable private schools to increase fees as they pleased. In the conveniently obscure technical jargon, it would 'remove disincentives to private investment in education'.[13] The ideology of school choice was used by the proponents of the unlevel playing field to mask the real objective of the policy: to allow non-government schools to raise as much money from parents as possible, while safeguarding and growing their public funding.

In 2000, David Kemp had trumpeted an announcement by Melbourne's Wesley College that the school was going to cut fees in response to his new policy.[14] But a decade later, Wesley's fees had not gone down; instead, they had doubled – a revealing indication of the real impact of the Howard Government's school funding arrangements.[15] By the time of the Gonski review, it was manifestly clear that school fees were going up, not down, and across the board private schools were becoming less and less affordable for low-income families than ever. Choice in schooling was not a reality for working-class Australians.

But the failure of Kemp's policy did not lead to the issuing of retractions, to calls for a change of direction, or to efforts to redress the situation. The Independent Schools Council, despite its statements a decade earlier, lobbied for the continuation of the policy that had produced the fee explosion. During the Gonski review process, their clear priority was to ensure that independent schools had complete freedom in setting fees and the capacity to maximise revenue from private sources. It was as though their earlier proclamations, along with those of David Kemp and John Howard, had vanished without a trace.[16]

The Gonski review did not call out the glaring gap between the policy's stated purpose and its actual effect. There was no examination of whether increasing public funding to private schools was actually reducing fees and expanding choice. The myth that more public funding for non-government schools, without any accompanying conditions, is sufficient for producing increased choice remained unchallenged. The Gonski review recommended that public funding continue to be provided with no strings attached, in the manner that David Kemp and John Howard had devised

– just as the proponents of the unlevel playing field demanded. The exclusion of the poor from non-government schools remained largely unacknowledged and entirely unaddressed.

Serving God and Mammon: the fee-paying coalition of non-government schools

Ever since the advent of state aid in the 1960s, the second unlevel playing has been sustained by what Gough Whitlam described as an alliance 'between God and Mammon'.[17] The powerful arguments for public funding of needy non-government schools have always been mobilised as part of a package which also included state support for wealthy, high-fee schools. In 1963, this was manifest in Prime Minister Menzies' insistence that all schools would be entitled to capital grants from the Commonwealth, and that anything else would be discriminatory. It was equally evident in 1969 when Malcolm Fraser, as education minister in the Gorton Government, introduced recurrent funding of all non-government schools on a uniform per-capita basis. It meant that the Commonwealth would treat exclusive Protestant schools, like the one Fraser had attended, as equally deserving of state support as St Brigid's Primary School in Goulburn. Thus the enduring grievances of the first unlevel playing field were used to create the second unlevel playing field.

Whenever taxpayer funding of wealthy and exclusive private schools has been questioned over the last half century, their poor cousins and alliance partners have played a decisive role in staving off the threat. In 1973, when the Karmel report recommended that the funding Fraser had introduced for exclusive Protestant schools be withdrawn, one of the fiercest critics was Catholic intellectual BA Santamaria. Santamaria fulminated against the logical application of a needs-based approach to the point of suggesting that, if the cuts went ahead, poor Catholic schools should hand over their public funding to much wealthier Protestant schools.[18]

In 1984, after Labor returned to government, Education Minister Susan Ryan attempted to impose relatively minor reductions to the 41 wealthiest schools in the country. Her advisor at the time, Dean Ashenden, recalls sitting with the minister in the back of a Commonwealth car in Ballarat, as it was rocked back and forth by an irate crowd of angry parents. The irony was that they were Catholics, and the cuts were not going to affect the schools their children attended. But they were fighting for the principle around which the fee-paying coalition united, then as now: no private school should lose a dollar of public funding.

In 2004, when the Labor Opposition announced it would increase funding in the hundreds of millions to needy non-government schools, it was again met with a united front of opposition from the fee-paying coalition. The Catholic Archbishop of Sydney, George Pell, joined with the Anglican Archbishop, Peter Jensen, to denounce Labor's policy for the same reasons as Santamaria had in 1973. Labor's needs-based funding would entail funding cuts at private schools that already enjoyed income far higher than the common resource standard. Therefore, from their perspective, the benefits of Labor's policy for needy non-government schools were of no interest.

In 2010, the 'no school loses a dollar' demand reflected exactly the same strategy and the same priorities. As always, the common objective of the fee-paying coalition privileged the interests of the wealthy over the poor. In refusing to accept even a funding freeze at the wealthy schools, the private school lobbies ensured that any effort to bring underfunded non-government schools up to an adequate level of resourcing would be delayed, possibly endlessly – just as it had in 1973, 1984 and 2004. And once again, the interventions of Catholic figures, like George Pell and Stephen

Elder, were absolutely critical to ensuring the wealthiest schools in the country continued to get increasing taxpayer support.

There have always been sincere voices within Catholic education who have resisted the priorities of the fee-paying coalition, and insisted that Catholic schools should embody a 'preferential option for the poor'. In 1973, Father Frank Martin, a member of the Interim Committee of the Schools Commission, spoke out in support of needs-based funding and against continuing grants for the wealthiest schools in the country as advocated by Santamaria.[19] In 2004, the Catholic Education Commission of Victoria, under a very different kind of leadership to the Gonski era, published *The Affordability of Catholic Schools in Victoria*, a far-reaching examination of the issue.[20] And in the same year, the National Catholic Education Commission chairman Monsignor Tom Doyle enthusiastically welcomed the Labor Opposition's school funding policy because it directed more funding to the neediest students.[21]

But these voices have always been sidelined, as was starkly illustrated in 2004. And by the time of the Gonski review, they had effectively been silenced. The head of St Vincent de Paul, John Falzon, was a vocal supporter of Gonski, but he was from outside Catholic education. His support reflected a frank recognition of the fact that the disadvantaged children his organisation served overwhelmingly attended public schools. By the time of Gonski, Catholic schools had largely become middle-class schools, defined by the fact they charged fees as much as their ostensible mission. The priorities of the Catholic leadership reflected the broader priorities of the fee-paying coalition: preserving the advantages that accrue to some via the unlevel playing field. Making choice a reality for working-class Australians did not even get a look-in.

In the Gonski era, the only non-government school organisation that made a concerted effort to address the lack of real choice was Christian Schools Australia. It explicitly acknowledged that even relatively low fees could be prohibitive for low-income families. And so it called for full public funding for schools it represented, on the basis that those schools would then become free, along with inclusive enrolment policies. The proposal thus indicated a willingness to forsake the advantages of the unlevel playing field, and represented an honest reckoning with the reality that existing arrangements were not providing choice to many.

But as long as debate and disagreement remained contained within the assumptions of the Karmel paradigm, the Gonski panel could hear the Christian Schools proposal without ever taking it seriously, or responding to the questions it raised. In the sphere of mainstream debate, it was simply understood that it wouldn't be fiscally viable to fully publicly fund all schools, or even some of the schools that currently rely on fee income. The idea could be dismissed without being seriously considered.

Of course, even if was not affordable to fully fund all schools, there was another question implicit in the Christian Schools proposal. Why are parents who choose a religious option the ones required to cover part of the cost of their child's education out of their own pockets? Historically, we know why. The explanation is encapsulated in the Goulburn moment and the rationalisation of state aid in terms of easing pressure on education budgets. But in point of logic, the answer is less clear. Parents who choose a school with a specific religious or educational ethos are effectively subject to a 'capacity to pay' test, while parents who choose a secular, state-run school are not – even though parents in the second group sometimes have a greater capacity to pay than those in the first. Parents who want their children to attend a school that reflects their conscientiously held beliefs effectively face a financial penalty, the loss of the entitlement to a fully publicly funded education. This penalty is rarely, if ever, justified – it is just the residue of the first unlevel playing field, which once meant poor Catholics received no public support for their children's education at all. In practice, this means that the poor religious have to pay out of their own pockets for their children's education, while rich atheists don't. Where religious schools were receiving 80 or 90 per cent of the public funding of state schools, these parents could well ask 'Why not 100 per cent?' This question was implicit in Christian Schools Australia's submission to the Gonski review. But it remained unanswered, and the assumptions that only secular schools can be free and religious schools must charge fees remained unexamined.

These unexamined assumptions had political consequences. They helped ensure that the powerful fee-paying coalition, the alliance between God and Mammon, that has sustained the unlevel playing field for half a century was preserved intact. Because the act of paying for a service carries with it the promise of a benefit in return. So, requiring some parents to pay for their children's education engenders the expectation that the schools their children attend will enjoy an advantage over the schools where parents don't have to pay. It is hardly surprising if parents who pay a private contribution out of their own pockets expect their children will enjoy a better resourced education. Why *else* should they have to pay school fees while their neighbours don't, they can reasonably ask. So to require some parents to pay fees, while others don't, is to practically enlist them in the cause of the unlevel playing field. The silence that greeted the Christian Schools Australia submission illustrated how little promise there was in pursuing a different agenda. It indicated that even those religious organisations and schools that might have desired a more inclusive and fair system had few options available to them. The default was to fall in line with the agenda of the fee-paying coalition.

A renovation or a revolution?

When Labor came to government in late 2007, its strategy was to accept the fee-paying coalition as a fact of electoral life, and then pursue school funding reform within the constraints that the proponents of the unlevel playing field would permit. It was this strategy which meant that Julia Gillard was so often left with a choice between Scylla and Charybdis, between the lesser of two evils – either conceding an indefensible policy position or attempting the politically impossible. It led the Labor Government into a world of unseemly contradictions: promising increases to overfunded schools, while trying to fund schools consistently; guaranteeing that each school sector would keep their share of the funding pie while attempting to deliver a needs-based system. It was why Labor's funding model ended up replicating so many of the flaws of the funding arrangements it replaced.

Once Gillard chose to pursue reform on this terrain, she did about as well as anybody might have. At various points, it was possible to believe she had somehow squared the circle. This was most strikingly the case after Labor had lost government: first Abbott's backdown at the end of 2013 and then Turnbull's embrace in the middle of 2017. But it's now evident that these were a series of tactical successes in a slowly unfolding strategic failure. Achieving an equitable school funding system was never possible on the terrain on which Labor chose to fight.

In an effort to suppress decades-old conflicts, the stewards of the Gonski process acquiesced in the demand that no school lost a dollar. But this effectively meant that the purpose of public funding, and the nature of our dual system of schools, would remain unexamined. The Gonski review was a creature of this strategy, and a particular sort of political compromise was designed into its composition. As a result, all the big questions remained unaddressed. Is it fair or appropriate for governments to support resource advantages at some schools that are inaccessible to many? Do private schools really save taxpayers money? If so, how much? And is it a smart way to do so? Why does the choice of a religious school entail the loss of an entitlement to a fully publicly funded education? Why don't schools that are mostly publicly funded face corresponding public obligations?

The rationale for the unlevel playing field, and the claims that it serves the public interest, remained unchallenged. Its beneficiaries continued to be able to hide behind claims that they were really doing taxpayers a favour – and that choice and competition, Australian-style, was benefiting everyone. Meanwhile, the proponents of change were unable to make inroads into the fee-paying coalition – the alliance between God and Mammon. The leaders of this alliance constantly put Mammon first. But the poor religious had, and continue to have, nowhere else to go. So their legitimate demands continued to be employed to justify the resource disparities and segregation that increasingly characterised the unlevel playing field. Thus the ultimate political consequence of the Gillard strategy was to strengthen the hand of those who wanted to sabotage the whole reform project.

Gonski failed because it was a symptom of the Karmel paradigm, not a solution to it. For half a century, we have attempted to implement needs-based funding, and for half a century we have failed. We have succeeded only in proving that needs-based funding is practically impossible in a hybrid system in which some schools are free and others charge fees. The mistake of the reformers a decade ago was to persevere in this failed endeavour, to attempt to renovate the Karmel paradigm rather than knocking it down and starting from scratch.

As a result, the entire reform effort was premised on a series of assumptions that would ensure its failure. While nominally pursuing needs-based funding, we remained committed to providing some schools with more resources than others, and providing public subsidies without any commensurate obligations. The unlevel playing field was preserved intact, and we failed to address the root causes of inequality and underperformance in our schools. It's difficult to overstate our lack of progress. Years ago, Julia Gillard declared that demography is not destiny.[22] She was wrong then, and even more so today. Demography *need not* be destiny, but it substantially is. Improving equity in schooling is the best way to ensure that demography doesn't *become* destiny.

Despite the failure of Gonski, it did evidence the potential to transcend the Karmel paradigm, embodied in the idea of sector-blind, needs-based funding. To finally realise the transformative potential of the last decade, we need to imagine a truly needs-based and sector-blind funding system. This would be a school system in which governments do not assist some children in enjoying greater opportunity than others. But it would also ensure that the entitlement to a fully publicly funded, free education extended across all schooling sectors. In other words, we need to finally solve the problem that first arose in the nineteenth century and has dogged us ever since: how do we reconcile our shared commitment to the universal provision of education with a diversity of views about what that education should involve? Much of our final chapter is about what needs to change. What arrangements could replace what we have? Can we sufficiently think outside the constraints of the Karmel paradigm?

2020: LIFE BEYOND SCHOOL

So how had the Gonski era shaped the lives of Kim and Maria? Kim went straight into university – her parents could afford the fees and she lived on campus. Maria, meanwhile, had fewer choices and took a number of casual jobs in Rivertown, separated by periods of unemployment and a lack of direction.

Both girls heard snippets of news about their old primary school classmates. Their little school was now even smaller, the town still in slow decline. Most teachers lived in Rivertown and commuted out and back each day. The pathways taken by the girls' classmates seemed to depend on the high school they chose or could afford. The schools had become known as the 'exculsive', the 'OK' and the 'don't go there!'

Maria's school was always much better than the local gossip would ever concede, but everything seemed to fall short: the funding, the supply of teachers, the support for the strugglers, even the patchy carpet in the classrooms that didn't go wall to wall. Would it ever change? (*To be continued …*)

10

Levelling the playing field

> The current structure of Australian education with one free, publicly funded sector and another sector that receives public funding but charges fees to parents sets us apart from most other countries around the world. We are structurally unique, and not in a good way … [O]ne idea to improve Australia's equity problem is for governments to fully publicly fund all schools including those that are operated by the non-government sector.[1]
>
> *Adrian Piccoli, former NSW education minister, 2020*

Thinking outside the Karmel paradigm

When Adrian Piccoli suggested that we should publicly fund all primary schools in Australia, he knew that he was challenging the structures and interests that define Australia's whole framework of schools. 'I have been a minister and I know that structural reform is hard', he said. 'While there is constant public and political demand to "fix" Australian education, the necessary structural changes are always off the table because the existing structures are so entrenched … It's like telling someone to renovate a house, but only allowing them to change the carpet.'[2]

Piccoli wanted to shake up the debates about schools and funding by injecting ideas which the main players had long ruled were off-limits – and which were certainly outside the Karmel paradigm. Schools in all sectors would be entitled to full public funding on condition that they would no longer charge fees, hence all fully-funded schools would be free. In return, all fully funded schools would be obliged to enrol applicants on a common and inclusive basis. They would be allowed to preserve their special ethos, but if they charged fees, they would cease receiving public funding. The fee versus free division of Australia's schools would come to an end.

The significance of Piccoli's proposal is that it came at a time when most seemed to believe that the big school funding issues had been settled once and for all. This book demonstrates that they weren't, and still aren't. We need new conversations that might take us closer to a lasting settlement. This chapter is about those conversations – how they might begin, and what they could include. Like Adrian Piccoli, we have our preferred solutions, suggestions which are about provoking debate rather than closing off options. Simply having everything on the table would represent a long-overdue departure from the Karmel paradigm. And it often has to start with someone kicking open doors which usually remain closed, just as Piccoli did in 2020.

Piccoli's proposal was significant at a number of levels. After years of deficient reviews and stalled efforts at reform, here were proposals from someone well regarded and who straddled the usual divides in the funding debates. Here was someone who would challenge the Karmel paradigm, envisaging that a truly sector-blind, needs-based reform would entail moving beyond the premises of Gonski. Here was a major character from the Gonski dramas arguing that it was time to look beyond Gonski. He said what we, as authors of this book, believe: there is no point in waiting for Gonski. It was never going to fix the problem of the unlevel playing field.

We did it our way: some international comparisons

Adrian Piccoli's observations echoed those from the past. This book started with Jean Blackburn's comments that Australia's arrangement of schools had become a kind of wonder at which people in other countries gape.[3] After half a century, Piccoli was able to observe that we are structurally unique – and not in a good way – issuing an invitation to look at the international experience and look at Australia from afar.

There were other times when we could have done that. Early in the Gonski review, there was good reason to believe that Australia might learn from other countries. The Discussion Paper issued early in 2010 certainly suggested that the review should look at what lessons can be learnt from overseas and domestic funding models. That could have sent the review searching for wider solutions, but it didn't expand on such opportunities.

As a consequence, Australia never questioned our existing mindset, continuing to believe that our extraordinary situation was just the way the world is. Systems developed in other countries should not be cut and pasted into Australia, but what many have done elsewhere would come as a revelation, including to the protagonists in our home-grown debates.

The closest contrast to Australia is just across the Tasman Sea. In the 1960s, Catholic schools in both Australia and New Zealand faced serious financial problems, and approached governments for public funding. In return for getting most of their funding from the state, New Zealand Catholic schools can't charge admission fees, but they maintain their special character as church schools and own their land and buildings. All government and integrated schools in New Zealand are equally subject to the same legislation and regulations, including in such matters as the enrolment, suspension and expulsion of students. Private schools, which enrol 5 per cent of students, exist outside the system. It is far from perfect: enrolment regulations are less effective than at first envisaged in 1975, and fees have also crept back in, albeit at much lower levels than fees in Australia.

While New Zealand is closer, Canada might be a better overseas example, being a federal system of government in a country which demographically has more in common with Australia. When the Dominion of Canada was established in 1867, the enabling legislation protected existing schools that served minority religious and linguistic communities. In the process, full public funding was guaranteed to most church schools. In three Canadian provinces – Alberta, Ontario and Saskatchewan, Catholic schools have a fully Catholic character in terms of school curriculum and culture, but enrol all applicants and do not charge fees. The ability of Catholic families to choose such schools in these provinces partly explains why fully publicly funded schools in Canada enrol over 90 per cent of students. Similar developments in other countries reinforce contrasts with Australia. Scotland, England, France, the Netherlands and Belgium are examples of countries which have found ways to accommodate church schools as part of the universal provision of free school education.

Overseas contrasts should not invite any cultural cringe about Australia's school systems. Nor do *all* these countries outpace Australia in school achievement – more on that later. Nor did they create their systems without considerable angst having to resolve big challenges and, although nothing could match the visceral war of words that has raged in Australia for close to 200 years. Most important, the lessons from overseas simply suggest that doing it our way, creating the inequitable and mediocre system we now have, is not much to celebrate.

A conversation we have to have

We argue that it is now time to have the debates we have been avoiding for decades and confront the questions we have been avoiding for half a century. Our deterioration in equity and excellence is a slow-moving disaster; there is no pivotal moment or catastrophe to spur action. In recent times, Piccoli's proposal is the only suggestion that would fundamentally address the sinking foundations of Australian education. So, let's build on that. There is more to Piccoli's suggestion than received attention at the time. The fact that schools would be fully funded on condition that they would no longer charge fees would immediately open a choice of schools to poor families who otherwise find a religious school out of reach. It would eventually achieve a more balanced distribution of more able and less able students in all sectors.

This better balance of students would increase the diversity of enrolments (including, potentially, culturally) in all schools. Given the strong family and school SES impact on student achievement, it would, over time, reduce the academic as well as the SES gaps between schools. Critically, the contrasting impact of *peers* on student achievement, currently further advantaging some schools and disadvantaging others, would also reduce. In effect, it would address the critical problem that the Gonski review identified but failed to tackle. It would increase the likelihood that disadvantaged students would find themselves in a school, regardless of sector, which would have the features essential to lifting their horizons and chance of success.

With a greater range of students, each school would need to have a more diverse and richer curriculum. A better spread of achieving students would have an impact on teacher morale and retention. More students would be in schools with peers who set high goals for themselves, including in post-school learning and careers. Their school would have an essential critical mass of these aspiring students, big enough to impact on the culture of the classroom and the school. Classrooms would be characterised by stronger norms around engagement and learning and classes would be less likely to be distracted by larger than usual numbers of strugglers. The focus of some existing school reforms is on creating these scenarios, but they are constantly derailed by the ever-increasing concentration of disadvantage in schools and increasing gaps between high and low achievers.

Are there places where a better balance of students between schools delivers such dividends promised by a better distribution of students? Comparisons between countries have to be made with care and need to allow for often vast structural, economic, social and demographic differences. However, Australia does have much in common with Canada, including a relatively small but widely distributed population, a large proportion of students from immigrant backgrounds and a similar impact of colonisation on Indigenous people. Both have resource-based economies and similar levels of poverty and income inequality. As previous research indicates, in comparing the relationship between school SES and educational achievement in Australia and Canada, we are at least comparing 'apples with apples'.[4]

Two Murdoch University academics, Laura Perry and Andrew McConney, explored the relationship between school SES on achievement in mathematics and reading in both countries, and concluded that student outcomes are more equitable in Canada than in Australia. Achievement gaps are smaller in Canada. Their findings indicate that, in terms of the average SES of the school, where one goes to school seems less important in Canada than in Australia. Perry and McConney suggest that this may be due to differences in the way the two education systems are funded and structured. 'Compared to Canada', they write, 'the Australian system appears to be more suited to reproducing educational advantage rather than ameliorating it'. They conclude that educational marketisation in Australia has provided unequal access to resources and 'good' schools and has led to levels of social exclusion and segregation higher than in comparable, highly developed countries such as Canada.[5]

Are these differences reflected in recent findings about student achievement? In the 2018 Programme for International Student Assessment (PISA) tests run by the OECD, Canada outperformed Australia in all subject areas, just as it has in every round of PISA since the test's inception at the start of this century.[6] In maths, the difference between the average 15-year-old Australian and Canadian is equivalent to nearly two-thirds of a year of schooling. Canada's mean score of 520 in reading was the sixth highest among all participating countries and economies. Australia was in 16th place, on 503.[7] Significantly, the dominant place of free, comprehensive schools in Canada means that there is much less variation in the socio-economic composition of student populations between schools.[8] As a consequence, disadvantaged students tend to do much better; the gap between advantaged and disadvantaged students in Canada in 2018 PISA reading scores is 20 points below the gap in Australia.[9]

But it is about more than actual test scores. The PISA student questionnaire tells about differences in student expectations, sense of belonging at school, and the composition of school enrolments. When compared with Australia, disadvantaged students in Canada have higher expectations about post-school study. They are more likely to feel that they belong in school. When compared with disadvantaged Australian students, they are less likely to be concentrated in schools with other disadvantaged students. The OECD measures the variation in the socio-economic composition of student populations between schools. In the PISA 2018 survey, egalitarian Norway topped the world on this measure, at

91 per cent, meaning that one Norwegian school looks pretty much like the next in terms of the kids who go there. Peru was at the bottom, with 49 per cent, while Australia, at 76 per cent, was similar to the United States. At 85 per cent, Canada looked a lot more like Norway.[10]

For two countries that have much in common, the differences between Australia and Canada are concerning. So where does that leave us? It leaves Australia with a school system struggling on a perpetually unlevel playing field. At the very least we need to have a much closer and deeper look at Canada to see which among that country's outcomes are desirable and achievable, and how we might transition our school system towards those ends. If we don't, our original sin in creating an inclusive school system that wasn't, will be with us forever, along with the consequences that beggar our schools and leave us trailing behind similar countries. That doesn't mean we should transplant better systems from abroad, but we do need to be clear about what is wrong, what is possible and why it could work.

What is wrong? Essentially, we are captive to an assumption that some parents have to pay out of their own pockets for school education and others don't. In return, the payers want and expect something much better. In pursuit of this we've created a hierarchical system that delivers for some, but not for others, and it certainly doesn't deliver for the nation.

What is possible? Imagine a pitch like this from a politician made at election time: 'We don't think you should have to pay school fees anymore – and we're going to provide the public funding for your school so you don't have to. You have the right to choose your child's school, and you shouldn't be financially penalised for your choice. Your church has agreed because they want to serve everyone, including the poor'.

Why could this work? Such a proposition could create a

coalition between two opposing groups: those who want education to be free and those who want choice. It would cut across the secular-religious lines that have long defined debates and continually created advantages for some at the expense of others. Such a coalition would be a necessary precondition for fundamental change.

Time to spell it out

There is now an opportunity to better resolve issues around the role of public funding across all three sectors. Such funding should provide services for the good of the whole community, while minimising provision which discriminates against some. The public purpose is to ensure the free and universal provision of compulsory education.

Public funding = public obligations

Having criticised unstated assumptions, it is only fair that we should declare our own. The provision and funding of school education, in any ongoing way and however intentioned, should not unfairly advantage some sections of the community over others and/or at their expense. Our suggestions point to all publicly funded schools committing to a public contract of obligations and operation, one which models and promotes the publicness, as well as the individual benefits, of school education.

We propose that public funding be allocated in ways to ensure that all funded schools, regardless of sector, comply with this contract. In other words, contracted non-government schools that are funded by taxpayers would be available to all comers in the local area, like public schools, while retaining the ethos that defines their special character.

Public funding = public contract

What might a contract cover? It could start with where to open, fund and even close schools. Again, such an idea isn't new: Gonski proposed that School Planning Authorities be established in each state and territory to manage planning and development of new schools and major expansions of existing ones.[11] It didn't happen, but even that level of cooperation would open possibilities for better cross-sectoral coordination.

Such a contract could apply to practices relating to curriculum delivery and assessment, annual reporting, child protection and other social legislation. Other practices defined by a contract could include student enrolment practices, compliance with freedom of information legislation, and complaints procedures. At present, there are significant but unjustified variations between publicly funded schools in these areas, providing very visible evidence of the unlevel playing field.

Common student enrolment practices should be a core requirement. In overall terms, enrolment is currently impacted by critical discriminators such as fees and entrance tests – the key underpinnings of our unlevel playing field. That practice would cease for all fully funded schools. Government and contracted schools – the only ones receiving public funding – would not be permitted to charge fees or establish any tests or other selection criteria. The level of their public funding would be primarily determined by the learning needs of their enrolled students. If any school seeks or attracts additional private funding, they would lose their public funding. Current practices and the problems they create, along with solutions, are contained in Table 3.

Table 3
The level playing field in practice

Area of concern	Current practice	Resulting problems	Solutions
1. Funding	Most schools, including religious ones, are substantially publicly funded.	There is a mismatch between the extent of public funding of schools and the educational task they face.	Governments to meet all costs of all public and contracted non-government schools.
2. Distribution of funding	Public funding is loosely based on need; private funding isn't.	Levels of total per-student funding create anomalies by sector, location and SES.	Funding to all schools to be strongly driven by student need.
3. School fees	These are low and often optional for public schools, higher for most private schools.	These substantially drive the socio-educational status of, and gaps between, schools.	Abolish fees in all public and contracted schools.
4. Enrolment obligations	Most public schools have to be open to all. For various reasons, most private schools are not.	Unequal obligations create contrasting enrolment profiles, impacting on socio-economic profile of schools and sectors, and overall student achievement.	Make both public and contracted schools available and open to all (while making allowance for the special ethos of schools).
5. Enrolment practices	Zoning usually exists for most public schools; various enrolment criteria used by private schools.	Selective enrolment practices effectively restrict choice of schools in both public and private sectors.	Increase choice by removing enrolment discriminators for all schools receiving public funding.
6. Suspension and expulsion	Some schools can suspend and/or expel students far more easily than others.	Such differences have a distorting impact on perceptions of schools and subsequent school choice decisions.	All public and contracted schools to have comparable procedures and regulations.

Area of concern	Current practice	Resulting problems	Solutions
7. Opening, closing, expanding and consolidating schools	Decisions are made by disconnected school authorities.	Decisions impact on viability of other schools and on overall cost of schools.	Establish a School Planning Authority in each state as Gonski recommended.
8. Relevant legislation; e.g., freedom of information, public comment	There is some variation between public and private sectors.	Variations create unequal obligations and accountabilities.	Common regulation is needed across public and contracted schools.
9. School purpose and character	A financial penalty attaches to the choice of schools with a distinctive religious or educational ethos.	Charging of fees restricts choice of religious schools to better-resourced families.	All funded schools supported to develop their special character within a mutually supportive framework.
10. Student achievement	Achievement is disproportionately impacted by the social background of a student's peers and family.	Australia continues to be bedevilled by a long tail of educational underachievement.	More inclusive schools to reduce the impact of social background on learning outcomes.

But can we afford it?

The very idea of fully funding all schools which agree to abolish fees is still likely to illicit a chorus of claims that it would be too expensive. But as we know, several submissions to the Gonski review pointed out that the cost of public funding of private schools was, even back then, more than commonly believed. Chapter 9 revealed that, even at the time of the Gonski review, Goulburn's Catholic schools were close to receiving the same public funding as the town's public schools.

THE 'SAVING THE TAXPAYER' STORY ACROSS AUSTRALIA

Our argument that governments equivalently fund all students needs further explanation, because it underpins our policy suggestions. So, how much more would it cost if governments paid the annual schooling costs (the recurrent costs) for every private school student? There are at least three different calculations.[12]

1. If government funding had to *replace all the expenditure* on private school students, it would cost up to around $9 billion extra, the figure often cited by the Catholic and independent peak groups. But why would governments do this when public schools enrolling similar students produce much the same results for much less money?
2. A second and more common calculation reduces the cost to around $4 billion. This is based on the *average amount spent* on students in each sector. But for *public* schools this average is quite high. Their students have higher needs and cost more, due to things such as location, disability and level of family advantage. If the higher SES private school students all went to public schools, they certainly wouldn't cost the same as the existing public school average.
3. A more accurate calculation is based on the likely cost if all existing private school students were funded at the same level as public school students with similar levels of advantage and needs. Similar students = similar costs. This calculation brings the cost to less than $1 billion.

How similar is the public funding of schools that a *majority* of students attend? Table 4 shows schools in three ICSEA ranges between 950 and 1099. Almost two-thirds of *all* students attend the schools represented in the table.

Table 4
Government recurrent funding per student by sector and ICSEA band.

ICSEA category	Sector	Median govt funding	% of $ to govt schools	Median govt funding	% of $ to govt schools
		2011		2018	
ICSEA 950–999	Government	11,017	(100%)	14,270	**(100%)**
	Catholic	10,383	94.2%	15,536	**108.9%**
	Independent	9,445	85.7%	14,896	**104.4%**
ICSEA 1000–1049	Government	10,323	(100%)	12,888	**(100%)**
	Catholic	9,044	87.6%	12,988	**100.8%**
	Independent	8,705	84.3%	12,951	**100.5%**
ICSEA 1050–1099	Government	9,704	(100%)	11,630	**(100%)**
	Catholic	8,105	83.5%	10,966	**94.3%**
	Independent	7,909	81.5%	11,259	**96.8%**

SOURCE My School, 2011 & 2018.

Fast forward to 2019: the most recent funding data further dispels any notion that governments save money by funding the Catholic schools. Trinity Catholic College in Goulburn (ICSEA 1018) is well ahead in the total funding per student stakes – at $22 412, this is $7000 more than Mulwaree High School (ICSEA

969). In government funding alone, Trinity is not far behind the much lower ICSEA Goulburn High School (ICSEA 947), and is $2224 per student *ahead* of Mulwaree High (ICSEA 969).[13] In other words, if the 488 students at Trinity had been enrolled at Mulwaree High in 2019, governments would have saved over $1 million ($2224 x 488 students) in that year alone. Funding figures for the town's primary schools reveal proportional savings.

The annual savings – not costs – to governments, if the public schools enrolled all Catholic school students in the town, would have been close to $3 million.[14] The exact numbers might vary: Trinity has a low enrolment, hence poorer economies of scale and higher costs per student. But the higher ICSEA Trinity students, if enrolled at Mulwaree, would cost less than the average student at the public school. Note that the figures don't include capital costs, but $3 million each year would buy quite a few classrooms.

It seems that Goulburn has played two starring roles in the state aid saga: it symbolically began state aid, and now it serves to demonstrate what state aid has created. But over the years in between, the savings to the taxpayer argument has had an unrelenting grip on policy, and on the Gonski review itself. This powerful, but seriously dated, assumption has created a 'path dependency' trap, preventing any active consideration of a fuller range of policy options.

It is certainly possible to have the operational costs of most private schools funded by government. In recurrent funding terms, the majority of non-government schools in Australia are already 'government' schools. It was only a matter of time before someone like Piccoli was going to state the obvious. With funding data so readily available, anyone can use the My School website to check the dollar cost of schools. Additional public savings would be accrued if governments in the future were no longer funding schools with fees already over the resource standard, or if School

Planning Authorities, as proposed by Gonski, were able to achieve greater coordination around school openings and closures. Can we really continue what any hard-nosed review would clearly identify as ongoing waste and inefficiency?

Will it really improve schools and student achievement?

To this point, we have illustrated how other countries structure their schools differently and have elaborated on how one country, Canada, puts Australia in the shade, including in student achievement. We have stated our proposal and demonstrated that cost needn't be an obstacle. Proposals such as ours create the potential to reshape schools and the relations between them, particularly around competition, choice and, most importantly, learning.

As it is currently structured, choice impacts negatively on so much else we try to accomplish, especially improving overall student achievement. The fact that families usually have to pay for choice of schools has so many unintended consequences: a school hierarchy, social and achievement gaps, unequal calls on public funding, and – quite oddly – less choice than the choosers believe. But given that parents feel that their children may gain a benefit if they enrol in particular schools, school choice is here to stay. The answer is not to deny their preference, but to better manage the policy challenges it may create. The immediate challenge is how to engage in a debate about choice without lapsing back into various thoughtless responses ('I believe in choice') and accusations ('You don't').

Over the years, unregulated competition between, and choice of, schools in Australia has become a primary policy driver, especially in the way we provide and fund schools. Choice would certainly be enhanced if existing financial barriers were removed. It would mean that choice and money would no longer be joined at the hip. It would break down the current SES hierarchy of schools and minimise the social and educational damage it is currently creating. It would provide a better basis for debates about school quality.

The proposal to fully fund all schools also reflects advice given in recent studies by the OECD.[15] Firstly, the OECD suggests that the conditions under which private schools are publicly funded influence the ways in which school choice impacts the accessibility, quality, and equity of the school system. Australia has found that out the hard way. Secondly, where market mechanisms apply, oversight and governance arrangements must be in place to guarantee that every child benefits from accessible, high-quality education. Thirdly, the threat to equality can be mitigated if all publicly funded providers adhere to the same regulations regarding tuition and admissions policies, and compliance with these regulations is monitored. In effect, the OECD is advocating for a level playing field.

But there are even more benefits of a level playing field, especially around school quality. It could shift the way school choice and competition works, proving a boost to overall student achievement. At the moment, schools compete with each other for preferred students, and parents scramble up the school SES ladder in search of preferred peers. Those missing out in this competition are the families without the resources to choose and the schools without the resources to compete against the winning schools, fuelling the divisions which impact on overall achievement. If competition and choice could be disconnected from an ability to pay fees, the onus would be placed back on schools to offer an authentic choice based on educational quality and diversity. Innovation would be less about appearances and resources and more about meeting the needs and improving the outcomes for all students.

A more level playing field will create a stronger *educational* rationale for choice, including school strengths and specialisations, special programs, school-to-work opportunities, support for targeted groups of students, community links, and co-curricular opportunities. It would create a diversity of schools around learning and opportunities, with a potential to break down the current socio-educational hierarchy, all supported by resources for schools, regardless of sector, which would be allocated strictly according to need.

The potential to achieve this after the pandemic has almost certainly been enhanced by the rapid growth in online learning. Notwithstanding the short-term losses, especially for the most disadvantaged, there is a chance that back to normal could actually mean 'normal plus'. Students, teachers and parents know much more about multiple learning modes and platforms. There are many ways to 'do school' and organise classrooms, and the value of innovation will achieve wider recognition. Schools which were relatively unscathed during the pandemic already include those with a strong element of independent and research-based learning. The success of such schools, including Big Picture schools,[16] is especially illustrated by students' post-school destinations, including university[17] and a more seamless transition to work. Such success already challenges conventional views of what good schools should look like. The second Gonski review opened the door to such innovation, but the dominant culture of competition and choice makes schools reluctant to stray too far from conventional views of learning and teaching.

Conceptualising schooling differently also has the potential to enhance opportunities for gifted and talented students, without negatively impacting on other schools, as existing selective schools currently do. As indicated in chapter 8, bricks-and-mortar selective schools draw gifted students away from comprehensive local schools in all sectors, adding to a wider problem that far exceeds the benefits to some students. A well-reported variation of the existing selective school model is Aurora College, a virtual selective high school in New South Wales, serving students from rural areas.[18] Students attend their local high school but also log in to Aurora's online conferencing system each day for lessons.[19] Residential gatherings are held twice each year and students have access to specialised lessons and leading scholars.

There is substantial potential to expand such virtual models of schooling. Doing so would enable more schools to provide a richer, more diverse curriculum to more students. Rather than separating young people into different schools, digital platforms allow schools to provide additional opportunities, differentiating the curriculum without exacerbating educational and social division. In effect, the often-conflicting views of education as a collective good or a private and positional good can be reconciled.

The school sector politics

If establishing a level playing field could help address our most urgent educational challenges, the central question becomes whether it is politically possible. For some, it isn't. Adrian Piccoli's proposal that we should fully publicly fund non-government primary schools was met with declarations that 'it's never going to happen' from both sides of the sectoral divide. The CEO of Catholic Schools NSW, Dallas McInerney, dismissed Piccoli's proposal as a 'think tank fantasy'.[20] And on this point, the public education advocate, Trevor Cobbold, agreed. 'The proposal is … highly unrealistic', Cobbold wrote.

> It is impossible to believe that Catholic and Independent schools would ever agree not to charge fees as a condition for the increase in government funding because it would mean reducing their resource advantage over public schools … Why would they choose to give this up? They will never accept a reduction in income to the level of public schools. They will always insist on the right to charge fees to maintain their

> resource advantage and status. It is no surprise that the CEO of Catholic Schools NSW called the proposal a 'flight of fantasy.[21]

Cobbold is right that some in the private school sectors would view the idea of fully publicly funding most schools as threatening, as McInerney's reaction attests. Does this mean that the private school lobbies would put the kibosh on any such initiative, and that such proposals stand no more chance of success than the Gonski reforms? After all, as things stand non-government schools can have their cake and eat it too: they are publicly funded at very high levels, can charge fees and enrol who, and how, they wish.

The executive director of the National Catholic Education Commission, Jacinta Collins, indicates an openness to dialogue. 'You might do it if you could be assured you'd be able to maintain the autonomy you want in relation to your mission. If it was done in a way that could guarantee that you could better meet your mission around preferential option for the poor.'[22] In this context Collins mentions the fee concessions Catholic schools provide families with a health care card in states like South Australia. 'And in fact, they've made another interesting change there, too', she says. 'Catholic schools take wards of the state at no cost in an agreement with the state government. So there are ways that you could say, well, alright, we'll introduce full funding for students of a particular character, and that would make it more accessible.' 'Our mission is to provide a faith-based education, particularly for, or focused on, a preferential option for the poor', Collins says. 'And we do that well in a range of areas. We can do it better, particularly around urban centres.'

But despite such admirable work, it is government schools that still enrol most of the poor and the disadvantaged. If Catholic schools were fully publicly funded, low-income Catholic families would be better able to exercise their first preference for their children's education. This would surely appeal to Catholics – and other believers – for whom the under-representation of disadvantaged kids at their schools is a cause of unease. That's the first big potential attraction of the level playing field for the non-government sectors.

The second is less about ideals and more about organisational self-interest. Not all non-government schools and sectors are growing. The independent sector is, but mainly due to the increasing number of Islamic schools. My School shows that the number of Catholic schools in the lower to middle ICSEA ranges is falling: Catholic school enrolments in the lower ICSEA half of schools fell by 18 per cent between 2012 and 2018. Do their school authorities really want to dismiss out of hand a proposal to improve the access of their poorer parishioners to their schools? It would certainly provide an opportunity to reconnect with the demographic which, in relative terms at least, seems to be walking away from their schools.

As Jacinta Collins indicated, the potential stumbling block is the set of conditions which would accompany full funding. 'How we've been operating in Australia has been, in the main, fairly healthily pluralist', says Collins. 'And there's a reservation that we could end up moving away from that if we just accepted full government funding.'[23] The director of Public Policy at Christian Schools Australia, Mark Spencer, shares this reservation. Many of the schools he represents would prefer to have their 'funding capped, or take reduced funding, rather than interfere with the ability of our schools to determine and act in accordance with a vision and mission. We would always insist on the right to employ the staff, we want staff who share our faith and beliefs, that would be an absolute non-negotiable'.[24]

This insistence is unsurprising, but an abundance of international experience illustrates that it need not be an insuperable obstacle to reform. In comparable countries around the world, fully public funded church schools have control over their curriculum and school culture, indicating it is possible to agree on mutually satisfactory arrangements. Indeed, when Christian Schools Australia proposed full funding for its schools in its submission to the Gonski review in 2011, it was because they could see that across the Tasman full public funding had not compromised the autonomy of New Zealand church schools. And, as we have seen, New Zealand is far from the only example of such an accommodation.

But for some public education advocates, such as organisations like Save Our Schools and the Council for Defense of Government Schools, full public funding of religious schools is anathema. 'Private schools would ... insist on control of their curriculum to meet religious and other objectives', Trevor Cobbold writes. 'In particular, Catholic and other Christian schools in the public system would insist on being able to teach religion as part of their curriculum. For some, it includes not teaching evolution and refusing to teach proper sex education.'[25] This is a strange argument. The reality is that full public funding would change nothing on this score: it would neither grant religious schools any exemptions that they do not already have; nor would it restrict the autonomy they currently enjoy. Would church schools be able to teach religion? They have been for eons, so what would change? Would they have to teach evolution? Absolutely, if it is in the national curriculum. Would schools enjoy exemptions from the *Sex Discrimination Act*? Unless the legislation changes, no more or no less than they do at present.

For too long, we've allowed the religious question, which will always involve a degree of compromise, to obscure issues which are both more important and more susceptible to change. The reality is that public funding will continue going to schools that aren't secular, as has been the case for decades. The real question is whether, in facilitating choice and pluralism in our school system, we are also going to continue to promote the imbalance in resourcing and responsibilities that define the unlevel playing field.

If a proposal to fully publicly fund private schools became a serious possibility, it would immediately make clear what is really at stake. It would force private school parents, educators and authorities to ask: do we want to be part of an inclusive, pluralistic system of schools resourced and regulated on a common basis? Or do we want to demand taxpayer funding to provide our children with a better resourced and more exclusive education?

The non-government sectors, particularly the Catholics, would have to think very carefully. After all, this reform would represent a historic victory, finally comprehensively addressing the injustices that Bishops Goold and Vaughan railed against in the 1870s and 1880s, and Archbishop Mannix fought unsuccessfully over the first half of the 20th century. Conscientious choice of a religious school would no longer affect the entitlement to a fully publicly funded education.

And rejection could not be justified on the grounds of choice, because that's precisely what full funding provides. Abolishing fees would improve access to the religious poor. Nor could opponents of full funding appeal to affordability because they would be arguing against free and inclusive schooling for their own flock. Rejectionists would risk being seen by commentators, politicians, the electorate and their own constituencies as opposing the idea that the religious poor should have a place in their schools.

Once religious choice is taken out of the argument, opposition to the level playing field could be more clearly seen for what it is: a claim that governments should help some kids enjoy a better-resourced education at schools other kids can't enter, an argument that is really an unsustainable demand for public support to aid private advantage. Other countries don't do it; governments can't, and shouldn't have to try, to afford it. And absent the religious argument, those who pursue this unreasonable demand are much less likely to be buttressed by a broad-based coalition of church schools and organisations. Along with the increased exposure of the exceptional wealth of Australia's most exclusive private schools, the fairness, as well as the prudence, of continuing taxpayer support, would be likely to come under ever closer scrutiny.[26]

What about supporters of public education? If they choose to oppose full funding of church schools, the risk is that the real issues will continue to be obscured. Religion will continue to be the moral shield behind which dubious arguments about privilege hide. And they would be tacitly accepting a continuation of Australia's unworkable and regressive dual system of free and fee-charging taxpayer-funded schools – along with the configuration of political interests that sustains it. Trevor Cobbold argues that the additional investment in non-government schools, to bring them up to full public funding, 'would be better used to support under-funded public schools and disadvantaged students'.[27] But this is to rather miss the point. Public schools enrol over 80 per cent of disadvantaged students because they are the only schools required to provide a free education to all comers. In return for full funding, private schools would be required to accept the full range of public obligations that go with the money. And that would mean non-government schools would be free, funded and required to enrol a larger proportion of disadvantaged students.

A more even distribution of students would make a massive difference to the public school communities which have to do the heaviest lifting at the moment – especially the teachers who are overwhelmed by aggregating disadvantage, the ones who see their kids' futures shaped not by their well-prepared lessons but by the lessons from those around them. The additional investment in private schools would be the price of purchasing a level playing field, of winning essential structural change – rather than some additional resourcing to cope with never-ending structural failure.

Instead of a public, inclusive, free and secular school system, our current funding arrangements have now created many taxpayer-supported schools which are private, exclusive, fee-charging and religious, with fewer public obligations. Despite the best efforts of public education advocates, Australian governments have been unsuccessfully attempting to introduce needs-based funding for half a century. The question for those committed to the cause of public education is: what's going to change in coming years and decades? Why is it going to be different next time? It is hard to believe that there will be a more inspired campaign than 'I Give a Gonski' or a public policy review that will offer a stronger basis for change, or a Labor government more willing to stand up to powerful interest groups. For public education advocates, the challenge is to open a dialogue that stands a reasonable chance of making a breakthrough: of shifting debate beyond the Karmel paradigm and all the problems it has produced.

In transition: meeting the challenges

The impact on public schools

When Adrian Piccoli proposed the full public funding of all schools, he recognised the need for a graduated approach. His suggestion was to start with primary schools, the implication being that this is a big step and should be done in stages. While Piccoli's proposal and our elaboration are a disrupter, no one wants chaos.

Among public education advocates, those most concerned will point to a possible exodus from public schools created by parents who have long wanted to enrol their kids in non-government schools. In this scenario, any increased interest would see demand for places exceeding supply. Schools might try to apply selection criteria, just as many high-demand schools currently do. Along with this, many private schools may try to re-impose fees, just as New Zealand's integrated schools have, in one guise or another. They won't want to give up the edge they have gained, courtesy of an unbalanced public funding system combined with unregulated fees.

These are real issues. In the short term, the fear would be justified; after all, the whole objective is to make church schools just as accessible and inclusive as public schools. At the same time, they would still be church schools. The trappings of religious labels and practice may be less of an attraction when the social profile, and the achievement profile, of the school increasingly resembles that of the public school down the road. Already it is widely accepted that school achievement levels, which once seemed to be related to school sector, are overwhelmingly a product of who goes to which school. In the long run, it would mean that schools would be competing for enrolments on the basis of what they do, rather than on their attractive student profiles and resource advantages.

It is critical that such changes are only implemented after a thorough investigation of preferred models and how any transition process might work, partly taking up what seemed to be options in the early stages of the Gonski review. This work has to focus on enrolment and choice processes found in systems that are both equitable and achieving, including those mentioned earlier in this chapter. Australia has more than enough research capacity able to carry out such an investigation. Aside from the established public service, Australia has an alphabet soup of organisations, including the National Schools Resourcing Board (NSRB), the Australian Education Research Organisation (AERO), the Australian Curriculum, Assessment and Reporting Authority (ACARA) and the Australian Council for Educational Research (ACER) which should be put to work on this priority. There is a big existing investment in these bodies, and they could be powerfully utilised to evaluate where we are, how we compare and set new directions.

Commonwealth-state relations

Australia faces serious constitutional challenges impacting on schools. It may have been inevitable that the Commonwealth, the best resourced level of government, would fund schools, but it has created another Australian oddity, with the Commonwealth Government overwhelmingly resourcing non-government schools, while the states mainly support government schools. In such a context, achieving progress is difficult. To succeed, policy initiatives in education need to secure broad agreement from all governments at both levels, as well as from the school sectors. The failure of needs-based funding to ever arrive reflects the failure to accomplish this.

Our federal system will continue to present challenges. Arguments about the respective roles of the two levels of government is to a significant extent a proxy war about the relative funding of the public and private sectors. This is why any push for change has to secure widespread community support, strong enough to shift the priorities of government and minimise the opposition from sectional interests.

The impetus for change is critical. If there was broad agreement that private schools should be fully publicly funded, then there would not be the same ideological pressure on the Commonwealth to heavily favour the non-government sector. If sectoral hostilities could be defused, this would enable stronger support for doing what Gonski recommended: sharing the role of funding all schools. Inevitably the pressure to reach this point won't come from the political parties, the lobby groups or the various other advocates: it will only come from a growing realisation that what we have simply doesn't work.

Keep waiting for Gonski?

If we ever had the chance to design an education system afresh from the ground up, we'd never create what we have now. All we've done is carry forward what is a demonstrably flawed and even failed system, while promising and expecting different results – effectively acting out Albert Einstein's definition of insanity.

All other factors being equal, it should be easy to agree on how to reform Australia's structure of schooling. But all other factors aren't equal: those who benefit from current arrangements certainly won't want to disturb the status quo. In a speech in 2011, a politician who was to become a federal education minister expressed concern that the Gonski reforms to improve equity could 'compel non-government schools to take certain cohorts of students or lose school funding'.[28] Just like most of his Coalition colleagues and over half of Labor's federal front bench around that time, Alan Tudge himself attended schools with very few from those 'cohorts'.[29]

The status quo in Australian schooling has shifted over decades. A large slice of the current adult population attended schools with peers who, in one way or another, were selected. The narratives about inclusive and public education haven't been a big part of their lived school experience. It will take a lot to shift their thinking; having a more level playing field of schools might help. But are supporters of public education also able to re-think the future? How much energy is really being poured into finding different solutions to decades-old problems? Will doing the same thing for another decade produce a different result for public schools, or merely a playing field that is increasingly tilted against them?

Some urge patience and perserverence, including Tanya Plibersek:

> I think all big reforms take a long time and are two steps forward, one step back on occasion. And I think about Medicare obviously being a huge example of that. But others, superannuation, national disability insurance scheme, carbon pricing or action on climate change – all of these things are enormous changes to make to a society and an economy … and needs-based funding is absolutely in that vein.[30]

But comparing the lifetime of Medicare with the half-century attempt to introduce needs-based school funding doesn't offer much comfort. One happened and the other didn't. Medicare has survived and is embedded in Australian political culture; equity and needs-based funding in schooling have always remained a pipe dream. Why have their fates been so different? Because unlike Medicare, needs-based funding on a dual system of publicly funded schools was never going to happen.

But giving up on structural reform isn't an option because the costs and casualties continue to slowly mount. Julia Gillard announced the Gonski review in 2010. The strugglers who started school that year should be in Year 12 in 2022. What about those who didn't last the distance? There are scarce headlines about the kids who didn't get the support they needed and fell by the wayside. Schools face the problem that, while the impacts of growing inequity are substantial, the growth is quiet and incremental.

Doing little or nothing comes at a significant and increasing cost: a cost in lost opportunities; a cost to the future livelihood for children; and a social cost created by increasingly marginalised schools. Last but not least is the dollar cost, including the cost of lost productivity and the financial burden as the marginalised fall into the welfare net.

What will happen if we do little or nothing?

- If recent trends are any guide, the overall data about **student achievement** is not going to change anytime soon: the gap between high and low SES schools will continue to widen and reduce the potential of other school reforms to make a difference. Our social hierarchy of schools might protect the most advantaged students, but others won't be so fortunate. The already very slippery slope of inequity, explained in chapter 8, will continue to steepen. If we do nothing, we are in for another two decades of decline – for all the reasons given in this book.
- The forces at play described in chapter 8 will **continue to impact** on our schools. High SES schools will grow, but low SES schools will become even more disadvantaged. It took just a few years for students in the lowest SES quarter to rise from one-third to one half of the enrolment of our more disadvantaged schools. When the strugglers look around their classrooms, they'll find it harder than ever to see the advantaged and the aspirant. The newly appointed teacher in front of them probably won't last any longer than the previous one. What miracle strategy among what we call 'school reforms' is going to turn their lives around?
- As we have seen, the problems of **school funding** simply aren't resolved and other money problems will accumulate. In 2016, Adam Rorris found that Australia's failure to retain all students to the end of Year 12 schooling will generate direct financial costs of over $72 billion by 2070.[31] In 2018, the Public Education Foundation found that the costs of the students at the bottom falling further below those at the top between 2009 and 2015 was over $20 billion.[32] Yet we still spend in the wrong places: when funding from both public and private sources is considered, Australia currently

over-spends around $5 billion each year in recurrent funding, poorly targeted to schools already above the resource standard.[33]

- As the Gonski Institute for Education has reported, **enrolment shifts** towards higher SES schools also mean that the SES of school enrolments tend to be higher or lower than that of their local area.[34] Students in schools in northern Geelong, for instance, are even less advantaged on average than most people in the nearby low-income localities. In contrast, students in schools elsewhere in Geelong tend to be even more advantaged than are the people living nearby. This is apparent in so many places around Australia and has implications for both schools and communities, when the former no longer reflect the latter.
- If we do nothing, we'll place the livelihood of **our most vulnerable** young people at greater risk. As the authors of the most recent Mitchell Institute report attest, one quarter of Australian 11–12-year-olds don't have the literacy and numeracy skills they need.[35] The Australian Council for Educational Research (ACER) has reported that Australian students have a declining sense of belonging at school.[36] Students from low SES backgrounds are particularly affected.
- **Competition between schools**, as it operates at present, will continue to get in the way of authentic improvements in school quality and student outcomes. As research indicates, competing schools will continue to focus on attracting high-value students ahead of focusing on teaching and learning.[37] They will persist in chasing 'the same academic pot of gold',[38] while innovations to improve learning and student achievement will continue to take second place.[39] This will go on acting as a drag on improving overall student outcomes.

- Given that the foundations of our system lack sufficient equity, our most disadvantaged students and **schools remain vulnerable** to large-scale disruptions to student learning. While this was demonstrated during the COVID-19 pandemic, it can equally happen at other times of natural and human disasters. Resilience at such times is critical to capacity to cope. An OECD Working Paper from 2018 found that Australian students, especially those with low school socio-economic status, are already becoming less resilient.[40]

If we do nothing, our schools and systems will never be able to tick all the boxes needed for success. For simplicity, these boxes can be considered the seven 'E's. The first couple are *excellence* and *equity* – the twin holy grails of school education, coupled together because you can't sufficiently achieve the first without the second. Then comes *efficiency*: is our investment in schools delivering the best possible outcomes for a reasonable cost? Given the widespread concern about student achievement, it seems our spending on schools also lacks *effectiveness*: too much goes to well-resourced schools where it makes too little difference. The priority instead should be the schools where it has a better chance of lifting student outcomes. Our spending also lacks sufficient *efficacy*; it doesn't deliver what it is planned and claimed to do. In part this is because it doesn't reflect sufficient *evidence* about what works and what doesn't. And last, but by no means least, if and when we ever get it right, perhaps we'll see good policy that is *enduring*.

Looking forward

We wanted this book to be a narrative about incremental progress towards a comprehensive solution. But Gonski too closely resembled imperfect solutions of the past; and too many problems have remained unanswered. It's hardly sector-blind and needs-based, and its implementation ensured that some schools would continue to enjoy undeserved advantages over others – assisted and exacerbated by public funding. The playing field continued to tilt against the most disadvantaged, something that, just as it had in the past, continued to deny the justice and fairness they needed and deserved.

In 2022, we know much more about the impact of unequal chances, of inequity, on opportunities and achievement. As school practitioners and writers, we are both committed to improving schools, but also to improving the ground on which they operate. Context matters. We didn't invent the playing field metaphor, but it certainly describes the core problem, one which creates winners and losers among students, schools and communities. One thing is certain about an unlevel playing field: at least half the players will harbour a lingering resentment and will want to tilt it back in their favour. It has to be as level as possible; individual schools succeed or fail as part of a broader ecosystem.

We don't want to conclude this book with any restatements or summaries. They are sprinkled enough through the ten chapters. In this chapter, we have provided a glimpse of our school future if Australia drifts on with just more of the same. Why not end with a contrasting glimpse of how some of the schools mentioned in this book might fare if structural reform, true equity and excellence become a reality?

Picture this scene: in 2032, the 'Gonski schools', plus some others, might gather to compare notes on what eventually happened, not ten, but 20 years after the review.

'Losing our public funding came as a shock at first', the head of Geelong Grammar might say. 'But that $5000 or so per student was really only a bonus. Our parents picked up the tab and the school also saved costs by not having to complete all the paperwork that came with government funding. Like our companion schools overseas, we are now authentically and proudly a private and an independent school.'

The principal of Adelaide High School might add her perspective: 'Like some other schools, we were dragging in kids from all over Adelaide for this-and-that sought-after program. But the pandemic opened our eyes to online learning. Now they go to their local school, but log in to some of our lessons as well. So when the government clamped down on out-of-area enrolments all the students and schools had the best of both worlds'.

Sitting together might be the principals of the two schools, Villawood North Public School and Sacred Heart School, that David Gonski visited. Imagine the possible comments of 'Sister Therese', a beginning teacher at the time: 'We thought things would change, but we ended up further advantaged than your school, financially and in other ways. We helped some poor families but the fees really meant, as the bishops once lamented, that we weren't serving the poorest Catholics. Now we don't charge fees our poor parishioners are much more able to enrol their children here. We now fulfill the mission that the oldies used to talk about'.

The principal of Wagga Wagga's Mount Austin High School, meanwhile, might say: 'The local private schools used to do us in. One way or another, their unwanted kids would end up with us. Great kids, but they didn't do a lot for our results, while their departure made their previous school look better. But over time a fair set of rules, applied to all, has meant our school looks a lot more like the wider community. Opportunities for students considerably improved. The mix of enrolments in each of the Wagga schools seems to have evened out. We don't seem to have that same concentration of disadvantage that we had a decade ago, and this has helped lift results'.

The principal of one of the 'dumped-on' schools might go further: 'In those years, our school looked like the pits. But the extra funding and capital works have been strongly welcomed by parents and teachers. We now have the same rules as the two local competing schools. Years ago they'd say to their problem kids: if you can't follow our rules you'll have to go to *that* school. Not anymore'.

Over a few drinks, those at the gathering might agree that improvement started in the early 2020s. 'Maybe it was the drought', they'd muse, 'or the big fires and floods ... or the pandemic. But slowly we realised that, just like teachers in a tough school, we battle this together or we get done over separately. We better appreciated that our schools are neighbours, we could help each other, help create and sustain communities, and shape the nation'.

We can create something better for Australia's schools and kids.

2032

Separate from that gathering of 'Gonski schools', Kim and Maria would meet up for coffee in Rivertown. Kim was now a Melbourne solicitor and Maria ran a small aged care home which grew out of her own care for her grandparents. 'It's been a long haul, and I went off the rails a few times', Maria said, 'but I think kids have got it better now'. 'You just wouldn't recognise the local town's schools,' Maria continued. 'They used to cater for different ends of town and compete to get the best students. They are still different, but in ways that matter, and they are also better, and considered to be far more equal.'

Glossary

Advantaged and disadvantaged schools: while schools can be advantaged or disadvantaged in many ways, these terms, as used in this book, generally refer to a school's socio-educational advantage (SEA) described by its Index of Community Socio-Educational Advantage (ICSEA) value.

AGSRC: the Average Government School Recurrent Cost (AGSRC) measure was used to form the benchmark for Commonwealth recurrent school funding levels and was derived from average state government expenditure in government schools. It was the basis of Australian Government recurrent funding for government and non-government school students until 2013.

Catholic systemic schools: these are Catholic schools which belong to a system, and are run by Catholic education offices in each jurisdiction, as distinct from independent Catholic schools which are usually run by established religious orders.

'Gonski 2.0': in May 2017, the Turnbull Government announced new funding arrangements and a new review to be conducted, once again, by David Gonski. While 'Gonski 2.0' can refer to either announcement, in this book it is used to describe the Turnbull Government funding arrangements, legislated in the *Australian Education Amendment Bill 2017*.

ICSEA: the Index of Community Socio-Educational Advantage (ICSEA) is a scale that represents levels of educational advantage and reported on the My School website. Each school's ICSEA value represents the averaged socio-educational level for its enrolled students. ICSEA is calculated from factors shown to have an impact on student outcomes, such as parental education levels, parental occupation, school geographic location and proportion of Indigenous students. The average ICSEA is 1000. Almost two-thirds of all students attend schools in the range 950–1100. While schools can be advantaged or disadvantaged in many ways, in this book these labels refer to the level of advantage, as described by ICSEA, of school enrolments. (*See also* Percentile)

ICSEA quarters: My School shows the distribution of each school's enrolment across four socio-educational advantage (SEA) quarters. Q1 is the percentage of students from families in the lowest quarter. Q4 is the percentage from the highest quarter, with Q2 and 3 in between. The national average in each quarter is 25 per cent. The spread of a school's enrolment across these four quarters provides a more detailed picture of advantage and disadvantage.

Independent schools: independent schools are a sub-set of non-government schools that are not operated by a non-government system or authority.

Learning years: learning years describe the typical growth in achievement over one year for a nation's students. The Australian Council for Educational Research indicates that: 'For Australia, one year of schooling corresponds to around 33 points on the PISA reading literacy scale, around 28 points on the mathematical literacy scale, and around 27 points on the scientific literacy scale'. <www.acer.org/au/discover/article/pisa-2018-australian-students-performance>.

My School: My School is a website administered by the Australian Curriculum, Assessment and Reporting Authority which provides access to information about Australian schools. <www.myschool.edu.au/>.

NAPLAN: the National Assessment Program – Literacy and Numeracy (NAPLAN) is an annual assessment for Australian students in Years 3, 5, 7 and 9. <www.nap.edu.au/naplan>.

National minimum standards: national minimum standards describe some of the skills and understandings students can generally demonstrate at their particular year of schooling, in a specific subject area or domain. <www.nap.edu.au/results-and-reports/how-to-interpret/standards>.

NRIPS: this refers to Net Recurrent Income per Student, which is a key financial measure reported on My School and includes income from all sources. <www.acara.edu.au/reporting/national-report-on-schooling-in-australia/national-report-on-schooling-in-australia-2011/funding-Australias-schools/overview-of-my-school-financial-information>

Peer effects: in general terms, peer effects refer to the influences which a group (e.g., a school class) might have on an individual's behaviour or outcomes. In the school context, it refers to the impact, either direct or indirect, of the socio-educational advantage (SEA) level of the peers on individual students.

Percentile: the My School website also more broadly shows ICSEA as a percentile or decile. On My School, a percentile of 40 means that a school is more educationally advantaged than 40 per cent of all schools in Australia, and correspondingly more educationally disadvantaged than 60 per cent of all schools in Australia.

PISA: the Program for International Student Assessment (PISA) is an international assessment that measures 15-year-old students' reading, mathematics and science literacy every three years.

Private schools: this includes all non-government schools, both independent and Catholic schools.

Q1, Q2, Q3, Q4: *See* ICSEA quarters

Residualisation: this describes the process in which the main burden of educating children and youth from less well-off families has become increasingly concentrated, mainly but not solely, in public schools, and with particular impacts on those schools and their enrolled students.

SES and SEA: Socio-economic status (SES) is a measure of an individual's or family's economic and social position in relation to others. The measure commonly includes income, education and occupation. SES is commonly used to depict relative advantage in society as a whole. In the context of schools, socio-educational advantage (SEA) refers to relative advantage as calculated in each school's ICSEA value. The My School website uses SEA, while SES is in more common use as an indicator of relative advantage. There is reasonable alignment between the two measures, although SEA doesn't include measures of family income. For convenience, references in this book are to SES, unless in the specific context of My School data.

SRS: the Schooling Resource Standard (SRS) is an estimate of how much total public funding a school needs to meet its students' educational needs, and is based on recommendations from the Gonski review. The SRS is made up of a base amount for all primary and secondary students and needs-based loadings for student priority cohorts and disadvantaged schools. <www.dese.gov.au/quality-schools-package/fact-sheets/what-schooling-resource-standard-and-how-does-it-work>.

Select bibliography

ABC, 'Education, Environment and Equality', *Q&A*, 26 September 2016.

ABC, 'Former education union chief urges all sides to back Gonski 2.0', *7.30*, 20 June 2017.

Allen Consulting Group, *Governments working together: A better future for all Australians*, part of the Victorian Government's Shared Future project, 2004.

Ashenden, D, 'Could Turnbull give a Gonski?', *Inside Story*, 24 September 2015.

——, 'The educational consequences of the peace', *Inside Story*, 28 July 2016, <www.insidestory.org.au/the-educational-consequences-of-the-peace/>.

——, 'What is to be done about Australian schooling?', *Inside Story*, 3 December 2019.

Austin, AG, *Select Documents in Australian Education, 1788–1900*, Pitman Press, Sydney, 1963.

Australian Government, Review of Funding for Schooling: Discussion Paper and Draft Terms of Reference, 2010. <apo.org.au/sites/default/files/resource-files/2010-05/apo-nid21412.pdf>.

Benson, S, 'Labor victory fuelled by Catholic education backing', *The Australian*, 19 March 2018.

Bentley, T & Savage, GC, *Educating Australia: Challenges for the Decade Ahead*, Melbourne University Press, Melbourne, 2017.

Bonnor, C, 'My School, PISA and Australia's equity gap', *Inside Story*, 11 May 2011. <insidestory.org.au/my-school-pisa-and-australias-equity-gap>.

——, 'One league away from disaster', *Inside Story*, 9 September 2009. <insidestory.org.au/one-league-away-from-disaster>.

——, 'Separating Scholars: How Australia abandons its struggling schools – Discussion Paper,' Centre for Policy Development, January 2019.

Bonnor, C, Ho, C & Richards, G, 'A creeping Indigenous separation', Centre for Policy Development, February 2018.

Bonnor, C, Kidson, P, Piccoli, A, Sahlberg, P & Wilson, R, *Structural Failure: Why Australia keeps falling short of its educational goals*, UNSW Gonski Institute, Sydney, 2021.

Bonnor, C & Shepherd, B, 'Uneven playing field: The state of Australia's schools', Centre for Policy Development, June 2016.

Bonnor, C & Wilson, R, 'The school money-go-round,' *EdMediaWatch*, 2021.

Boston, K, 'Gonski review: Vision or hallucination', TJ Ryan Foundation, 14 February 2017.

——, speech to New South Wales Teachers Federation Conference, Sydney Town Hall, 29 June 2014. <www.nswtf.org.au/files/2014_06june_29_dr_ken_boston_speech.pdf>.

——, 'What Gonski really meant, and how that's been forgotten almost everywhere', *Inside Story*, 6 September 2016. <insidestory.org.au/what-gonski-really-meant-and-how-thats-been-forgotten-almost-everywhere>.

Browne, P, 'Latham's list was a hit in the polls', *Inside Story*, 27 August 2012. <insidestory.org.au/lathams-list-was-a-hit-in-the-polls/>.

Select bibliography

Campbell, C, Proctor, H & Sherrington, G, *School Choice: How parents negotiate the new school market in Australia*, Allen & Unwin, Sydney, 2009.

Cobbold, T, 'The state of school funding in Australia 2017', *Save our Schools*, June 2019. <saveourschools.com.au/wp-content/uploads/2019/06/The-State-of-School-Funding-in-Australia-2017-Update.pdf>.

Connors, L & McMorrow, J, *Imperatives in Schools Funding: Equity, sustainability and achievement*, Australian Council for Educational Research, Camberwell, Vic., 2015.

——, *New Directions in Schools Funding: A proposed model*, Faculty of Education and Social Work, University of Sydney, 2010.

Ferguson, J, 'Labor fires Catholic funding war', *The Australian*, 9 March 2018.

Ferrari, J, 'Gillard fails to back school funding recommendations', *The Australian*, 21 February 2012.

——, 'Howard wanted to wean schools off funds deal', *Weekend Australian*, 7 May 2011.

Freudenberg, G, *A Certain Grandeur: Gough Whitlam in politics*, Macmillan, South Melbourne, 1977.

Garrett, P, *Big Blue Sky*, Allen & Unwin, Sydney, 2016.

Gillard, J, 'A future fair for all: School funding in Australia', address to Sydney Institute, 15 April 2010.

——, 'A national plan for school improvement, speech to National Press Club', Department of Prime Minister and Cabinet, Canberra, 3 September 2012.

——, 'Address to the Independent Schools National Forum', Department of Prime Minister and Cabinet, Canberra, 20 August 2012. <pmtranscripts.pmc.gov.au/release/transcript-18746>.

——, *My Story*, Penguin Random House Australia, Melbourne, Kindle edition, 2014.

Gonski, D, Greiner, K, Boston, K, Lawrence, C, Tannock, P & Scales, B, *Review of Funding for Schooling: Emerging isssues paper*, Federal Department of Education, Employment and Workplace Relations, Canberra, 2010.

——, *Review of Funding for Schooling: Final report*, Federal Department of Education, Employment and Workplace Relations, Canberra, December 2011.

Goss, P, 'A simple and immediate fix for schools funding', *Australian Financial Review*, 22 September 2016. <grattan.edu.au/news/a-simple-and-immediate-fix-for-schools-funding/>.

——, 'Funding lavished on schools that need it least', *The Age*, 16 May 2018. <www.smh.com.au/education/lopsided-funding-gives-more-to-private-schools-that-need-it-least-20190514-p51ndt.html>.

Goss, P & Sonnemann J, *Circuit breaker: A new compact on school funding*, Grattan Institute, Melbourne, November 2016. <grattan.edu.au/wp-content/uploads/2016/11/881-Circuit-Breaker-New-Compact-replaced-3.pdf>.

——, 'Submission to the Senate Inquiry into the Australian Education Amendment Bill', Grattan Institute, Melbourne, 2017.

Greenwell, T, 'We wouldn't want to be where you guys are, that's for sure', *Inside Story*, 1 February 2017. <https://insidestory.org.au/we-wouldnt-want-to-be-where-you-guys-are-thats-for-sure>.

——, 'Why do Canada's schools outperform Australia's'? *Inside Story*, 9 April 2020. <https://insidestory.org.au/why-do-canadas-schools-outperform-australias/>.

Harrington, M, *Australian Government Funding for Schools Explained: 2013*, Social Policy Section, Parliamentary Library, 8 March 2013. <apo.org.au/node/33106>.

——, 'Schools funding legislation passed by Parliament – an update on the amendments', FlagPost (Parliamentary Library), 28 June 2017. <parlinfo.aph.gov.au/parlInfo/download/library/prspub/5364824/upload_binary/5364824.pdf;fileType=application%2Fpdf#search=%22library/prspub/5364824%22>.

Karmel, P, et al., *Schools in Australia: Report of the Interim Committee for the Australian Schools Commission*, Australian Government Publishing Service, Canberra, May 1973.

Karp, P, 'Catholic and independent schools given extra $4.6bn in funding peace deal', *The Guardian*, 20 September 2018. <www.theguardian.com/australia-news/2018/sep/20/catholic-and-independent-schools-given-extra-46bn-in-funding-peace-deal>.

Karvelas, P, 'Labor puts off schools funding battle for a year – ELECTION 2010', *The Australian*, 5 August 2010.

Keating, J, *Resourcing schools in Australia: A proposal for the restructure of public funding*, Foundation for Young Australians, Melbourne, 2010. <www.fya.org.au/app/theme/default/design/assets/publications/Keating-2010-Resourcing-Aust-Schools.pdf>.

Kelly, P, 'The real story behind the Gonski train wreck', *The Australian*, 4 December 2013.

Knott, M & Koziol, M, 'Gonski 2.0: the story of how the government got it done', *Sydney Morning Herald*, 24 June 2017. <www.smh.com.au/politics/federal/gonski-20-the-story-of-how-the-government-got-it-done-20170623-gwwwuk.html>.

Lamb, S, Huo, S, Walstab, A, Wade, A, Maire, Q, Doecke, E, Jackson, J & Endekov, Z, *Educational opportunity in Australia 2020: Who succeeds and who misses out*. Centre for International Research on Education Systems, Victoria University, for the Mitchell Institute, Melbourne, 2020.

Latham, M & Macklin, J, 'Great Australian Schools', Australian Labor Party, 15 September 2004. <drive.google.com/file/d/102uUIpArVXWBsDJaaZrbYWYXQHXaYvKv/view?usp=sharing>.

Macdonald, E, 'The genesis of state aid', *The Canberra Times*, 14 July 2012. <www.canberratimes.com.au/story/6168022/the-genesis-of-state-aid/#gsc.tab=0>.

Maiden, S, '3000 schools face funding cuts', *Herald Sun*, 19 August 2012.

Marginson, S, et al., 'Can we afford to continue funding private schools?', *Sydney Morning Herald*, 12 February 2012. <www.smh.com.au/education/can-we-afford-to-continue-funding-private-schools-20110211-1aqke.html>.

Marginson, S, 'Re-assessing Karmel: Results of the 1973 Education Settlement', *Progress in Political Economy*, no. 16, March 1984, pp. 15–33. <www.ppesydney.net/content/uploads/2020/04/Reassessing-Karmel-results-of-the-1973-education-settlement.pdf>.

McGowan, M, 'Bill Shorten pledges extra $250m for Catholic schools if Labor elected', *The Guardian*, 9 March 2018. <www.theguardian.com/australia-news/2018/mar/09/bill-shorten-pledges-extra-250m-for-catholic-schools-if-labor-elected>.

Murphy, K & Harrison, D, 'Gillard buys peace with private schools – and some grief', *The Age*, 5 August 2010.

New South Wales Department of Education and Communities, *Discussion Paper: Australian school funding arrangements*, NSW DEC, 2011. <drive.google.com/file/d/1cEUu9FUlTsmJHD2nGSDUdBK_dodkgLN0/view>.

Nous Group, *Schooling challenges and opportunities – A report for the Review of Funding for Schooling*, with the Melbourne Graduate School of Education (MGSE) and the National Institute of Labour Studies (NILS), August 2011.

O'Doherty, S & Spencer, M, *Review of Funding of Schooling Emerging Issues Paper: Response by Christian Schools Australia*, 31 March 2011. <drive.google.com/file/d/1H1KseAcqwNyveqtrctULx4H_shd0Diiw/view?usp=sharing>.

O'Kelly, G, 'Media release – Funding for Catholic Schools', Bishops Commission for Catholic Education, 15 July 2010.

Patty, A, 'Christian schools seek full public funding', *Sydney Morning Herald*, 1 April 2011. <www.smh.com.au/national/christian-schools-seek-full-public-funding-20110331-1cncu.html>.

——, 'How private schools owe taxpayer $2b', *Sydney Morning Herald*, 9 February 2008.

——, 'Parents bear the burden of surging private fees', *Sydney Morning Herald*, 23 January 2011. <www.smh.com.au/education/parents-bear-the-burden-of-surging-private-fees-20110122-1a0jq.html>.

——, 'School fees hit record highs', *Sydney Morning Herald*, 26 December 2009. <www.smh.com.au/education/school-fees-hit-record-highs-20091225-lezt.html>.

——, 'Show us the money, says Gonski review member', *Sydney Morning Herald*, 3 May 2012. <www.smh.com.au/national/show-us-the-money-says-gonski-review-member-20120502-1xzhq.html>.

Perry, L, 'To reduce inequality in Australian schools, make them less socially segregated', *The Conversation*, 20 April 2018. <theconversation.com/to-reduce-inequality-in-australian-schools-make-them-less-socially-segregated-95034>.

Perry, L & McConney, A, 'School socioeconomic composition and student outcomes in Australia: Implications for educational policy', *Australian Journal of Education*, ACER, Melbourne, vol. 54, no. 1, 2010, pp. 72–85.

Preston B, 'Residualisation: What's that?', *The Australian Teacher*, no. 8, May 1984. <barbaraprestonresearch.com.au/wp-content/uploads/1984-BPreston-Residualisation-in-Australian-Teacher.pdf>.

——, 'The social make-up of schools: A report prepared for the Australian Education Union', Barbara Preston Research, Canberra, 2018. <www.aeufederal.org.au/application/files/7115/2090/2405/Preston2018.pdf>.

Pell, G, 'Religion and culture: Catholic Schools in Australia', Keynote address to the 2006 National Catholic Education Conference, Sydney, 28 September 2006.

Reid, A, *Changing Australian Education: How policy is taking us backwards and what can be done about it*, Allen & Unwin, Sydney, 2019.

Ryan, C & Sibieta, L, 'A comparison of private schooling in the United Kingdom and Australia,' *The Australian Economic Review*, vol. 44, no. 3, September 2011, pp. 295–307.

Senate Select Committee on School Funding, 'Equity and excellence in Australian schools', Commonwealth of Australia, Canberra, 9 July 2014. <www.aph.gov.au/Parliamentary_Business/Committees/Senate/School_Funding/School_Funding/Report/index>.

Stevenson, A, 'Defer Gonski's funding reforms, private schools urge', *Sydney Morning Herald*, 22 May 2012. <www.smh.com.au/politics/federal/defer-gonskis-funding-reforms-private-schools-urge-20120521-1z1fj.html>.

Teese, R, 'From opportunity to outcomes: The changing role of public schooling in Australia and national funding arrangements', Centre for Research on Education Systems, University of Melbourne, 2011.

Thomson, S et al., 'Challenges for Australian Education: Results from PISA 2009', Australian Council for Educational Research, Melbourne, 2011. <www.acer.org/files/PISA-Report-2009.pdf>.

——, 'PISA 2015: A first look at Australia's results', ACER, 2016. <www.acer.org/au/discover/article/pisa-2015-australian-students-achievement>.

Thomson, S, De Bortoli, L, Underwood, C & Schmid, M, 'PISA in Brief: Student Performance', Australian Council for Educational Research, under contract with the Commonwealth of Australia as represented by the Department of Education, Canberra, 2019. <research.acer.edu.au/cgi/viewcontent.cgi?article=1036&context=ozpisa>.

Ting, I et al., 'Counting the cost of the education revolution', *ABC*, 22 November 2018. <www.abc.net.au/news/2018-11-22/counting-the-cost-of-the-education-revolution/10495756>.

Ting, I, Shatoba, K & Palmer, A, 'How the Catholic school system takes from the poor to give to the rich', *ABC News*, 4 September 2020.

Topsfield, J, 'School reforms delayed too long, says Lawrence', *The Age*, 26 May 2012. <www.theage.com.au/education/school-reforms-delayed-too-long-says-lawrence-20120525-1zadr.html>.

Turnbull, M, *A Bigger Picture*, Hardie Grant Books, Melbourne, 2020.

Watson, L & Ryan, C, 'Choosers and losers: The impact of government subsidies on Australian secondary schools', *Australian Journal of Education*, Melbourne, vol. 54, no. 1, 2011, pp. 86–107.

Whitlam G, *The Whitlam Government*, Viking Australia, Melbourne, 1985.

Wilkinson, I, Caldwell, B, Selleck, R, Harris, J & Dettman, P, *A History of State Aid to Non-Government Schools in Australia*, Educational Transformations Pty Ltd, for the Department of Education, Science and Training, Canberra, 2006.

Acknowledgments

The authors wish to thank the following people consulted during the writing of this book: Dean Ashenden, Jane Caro, Lyndsay Connors, Christine Goode, Peter Goss, John Hood, Paul Kidson, Jim McMorrow and Alan Reid.

Others who have given significant input are mentioned in the book. They include those interviewed, as well as the teachers and principals who contributed their reflections on the matters raised.

This book has been a two-year undertaking. We acknowledge long-suffering family and friends, particularly when 'lock-down' during the pandemic seemed to be accompanied by 'tune out'. We thank them for their insights, encouragement and constant support.

Tom would like to thank the ever-helpful librarians, building staff and baristas of the National Library of Australia. He also expresses gratitude for the kind encouragement, support and inspiration of colleagues at Hawker College, Canberra.

We acknowledge, and admire, the commitment and professionalism of the staff and associates of NewSouth Publishing.

Notes

Introduction

1 David Gonski, interview with the authors, 4 September 2020.

2 A Stevenson, 'Gap between poor and rich schools growing', *Sydney Morning Herald*, 17 October 2011. <www.smh.com.au/education/gap-between-poor-and-rich-schools-growing-20111016-1lrfh.html>.

3 Gonski 2020.

4 D Gonski, K Greiner, K Boston, C Lawrence, P Tannock & B Scales, *Review of Funding for Schooling: Final Report*, Australian Government, December 2011, p. 150.

5 Gonski 2020.

6 S Thomson, 'Aussie students are a year behind students 10 years ago in science, maths and reading', *The Conversation*, 3 December 2019. <theconversation.com/aussie-students-are-a-year-behind-students-10-years-ago-in-science-maths-and-reading-127013>.

7 S Thomson, L De Bortoli, C Underwood & M Schmid, 'PISA in Brief: Student Performance', Australian Council for Educational Research, under contract with the Commonwealth of Australia as represented by the Department of Education, 2019, p. 7. <research.acer.edu.au/cgi/viewcontent.cgi?article=1036&context=ozpisa>.

8 Thomson et al. 2019, p. 18.

9 T Cobbold, 'Public schools are defrauded by billions under new funding agreements', *Save our Schools*, 6 February 2019. <saveourschools.com.au/funding/public-schools-are-defrauded-by-billions-under-new-funding-agreements/>.

10 T Cobbold, 'Public schools face a funding crisis; Private schools are in clover', *Save our Schools*, June 2020, p. 7. <saveourschools.com.au/wp-content/uploads/2020/06/Public-Schools-Face-Funding-Crisis-1.pdf>.

11 I Ting, R Liu & N Scott, 'Counting the cost of the education revolution', *ABC News*, 30 June 2020. <http://www.abc.net.au/news/2018-11-22/counting-the-cost-of-the-education-revolution/10495756>.

12 Gonski 2020.

13 OECD, 'Equity in education: Breaking down barriers to social mobility', OECD Publishing, Paris, 2018, p. 122. <www.oecd-ilibrary.org/education/equity-in-education_9789264073234-en>.

14 Gonski et al. 2011, p. 150.

1 The original sin: where did Gonski come from?

1 D Ashenden, 'Political games hide hard facts of Gonski education reform', *Crikey*, 21 August 2012. <www.crikey.com.au/2012/08/21/political-games-hide-hard-facts-of-gonski-education-reform/>.

2 J Gillard, 'Howard's unfair school funding must go', 4 October 2001, 2010 Australian federal election campaign – House of Representatives election candidate websites, Canberra. <webarchive.nla.gov.au/awa/20040916101959/

http://pandora.nla.gov.au/pan/22624/20011114-0000/www.jgillard.com/textlnks/1wls.html>.

3 M Latham & J Macklin, 'Great Australian schools', Australian Labor Party policy document, Australian Labor Party, 15 September 2004. <drive.google.com/file/d/102uUIpArVXWBsDJaaZrbYWYXQHXaYvKv/view?usp=sharing>.

4 P Browne, 'Latham's list was a hit in the polls', *Inside Story*, 27 August 2012. <insidestory.org.au/lathams-list-was-a-hit-in-the-polls/>.

5 Browne 2012.

6 Browne 2012.

7 J Gillard, 'A future fair for all: School funding in Australia', address to Sydney Institute, 15 April 2010. <parlinfo.aph.gov.au/parlInfo/search/display/display.w3p;query=Id%3A%22media%2Fpressrel%2FVMGW6%22>.

8 Gillard 2010.

9 D Harrison, 'Schools will keep funding under review, Gillard says', *Sydney Morning Herald*, 16 April 2010. <www.smh.com.au/education/schools-will-keep-funding-under-review-gillard-says-20100415-shsd.html>.

10 D Harrison, 'Private schools fear funds freeze,' *The Age*, 17 April 2010. <www.theage.com.au/education/private-schools-fear-funds-freeze-20100416-skpc.html>.

11 S Ryan, *Catching the Waves: Life in and out of politics*, HarperCollins, Sydney, 1999, p. 229.

12 M Clark, 'No Gerard, schooling is not part of the social safety net: It is a public good', *Online Opinion*, 3 May 2012. <www.onlineopinion.com.au/view.asp?article=13574>.

13 P Moran, *History of the Catholic Church in Australasia*, Oceanic Pub. Co., Sydney, 1896, p. 875.

14 AG Austin, *Select Documents in Australian Education, 1788–1900*, Pitman Press, Sydney, 1963, p. 220.

15 Austin 1963, pp. 222–24.

16 I Wilkinson, B Caldwell, R Selleck, J Harris & P Dettman, *A History of State Aid to Non-Government Schools in Australia*, Educational Transformations Pty Ltd, Canberra, 2006, p. 6; Austin 1963, p. 208.

17 Austin 1963, pp. 237–38.

18 Austin 1963, p. 242.

19 Wilkinson et al. 2006, p. 16.

20 Wilkinson et al. 2006, p. 16.

21 L Connors & J McMorrow, *Imperatives in Schools Funding: Equity, sustainability and achievement*, Australian Council for Educational Research, Camberwell, Vic., 2015, p. 17. <research.acer.edu.au/aer/14/>.

22 G Freudenberg, *A Certain Grandeur: Gough Whitlam in politics*, Macmillan, South Melbourne, 1977, p. 24.

23 E Macdonald, 'The genesis of state aid', *Canberra Times*, 14 July 2012. <www.canberratimes.com.au/story/6168022/the-genesis-of-state-aid>.

24 K McQueen, 'The 1962 Goulburn Catholic school strike', *Education*, 12 February 2001.

25 J Warhurst, '50 years since Australia's "most poisonous debate"', *Eureka Street*, 9 July 2012. <www.eurekastreet.com.au/article/50-years-since-australia-s--most-poisonous-debate>.

26 McQueen 2001.
27 Macdonald 2012.
28 T Taylor, *Class Wars: Money, schools and power in Modern Australia*, eBook, Monash University Publishing, Melbourne, 2018, Loc. 832.
29 G Whitlam, *The Whitlam Government*, Viking, Ringwood, 1985, p. 309.
30 Whitlam 1985, p. 291.
31 Whitlam 1985, p. 300.
32 Whitlam 1985, p. 300.
33 Freudenberg 1977, p. 28.
34 Freudenberg 1977, p. 32.
35 Freudenberg 1977, p. 156.
36 Freudenberg 1977, p. 153.
37 P Karmel et al., *Schools in Australia: Report of the Interim Committee for the Australian Schools Commission*, Australian Government Publishing Service, Canberra, May 1973, p. 48.
38 Karmel et al. 1973, p. 53.
39 Karmel et al. 1973, p. 71.
40 Karmel et al. 1973, p. 71.
41 Karmel et al. 1973, p. 71.
42 Wilkinson et al. 2006, p. 63.
43 'Private schools welcome bills', *Canberra Times*, 17 December 1973.
44 Wilkinson et al. 2006, pp. 61–62.
45 Wilkinson et al. 2006, pp. 61–62.
46 Wilkinson et al. 2006, p. 63.
47 'Liberals foreshadow schools bill changes', *Canberra Times*, 6 December 1973.
48 'CP, DLP back Government', *Canberra Times*, 14 December 1973.
49 L Watson & C Ryan, 'Choosers and losers: The impact of government subsidies on Australian secondary schools', *Australian Journal of Education*, vol. 54. no. 1, 2011, p. 92.
50 Gonski et al. 2011, p. 15.
51 Connors & McMorrow 2015, p. 22.
52 Connors & McMorrow 2015, p. 27.
53 Gonski et al. 2011, p. 15.
54 D Ashenden, 'The educational consequences of the peace', *Inside Story*, 28 July 2016. <insidestory.org.au/the-educational-consequences-of-the-peace/>.
55 Ashenden 2012.
56 Wilkinson, et al. 2006, pp. 61–62.
57 Connors & McMorrow 2015, p. 30.
58 Ross Gittins, quoted in Connors & McMorrow 2015, p. iv.
59 C Campbell, H Proctor & G Sherington, *School Choice: How parents negotiate the new school market in Australia*, Allen & Unwin, Sydney, 2009, p. 164.
60 Karmel et al. 1973, p. 13.
61 Karmel et al. 1973, p. 74.
62 DC Hallin, *The Uncensored War: The media and Vietnam*, University of California Press, Berkeley, 1989, p. 117.
63 Ryan 1999, p. 230.
64 Australian Government, *Review of Funding for Schooling: Discussion Paper and Draft Terms of Reference, 2010*, Australian Government, Canberra, 2010, p. 14.

65 Australian Government 2010, p. 4.
66 Bill Scales, interview with the authors, 13 April 2021.
67 David Gonski, interview with the authors, 4 September 2020.

2 Needs-blind and sector-based: the 'no school loses a dollar' saga

1 J Gillard, 'A future fair for all: School funding in Australia', address to Sydney Institute, 15 April 2010. <parlinfo.aph.gov.au/parlInfo/search/display/display.w3p;query=Id%3A%22media%2Fpressrel%2FVMGW6%22>.
2 J Gillard, 'Address to the Independent Schools National Forum', Department of Prime Minister & Cabinet, 20 August 2012. <https://pmtranscripts.pmc.gov.au/release/transcript-18746>.
3 Gillard 2010.
4 D Harrison, 'Private schools fear funds freeze', *The Age*, 17 April 2010. <www.theage.com.au/education/private-schools-fear-funds-freeze-20100416-skpc.html>.
5 Australian Curriculum, Assessment and Reporting Authority, My School, ACARA, 2011.
6 J Ferrari, 'Catholic schools "under threat"', *The Australian*, 15 July 2010; Greg O'Kelly, 'Funding for Catholic Schools', Australian Catholic Bishops Conference, 2010.
7 O'Kelly 2010.
8 K Murphy & D Harrison, 'Gillard buys peace with private schools – and some grief', *The Age*, 5 August 2010.
9 J Gillard, *My Story*, Penguin Random House Australia, Melbourne, Kindle edition, 2014, location 4125.
10 Murphy & Harrison 2010.
11 Angelo Gavrielatos, interview with the authors, 4 September 2020.
12 Gillard 2014, location 4131.
13 D Gonski, K Greiner, K Boston, C Lawrence, P Tannock & B Scales, *Review of Funding for Schooling: Final report,* Federal Department of Education, Employment and Workplace Relations, Canberra, 2011, p. 231. <www.dese.gov.au/school-funding/resources/review-funding-schooling-final-report-december-2011>.
14 Independent Schools Council of Australia, 'Submission: Review of funding for schooling', ISCA, March 2011, p. 1. <isa.edu.au//wp-content/uploads/2017/02/ISCA-Funding-Review-Submission-31-March-2011-1.pdf>.
15 National Catholic Education Commission, 'Submission to the Review of Funding for Schooling', NCEC, 31 March 2011, p. 11.
16 M Green, 'Review of Funding for Schooling Response', Independent Schools Victoria, p. 35. <www.is.vic.edu.au/independent/pubs/review_of_funding_for_schooling_response.pdf>.
17 I Ting, R Liu & A Palmer, 'Counting the cost of the education revolution', *ABC News*, 30 June 2020. <www.abc.net.au/news/2018-11-22/counting-the-cost-of-the-education-revolution/10495756>.
18 D Kemp, 'Major reform of non-government school funding', media release, 11 May 1999.

19 A Probyn, 'Wesley funding windfall', *Herald Sun*, 31 August 2000; N Craig, 'Our richest schools raise fees by 91%', *The Age*, 16 January 2011. <www.theage.com.au/national/victoria/our-richest-schools-raise-fees-by-91-percent-20110115-19s1g.html>.
20 My School 2011.
21 Gillard 2010.
22 C Ryan & L Sibieta, 'A comparison of private schooling in the United Kingdom and Australia', *The Australian Economic Review*, vol. 44, no. 3, September 2011, pp. 295–307.
23 Ryan & Sibieta 2011.
24 Independent Schools Council of Australia 2011, p. 5.
25 J Keating, 'Resourcing schools in Australia: A proposal for the restructure of public funding', The Foundation for Young Australians, 2010, p. 37; Senate Select Committee on School Funding, 'Equity and excellence in Australian schools', Commonwealth of Australia, Canberra, 9 July 2014, p. 9. <www.aph.gov.au/Parliamentary_Business/Committees/Senate/School_Funding/School_Funding/Report/index>.
26 Carmen Lawrence, interview with the authors, 20 August 2020.
27 Gonski et al. 2011, p. 84–85.
28 Gonski et al. 2011, p. 85.
29 Gonski et al. 2011, pp. xvii, xxiv, 177.
30 Gonski et al. 2011, p. 176.
31 A White & F Carruthers, 'Private schools won't suffer: Gonski', *Australian Financial Review*, 24 February 2012.
32 Independent Schools Council of Australia, 'Gonski recommendations deserve further consideration', media release, 28 February 2012. <isa.edu.au//wp-content/uploads/2016/12/Gonski-Recommendations-Deserve-Futher-Consideration.pdf>
33 G Newcombe, 'Gonski: a job well done but will it bear fruit?', Association of Independent Schools of NSW, blog post, 24 February 2012. <web.archive.org/web/20140912021647/http://www.aisnsw.edu.au/Publications/Blog/ViewBlogPost.aspx?ID=8>.
34 T Temby, 'Families must come first in new school funding model', media release, National Catholic Education Commission, 20 February 2012. <www.ncec.catholic.edu.au/news-events/media-releases/153-families-must-come-first-in-new-school-funding-model/file>.
35 C Pyne, 'Gonski review: Christopher Pyne doorstop', *YouTube*, 20 February 2012. <www.youtube.com/watch?v=7Nt_sLqj7Iw>.
36 P Kelly, 'Wait for the uproar on a grand political bargain', *The Australian*, 21 February 2012.
37 J Topsfield, 'Private schools cash in above base grade', *The Age*, 22 February 2012. <www.theage.com.au/politics/federal/private-schools-cash-in-above-base-grade-20120221-1tltg.html>.
38 Gonski et al. 2011, p. 64.
39 A Patty, 'How private schools owe taxpayer $2b', *Sydney Morning Herald*, 9 February 2008.
40 Patty 2008.

41 D Gonski, K Greiner, K Boston, C Lawrence, P Tannock & B Scales, *Review of Funding for Schooling: Emerging issues paper,* Federal Department of Education, Employment and Workplace Relations, Canberra, 2010, p. 19.

42 J Ferrari, 'Howard wanted to wean schools off funds deal', *The Australian*, 7 May 2011.

43 Gonski et al. 2011, p. 84.

44 Gonski et al. 2011, p. 82.

45 Gonski et al. 2011, p. 208.

46 J McTernan, written correspondence with the authors, 2021.

47 A Patty, 'Gonski Report not government policy, insists Garrett', *Sydney Morning Herald*, 29 March 2012. <www.smh.com.au/national/gonski-report-not-government-policy-insists-garrett-20120329-1w0jj.html>; A Patty, 'Gonski: top losing schools named', *Sydney Morning Herald*, 23 April 2012. <www.smh.com.au/education/gonski-top-losing-schools-named-20120422-1xf71.html>.

48 A Stevenson, 'Defer Gonski's funding reforms, private schools urge', *Sydney Morning Herald*, 22 May 2012. <www.smh.com.au/politics/federal/defer-gonskis-funding-reforms-private-schools-urge-20120521-1z1fj.html>.

49 Stevenson 2012.

50 S Maiden, '3000 schools face funding cuts', *Herald Sun*, 19 August 2012.

51 T Abbott, 'Address to the Association of Heads of Independent Schools', 20 August 2012. <isa.edu.au/wp-content/uploads/2017/02/The-Hon-Tony-Abbott-MHR-Address-to-NEF.pdf>.

52 J Topsfield, 'Schools jittery as Gillard delays education reforms,' *The Age*, 18 August 2012. <www.theage.com.au/education/schools-jittery-as-gillard-delays-education-reforms-20120817-24e6q.html>.

53 J Gillard, 'Address to the Independent Schools National Forum', Department of Prime Minister & Cabinet, 20 August 2012. <pmtranscripts.pmc.gov.au/release/transcript-18746>.

54 Independent Schools Council of Australia, 'Government commits to increased independent school funding', media release, 20 August 2012. <isa.edu.au//wp-content/uploads/2016/12/Media-Release-2012-20-August-Government-Commits-to-Increased-Independent-School-Funding-.pdf>.

55 Editorial, 'Class warfare has no place in our nation's schools', *Daily Telegraph*, 21 August 2012. <www.dailytelegraph.com.au/news/opinion/class-warfare-has-no-place-in-our-nations-schools/news-story/9d30e4cda9027b9e0955ca1b1911f0cc>.

56 Peter Garrett, interview with the authors, 18 September 2020.

57 Angelo Gavrielatos, interview with the authors, 4 September 2020.

58 K Boston, Speech to NSWTF conference, 29 June 2014. <www.nswtf.org.au/files/2014_06june_29_dr_ken_boston_speech.pdf>.

59 Boston 2014.

60 ABC, 'Education, environment and equality', *Q&A*, 26 September 2016. <www.abc.net.au/qanda/education-environment-and-equality/10652014>.

61 T Cobbold, 'Labor is a specialist in special deals for private schools', *Save our Schools*, 22 March 2018. <saveourschools.com.au/funding/labor-is-a-specialist-in-special-deals-for-private-schools/>.

3 The unlevel playing field: what Gonski found

1 D Gonski, K Greiner, K Boston, C Lawrence, P Tannock & B Scales, *Review of Funding for Schooling: Final report,* Federal Department of Education, Employment and Workplace Relations, Canberra, 2011, p. 124. <www.dese.gov.au/school-funding/resources/review-funding-schooling-final-report-december-2011>.
2 Australian Government, 'Review of Funding for Schooling: discussion paper and draft terms of reference', Department of Education, Employment and Workplace Relations, Canberra, 2010, p. 4.
3 G Masters, 'Review pointing in the right direction', *The Age*, 27 February 2012, <www.theage.com.au/education/review-pointing-in-the-right-direction-20120224-1ttck.html>; Gonski et al. 2011, p. 20.
4 Gonski et al. 2011, p. 21.
5 Gonski et al. 2011, p. 114.
6 J Ferrari, 'System widening the divide', *The Australian*, 8 December 2010.
7 A Horin, 'Let's demonstrate a little class and give every child a fair go', *Sydney Morning Herald*, 5 December 2009. <www.smh.com.au/politics/federal/lets-demonstrate-a-little-class-and-give-every-child-a-fair-go-20091204-kaug.html>; K Arlington, 'Children less likely to make the grade if their parents left school early', *Sydney Morning Herald*, 24 January 2012. <https://www.smh.com.au/education/children-less-likely-to-make-the-grade-if-their-parents-left-school-early-20120123-1qe1f.html>.
8 Gonski et al. 2011, p. 113.
9 Gonski et al. 2011, p. 28.
10 D Gonski, K Greiner, K Boston, C Lawrence, P Tannock & B Scales, *Review of Funding for Schooling: Emerging issues paper,* Federal Department of Education, Employment and Workplace Relations, Canberra, 2010, p. 18.
11 K Boston, interview with the authors, 6 August 2020.
12 Gonski et al. 2011, p. 23.
13 Gonski et al. 2011, p. 25.
14 S Thomson, et al., *Challenges for Australian Education: Results from PISA 2009*, Australian Council for Educational Research, 2011, p. 278. <www.acer.org/files/PISA-Report-2009.pdf>.
15 Gonski et al. 2011, pp. 26–27.
16 NSWDEC, *Australian School Funding Arrangements: Discussion paper*, Department of Education and Communities, 2011.
17 NSWDEC 2011, p. 11.
18 NSWDEC 2011, p. 12.
19 L Perry & A McConney, 'School socio-economic composition and student outcomes in Australia: Implications for educational policy', *Australian Journal of Education*, vol. 54, no. 1, 2010, pp. 82–83. <research.acer.edu.au/aje/vol54/iss1/5>.
20 Gonski et al. 2011, p. 124.
21 B Roebuck, B Harper, P Morgan & anonymous, written correspondence with the authors, October 2021.
22 C Campbell, H Proctor & G Sherington, *School Choice: How parents negotiate the new school market in Australia*, Allen & Unwin, Sydney, 2009, p. 146.
23 Campbell et al. 2009, p. 150.

24 R van Ewijk & P Sleegers, 'The effect of peer socioeconomic status on student achievement: a meta-analysis', *SSRN*, 1 April 2009. <papers.ssrn.com/sol3/papers.cfm?abstract_id=1402645>.
25 R Teese, 'From opportunity to outcomes: The changing role of public schooling in Australia and national funding arrangements', University of Melbourne Centre for Research on Education Systems, Melbourne, 2011, p. 64. <apo.org.au/sites/default/files/resource-files/2011-09/apo-nid27999.pdf>.
26 Thomson et al. 2009, p. 289.
27 Gonski et al. 2011, p. 124.
28 Gonski et al. 2011, p. 126.
29 Gonski et al. 2011, p. 9.
30 Gonski et al. 2011, p. 10.
31 Australian Curriculum, Assessment and Reporting Authority, My School, ACARA, 2011.
32 My School 2011.
33 J Lee, 'Wrong side of the tracks in Geelong makes all the difference for children's futures', *The Age*, 21 January 2012. <www.smh.com.au/education/wrong-side-of-the-tracks-in-geelong-makes-all-the-difference-for-childrens-futures-20120120-1qa8v.html>.
34 My School 2011.
35 'Parents face SOS plea as battlers left behind', *Sydney Morning Herald*, 11 August 2004. <www.smh.com.au/national/parents-face-sos-plea-as-battlers-left-behind-20040811-gdjj0e.html>.
36 G Pell, 'Religion and culture: Catholic Schools in Australia', keynote address to the 2006 National Catholic Education Conference, Sydney, 28 September 2006.
37 My School 2011.
38 Gonski et al. 2011, pp. 11–13.
39 T Cobbold, G Newcombe, J McMorrow & S Marginson, 'Can we afford to continue funding private schools?', *Sydney Morning Herald*, 12 February 2011. <www.smh.com.au/education/can-we-afford-to-continue-funding-private-schools-20110211-1aqke.html>.
40 Gonski et al. 2011, p. 10.
41 My School 2011.
42 My School 2011.
43 My School 2011.
44 Watson & Ryan, 'Choosers and losers: The impact of government subsidies on Australian secondary schools', *Australian Journal of Education*, vol. 54, no. 1, 2010, p. 93. <research.acer.edu.au/aje/vol54/iss1/6>.
45 Gonski et al. 2011, p. 13.
46 OECD, *Balancing School Choice and Equity: An international perspective based on PISA*, OECD Publishing, Paris, 2019. <www.oecd.org/education/balancing-school-choice-and-equity-2592c974-en.htm>.
47 C Bonnor, 'My School, PISA and Australia's equity gap', *Inside Story*, 11 May 2011. <insidestory.org.au/my-school-pisa-and-australias-equity-gap/>.
48 B Preston, 'Submission to the Review of Funding for Schooling (Gonski review)', Barbara Preston Research, 11 April 2011, p. 5. <www.barbaraprestonresearch.com.au/wp-content/uploads/2011-BPreston-Submission-to-Review-of-Funding-for-Schooling-.pdf>.

49 J Keating, 'Priorities in education', *Online Opinion*, 8 February 2008. <www.onlineopinion.com.au/view.asp?article=6967&page=0>.
50 T Bentley & G Savage (eds), *Educating Australia: Challenges for the decade ahead*, Melbourne University Press, Melbourne, Vic., 2017, p. 424.
51 B Preston, 'Residualisation, what's that?', *The Australian Teacher*, May 1984. <barbaraprestonresearch.com.au/wp-content/uploads/1984-BPreston-Residualisation-in-Australian-Teacher.pdf>.
52 Gonski et al. 2011, p. 30.
53 Gonski et al. 2011, p. 13.
54 C Bonnor, 'One league away from disaster', *Inside Story*, 9 September 2009. <insidestory.org.au/one-league-away-from-disaster/>.
55 Watson & Ryan, 2010, p. 101.
56 Gonski et al. 2011, pp. 11–13.
57 D Harrison, 'School funding review considers strict obligations', *Sydney Morning Herald*, 23 December 2010. <www.smh.com.au/education/school-funding-review-considers-strict-obligations-20101222-195my.html>.
58 Terry Moran, correspondence with the authors, 12 August 2020.
59 MA O'Loughlin et al., 'Governments working together: A better future for all Australians', The Allen Consulting Group, 2004, p. 162.
60 O'Loughlin et al. 2004, p. 162.
61 O'Loughlin et al. 2004, p. 162.
62 L Connors & J McMorrow, 'New directions in school funding: A proposed model,' Faculty of Education and Social Work, University of Sydney, Sydney, 2010, p. 3.
63 Connors & McMorrow 2010, p. 86.
64 Connors & McMorrow 2010, p. 96.
65 DEEWR Briefing No. BR10-003929, 'Third meeting of the panel for the Review of Funding for Schooling', DESE FOI, February 2021.
66 J Keating, 'Resourcing schools in Australia: A proposal for the restructure of public funding', The Foundation for Young Australians, 2010.
67 Keating 2010, p. 31.
68 Gonski et al. 2011, p. 226.
69 B Smith, 'State school heads in funding push', *The Age*, 2 October 2008. <www.theage.com.au/national/state-school-heads-in-funding-push-20081001-4s1v.html>.
70 S O'Doherty & M Spencer, 'Review of Funding of Schooling: Emerging Issues Paper – Christian Schools Australia', 31 March 2011, p. 13. <drive.google.com/file/d/1H1KseAcqwNyveqtrctULx4H_shd0Diiw/view?usp=sharing>; A Patty, 'Christian schools seek full public funding', *Sydney Morning Herald*, 1 April 2011.
71 O'Doherty & Spencer 2011, p. 9.
72 O'Doherty & Spencer 2011, p. 13.
73 O'Doherty & Spencer 2011, pp. 13–14.
74 K Boston, Speech to NSWTF conference, 29 June 2014, pp. 5–6. <www.nswtf.org.au/files/2014_06june_29_dr_ken_boston_speech.pdf>.
75 'Review of SES funding arrangements for non-government schools', Commonwealth Department of Education, Canberra, 2006.
76 A Patty, 'School fees hit record highs', *Sydney Morning Herald*, 26 December 2009. <www.smh.com.au/education/school-fees-hit-record-highs-20091225-lezt.html>.

77 A Patty, 'Parents bear the burden of surging private fees', *Sydney Morning Herald*, 23 January 2011. <www.smh.com.au/education/parents-bear-the-burden-of-surging-private-fees-20110122-1a0jq.html>.
78 T Cobbold, 'Fee and funding increases give elite private schools a massive resource advantage', *Save our Schools*, 25 January 2011. <saveourschools.com.au/funding/fee-and-funding-increases-give-elite-private-schools-a-massive-resource-advantage/>.
79 J Ferrari, 'Richest schools add higher fees to funding pool', *The Australian*, 20 December 2010.
80 D Kemp, 'Major reform of non-government school funding', media release, 11 May 1999.
81 Ferrari 2010.
82 Patty 2009.
83 Ferrari 2010.
84 Ferrari 2010.
85 Gonski et al. 2011, p. 76.
86 Gonski et al. 2011, p. 79.
87 Gonski et al. 2011, p. 177.
88 Gonski et al. 2011, p. 79.
89 G Newcombe, 'Gonski: a job well done but will it bear fruit?', Association of Independent Schools of NSW, blog post, 24 February 2012. <web.archive.org/web/20120321063327/http://aisnsw.edu.au/Publications/Blog/ViewBlogPost.aspx?ID=8>.
90 David Gonski, interview with the authors, 4 September 2020.
91 Gonski et al. 2011, p. xxxii.
92 Gonski et al. 2011, p. 127.
93 Gonski et al. 2011, p. 127.
94 Teese 2011, pp. 65, 66.
95 Gonski et al. 2011, p. 208.
96 Gonski et al. 2011, p. 175.
97 O'Loughlin et al. 2004, p. 162.
98 Gonski et al. 2011, p. 188.
99 Gonski et al. 2011, p. 127.

4 A troubled birth (2012)

1 Peter Garrett, interview with the authors, 18 September 2020.
2 David Gonski, interview with the authors, 4 September 2020.
3 H Proctor, 'Top marks to Gonski review for its focus on children, schools and teachers', *Sydney Morning Herald*, 24 February 2012.
4 A Patty & K Arlington, 'O'Farrell backs Gonski as fears rise over funding cuts', *Sydney Morning Herald*, 17 April 2012. <www.smh.com.au/education/ofarrell-backs-gonski-as-fears-rise-over-funding-cuts-20120416-1x3qt.html>.
5 AEU Federal, 'Politicians must commit to funding boost for public schools', Australian Education Union, 19 February 2012; AEU Federal, 'Ministers must support Gonski funding reforms', Australian Education Union, 5 April 2012.
6 Angelo Gavrielatos, interview with the authors, 4 September 2020.

7 PMO, 'Gonski review; Australian Labor Party', transcript of joint press conference, Canberra, 20 February 2012. <parlinfo.aph.gov.au/parlInfo/download/media/pressrel/1436897/upload_binary/1436897.pdf>.

8 J Ferrari, 'Gonski's $5bn blueprint to arrest student decline, Gillard fails to back school funding recommendations', *The Australian*, 21 February 2012.

9 J Ferrari, 'Good delivery, but PM's response the catch', *The Australian*, 21 February 2012.

10 J Gillard, 'Transcript of joint doorstop interview, Western Sydney', Department of Prime Minister and Cabinet, Canberra, 21 February 2012. <pmtranscripts.pmc.gov.au/release/transcript-18398>.

11 J Gillard, 'Towards a new school funding system', Department of Prime Minister and Cabinet, Canberra, 20 February 2012. <pmtranscripts.pmc.gov.au/release/transcript-18397>.

12 P Garrett, *Big Blue Sky: A memoir*, Allen & Unwin, Sydney, 2016, p. 420.

13 A Patty, 'Show us the money, says Gonski review member', *Sydney Morning Herald*, 3 May 2012. <www.smh.com.au/national/show-us-the-money-says-gonski-review-member-20120502-1xzhq.html>.

14 J Topsfield, 'School reforms delayed too long, says Lawrence', *The Age*, 26 May 2012. <www.theage.com.au/education/school-reforms-delayed-too-long-says-lawrence-20120525-1zadr.html>.

15 Mark Robinson, written correspondence with authors, 25 May 2021.

16 Angelo Gavrielatos, interview with the authors, 4 September 2020.

17 Gavrielatos 2020.

18 AEU Federal, 'New campaign for action on the Gonski review', Australian Education Union, 17 June 2012. <web.archive.org/web/20120717035959/http:/www.aeufederal.org.au/Media/MediaReleases/2012/1706.pdf>.

19 B Hall, 'MPs back reforms on school cash', *Sydney Morning Herald*, 22 June 2012. <www.smh.com.au/politics/federal/mps-back-reforms-on-school-cash-20120621-20qwp.html>.

20 Hall 2012.

21 J Ferrari, 'Overhaul of schools to cost $6.5bn – Labor to act on Gonski reforms', *The Australian*, 23 June 2012.

22 Ferrari 23 June 2012.

23 Ferrari 23 June 2012.

24 B Jabour, 'Gillard grilled and heckled at community cabinet', *Sydney Morning Herald*, 11 July 2012. <www.brisbanetimes.com.au/national/queensland/gillard-grilled-and-heckled-at-community-cabinet-20120711-21ul8.html>.

25 J Gillard, *My Story*, Penguin Random House, Melbourne, Kindle edition, 2014, location 4173.

26 Peter Garrett, interview with the authors, 18 September 2020.

27 Gillard 2014, location 4189.

28 R Denniss, 'Peter Costello's five most "profligate" decisions as treasurer cost the budget $56bn a year', *The Guardian*, 15 April 2015. <www.theguardian.com/commentisfree/2015/apr/15/peter-costellos-five-most-profligate-decisions-as-treasurer-cost-the-budget-56bn-a-year>.

29 J Ferrari, 'Backdown on national school "league tables"', *The Australian*, 13 May 2008.

30 D Harrison, 'Government told to delay teacher bonuses', *Sydney Morning Herald*, 18 November 2011; J Ferrari, 'Proposal to give principals, school councils power to hire teachers – Gillard plan to liberate schools', *The Australian*, 30 December 2010.
31 ABC, 'Six billion dollar education reform', *Lateline*, 3 September 2012. <web.archive.org/web/20160731040924/http://www.abc.net.au/lateline/content/2012/s3582150.htm>; ABC, 'Pyne denies public schools will suffer', *AM*, 13 November 2013. <www.abc.net.au/am/content/2013/s3902332.htm>; ABC, 'Teacher training to be reviewed', *Lateline*, 19 February 2014. <web.archive.org/web/20160731032621/http://www.abc.net.au/lateline/content/2013/s3948371.htm>.
32 B Jensen, 'Wrong fix for failing schools', *The Australian*, 23 February 2013.
33 M Latham, 'Christopher Pyne's school lunch', *Australian Financial Review*, 11–12 August 2012.
34 J Gillard, 'Address to the Independent Schools National Forum', Department of Prime Minister and Cabinet, Canberra, 20 August 2012. <pmtranscripts.pmc.gov.au/release/transcript-18746>.
35 Garrett 2020.
36 J Irvine & N Chrysanthos, 'Federal government should get out of school funding, says former top bureaucrat', *Sydney Morning Herald*, 17 February 2020. <www.smh.com.au/national/federal-government-should-get-out-of-school-funding-says-former-top-bureaucrat-20200217-p541kz.html>.
37 Garrett 2016, p. 404.
38 Australian Senate, Senate Education and Employment Legislation Committee, 4 June 2015. <https://parlinfo.aph.gov.au/parlInfo/download/committees/estimate/21504c01-9ee5-46e0-b21f-3240b4da0b70/toc_pdf/Education%20and%20Employment%20Legislation%20Committee_2015_06_04_3491_Official.pdf>.
39 Productivity Commission, 'Report on Government Services 2015, Volume B: Child care, education and training', January 2015. <www.pc.gov.au/research/ongoing/report-on-government-services/2015/childcare-education-and-training/download-the-volume/rogs-2015-volumeb-child-care-education-and-training.pdf>.
40 Productivity Commission 2015, Table 4A17.
41 T Cobbold, 'Federal Education Dept Befuddled by Pyne's Funding Increase Claims', *Save our Schools*, 15 June 2015. <saveourschools.com.au/funding/federal-education-dept-befuddled-by-pynes-funding-increase-claims-2/>.
42 D Gonski, K Greiner, K Boston, C Lawrence, P Tannock & B Scales, *Review of Funding for Schooling: Final report*, Federal Department of Education, Employment and Workplace Relations, Canberra, 2011, p. 13.
43 L Connors & J McMorrow, *Imperatives in Schools Funding: Equity, sustainability and achievement*, Australian Council for Educational Research, Camberwell, Vic., 2015, p. 27.
44 J Gillard, 'Howard's unfair school funding must go', 4 October 2001, 2010 Australian federal election campaign – House of Representatives election candidate websites – Australian Internet Sites. <webarchive.nla.gov.au/awa/20040916101959/http://pandora.nla.gov.au/pan/22624/20011114-0000/www.jgillard.com/textlnks/1wls.html>.

45 Gonski et al. 2011, p. 65.
46 Gonski et al. 2011, p. 66.
47 Gonski et al. 2011, p. 61.
48 Gonski et al. 2011, p. 62.
49 Gonski et al. 2011, p. 171.
50 AIS, 'AIS concerns about Gonski funding model', Association of Independent Schools of NSW, news, 27 June 2012. <web.archive.org/web/20120627182658/http:/www.aisnsw.edu.au/Publications/News/Pages/AIS-concerns-about-Gonski-funding-model.aspx>.
51 A Patty, 'Gonski: top losing schools named', *Sydney Morning Herald*, 23 April 2012. <www.smh.com.au/education/gonski-top-losing-schools-named-20120422-1xf71.html>.
52 C Pyne, 'More evidence of new private school hit list', media release, 23 April 2012. <www.pyneonline.com.au/media-centre/media-releases/more-evidence-of-new-private-school-hit-list>.
53 B Hall, 'Garrett pushes for reforms to improve "shameful" results', *Sydney Morning Herald*, 24 May 2012. <www.smh.com.au/politics/federal/garrett-pushes-for-reforms-to-improve-shameful-results-20120523-1z5m6.html>.
54 Gonski et al. 2011, p. 51.
55 Gonski et al. 2011, p. 38.
56 S Thomson et al., *Challenges for Australian Education: Results from PISA 2009*, Australian Council for Educational Research, 2011, p. 278. <www.acer.org/files/PISA-Report-2009.pdf>.
57 B Roebuck, J Frew, B Harper, P Morgan, Written correspondence with the authors, October 2021.
58 Garrett 2020.
59 Garrett 2016, p. 419.
60 Gillard 2012.
61 J Gillard, 'Transcript of interview with Fran Kelly', Department of Prime Minister and Cabinet, Canberra, 15 April 2013. <pmtranscripts.pmc.gov.au/release/transcript-19237>.
62 J Gillard, 'A national plan for school improvement, speech to National Press Club', Department of Prime Minister and Cabinet, Canberra, 3 September 2012. <pmtranscripts.pmc.gov.au/release/transcript-18776>.
63 B Daniels, 'Gonski Recommendations Deserve Further Consideration', Independent Schools Council of Australia, 28 February 2012. <isa.edu.au//wp-content/uploads/2016/12/Gonski-Recommendations-Deserve-Futher-Consideration.pdf>.

5 A new national consensus? (2013)

1 E Griffiths, 'Tony Abbott says Coalition will honour Gonski school funding plan for four years', *ABC News*, 2 August 2013. <www.abc.net.au/news/2013-08-02/coalition-to-support-gonski-school-funding/4861102>; J Ferrari, 'Coalition joins Labor's Gonski "unity ticket"', *Weekend Australian*, 3 August 2013.
2 Australian Education Union – Federal Office, 'No surprises, no excuses? Abbott flounders on Gonski promises', media release, AEU, 1 December 2013. <web.archive.org/web/20140126042618/http:/www.aeufederal.org.au/Media/MediaReleases/2013/0112.pdf>.

3 T Bentley, 'Gonski: Christopher Pyne should know that Australia isn't England', *The Guardian*, 30 November 2013. <www.theguardian.com/commentisfree/2013/nov/30/gonski-christopher-pyne-should-know-that-australia-isnt-england>.
4 Senate Select Committee on School Funding, 'Equity and excellence in Australian schools', Commonwealth of Australia, Canberra, 9 July 2014, pp. 151–52. <www.aph.gov.au/Parliamentary_Business/Committees/Senate/School_Funding/School_Funding/Report/index>.
5 A Patty & S Nicholls, 'Schoolyard brawl', *Sydney Morning Herald*, 15 September 2012. <www.smh.com.au/national/nsw/schoolyard-brawl-20120914-25xq2.html>.
6 A Patty, 'Piccoli wins support to close gap', *Sydney Morning Herald*, 16 April 2011.
7 Adrian Piccoli, interview with the authors, 3 August 2020.
8 Piccoli 2020.
9 Piccoli 2020.
10 Piccoli 2020.
11 T McIlroy, 'Quick guide to Morrison's rorts scandals', *Australian Financial Review*, 28 February 2020.
12 Piccoli 2020.
13 Piccoli 2020.
14 Australian Education Union – Federal Office, 'Premier Newman would be mad to knock Gonski back – for Ashgrove schools alone', media release, AEU, 16 July 2013. <web.archive.org/web/20140205204508/http://www.aeufederal.org.au/Media/MediaReleases/2013/1607.pdf>.
15 Australian Education Union – Federal Office, 'Whether or not a school gets Gonski funds should not depend on which side of the Murray you live: AEU', media release, AEU, 17 May 2013. <web.archive.org/web/20150318070947/http://www.aeufederal.org.au/Media/MediaReleases/2013/1705.pdf>.
16 J Ferrari, 'School funding hold-outs will pass up $27bn', *The Australian*, 30 July 2013.
17 Piccoli 2020.
18 Piccoli 2020.
19 A Patty, S Nicholls & P Coorey, 'O'Farrell takes axe to education', *Sydney Morning Herald*, 12 September 2012. <www.smh.com.au/education/ofarrell-takes-axe-to-education-20120911-25qof.html>.
20 Patty, Nicholls & Coorey, 2012.
21 Piccoli 2020.
22 Angelo Gavrielatos, interview with the authors, 4 September 2020.
23 P Garrett, *Big Blue Sky: A memoir*, Allen & Unwin, Sydney, 2016, pp. 401–402.
24 T Cobbold, 'Private school funding is corrupted by special deals', *Save our Schools*, November 2016. <saveourschools.com.au/wp-content/uploads/2018/06/Private-School-Funding-Is-Corrupted-by-Special-Deals.pdf>.
25 National Commission of Audit, 'Towards responsible government: the report of the National Commission of Audit', Australian Government, Canberra ACT, 2014, vol. 1, p. 266. <web.archive.org/web/20150103093304/http://www.ncoa.gov.au/report/docs/appendix_volume%201.pdf>.
26 T Cobbold, 'Wealthy private schools walk away from Pyne's train wreck with millions in over-funding', *Save our Schools*, 9 June 2014. <saveourschools.com.au/funding/wealthy-private-schools-walk-away-from-pynes-train-wreck-with-millions-in-over-funding/>.

27 Cobbold 2016.
28 P Goss & J Sonnemann, 'Circuit breaker: A new compact on school funding', Grattan Institute, November 2016, p. 22.
29 Peter Garrett, interview with the authors, 18 September 2020.
30 J Topsfield, 'PM gives Catholics funding assurance', *Sydney Morning Herald*, 19 April 2013. <www.smh.com.au/politics/federal/pm-gives-catholics-funding-assurance-20130418-2i327.html>.
31 Senate Select Committee on School Funding, 'Report, Chapter 5: Rudd/Gillard Governments' school funding reforms', Parliament of Australia, Canberra, 2014. <www.aph.gov.au/Parliamentary_Business/Committees/Senate/School_Funding/School_Funding/Report/c05>.
32 Cobbold 2016, p. 16.
33 Senate Select Committee on School Funding, 'Equity and excellence in Australian schools', Commonwealth of Australia, 9 July 2014, p. 63. <www.aph.gov.au/Parliamentary_Business/Committees/Senate/School_Funding/School_Funding/Report/index>; Australian Government, Australian Education (SES Scores) Determination 2013, Compilation No. 4; Australian Education Bill 2013, p. 56. <parlinfo.aph.gov.au/parlInfo/download/legislation/bills/r4945_third-reps/toc_pdf/12229b01.pdf>.
34 B Daniels, 'Independent Schools Council welcomes agreement on Better Schools', Independent Schools Council of Australia, media release, 10 July 2013. <isa.edu.au/wp-content/uploads/2016/12/Media-Release-2013-10-July-Independent-School-Council-Welcomes-Agreement-on-Better-Schools-.pdf>.
35 R Fox, 'Funding reform directions', National Catholic Education Commission, media statement, 3 July 2013. <web.archive.org/web/20140127033406/http:/www.fundinginfo.catholic.edu.au/_uploads/_cknw/files/130703%20%20NCEC%20Media%20Statement%20on%20funding%20reform.pdf>.
36 Catholic Communications, Sydney Archdiocese, 'Catholic school sector signs onto Gonski and keeps autonomy', media release, 23 July 2013.
37 J Topsfield & B Preiss, 'Victoria signs on but deal has a cost', *The Age*, 5 August 2013. <www.smh.com.au/politics/federal/victoria-signs-on-but-deal-has-a-cost-20130804-2r7q4.html>.
38 J Norman, 'Coalition backflips on school funding', *ABC PM*, 2 August 2013. <www.abc.net.au/pm/content/2013/s3817208.htm> .
39 E Griffiths, 'Tony Abbott says Coalition will honour Gonski school funding plan for four years', *ABC News*, 2 August 2013. <www.abc.net.au/news/2013-08-02/coalition-to-support-gonski-school-funding/4861102>; J Ferrari, 'Coalition joins Labor's Gonski "unity ticket"', *Weekend Australian*, 3 August 2013.
40 L Wilson, 'Back to drawing board for Gonski – ALP plan a shambles: Pyne', *The Australian*, 25 November 2013.
41 A Patty, 'Barry O'Farrell criticises Christopher Pyne over Gonski', *Sydney Morning Herald*, 26 November 2013. <www.smh.com.au/national/nsw/barry-ofarrell-criticises-christopher-pyne-over-gonski-20131126-2y7fu.html>.
42 'States say Christopher Pyne has dropped public schools bombshell in heated education meeting', *ABC News*, 29 November 2013. <www.abc.net.au/news/2013-11-29/pyne-drops-education-overhaul-bombshell-on-states-during-heated/5124968>.

43 Australian Education Union - Federal Office, 'No surprises, no excuses? Abbott flounders on Gonski promises', media release, AEU, 1 December 2013. <web.archive.org/web/20140126042618/http:/www.aeufederal.org.au/Media/MediaReleases/2013/0112.pdf>.
44 P Kelly, 'The real story behind the Gonski train wreck', *The Australian*, 4 December 2013.
45 D Shanahan, 'Abbott loses his carbon tax edge', *The Australian*, 10 December 2013.

6 A mixed-up kid (2014–16)

1 I Ting, R Lui & N Scott, 'Counting the cost of the education revolution', *ABC News*, 22 November 2018. <www.abc.net.au/news/2018-11-22/counting-the-cost-of-the-education-revolution/10495756>.
2 Australian Curriculum, Assessment and Reporting Authority, My School, ACARA, 2011 & 2017.
3 My School 2011 & 2017.
4 My School 2013 & 2017.
5 My School 2013 & 2017.
6 My School 2013 & 2017.
7 Ting et al. 2018.
8 C Bonnor & R Wilson, 'The school money-go-round', *EdMediaWatch*, 2021. <edmediawatch.com.au/>.
9 T Cobbold, 'The state of school funding in Australia, 2017,' *Save our Schools*, June 2019, p. 12. <saveourschools.com.au/wp-content/uploads/2019/06/The-State-of-School-Funding-in-Australia-2017-Update.pdf>.
10 L Connors & J McMorrow, *Imperatives in Schools Funding: Equity, sustainability and achievement*, Australian Council for Educational Research, Camberwell, Vic., 2015, p. 27.
11 Connors & McMorrow 2015, p. 29.
12 J Ferrari, 'School funding hold-outs will pass up $27bn', *The Australian*, 30 July 2013; M Harrington, Parliamentary Library, *Funding the National Plan for School Improvement: An explanation*, June 2013, p. 6.
13 C Pyne, 'School funding', press conference, 26 November 2013. <ministers.dese.gov.au/pyne/press-conference-parliament-house>.
14 T Abbott, joint press conference, PM transcripts, Department of the Prime Minister and Cabinet, 2 December 2013. <pmtranscripts.pmc.gov.au/release/transcript-23134>.
15 ABC, 'Christopher Pyne discusses proposed changes to education funding', *Lateline*, 20 May 2014. <www.abc.net.au/lateline/students-should-contribute-to--own-education/5466486>.
16 C Pyne, 'Matters of public importance', House of Representatives Hansard, Commonwealth of Australia, 3 December 2013, p. 1421. <parlinfo.aph.gov.au/parlInfo/download/chamber/hansardr/af7f2b6d-1ae3-4be8-ac66-e69bab8105a8/toc_pdf/House%20of%20Representatives_2013_12_03_2131_Official.pdf;fileType=application%2Fpdf>.
17 T Cobbold, 'Pyne's opportunistic support of states' rights has sabotaged Gonski', *Save our Schools*, 25 February 2014. <saveourschools.com.au/funding/pynes-opportunistic-support-of-states-rights-has-sabotaged-gonski/>.

18 My School 2013 & 2017.
19 My School 2013 & 2017.
20 Cobbold 2019, p. 15.
21 Cobbold 2019, p. 10.
22 J Ryan, 'Gonski: A wasted opportunity for NT schools?', AEUNT, 22 January 2016. <aeunt.org.au/news/gonski-a-wasted-opportunity-for-nt-schools/>
23 Cobbold 2019, p. 15.
24 SSTUWA, 'Report reveals WA has highest student–teacher ratios in the country', 22 February 2017. <web.archive.org/web/20170225054059/http:/www.sstuwa.org.au/news-home/2015/report-reveals-wa-has-highest-student-teacher-ratios-country>.
25 SSTUWA 2017.
26 T Cobbold, 'The facts about school funding in NSW', *Save our Schools*, 26 June 2019. <saveourschools.com.au/funding/the-facts-about-school-funding-in-nsw/>.
27 Senate Select Committee on School Funding, 'Equity and excellence in Australian schools', Commonwealth of Australia, 9 July 2014, p. 26. <www.aph.gov.au/Parliamentary_Business/Committees/Senate/School_Funding/School_Funding/Report/index>.
28 Cobbold 2019, p. 3.
29 My School 2014 & 2017.
30 My School 2011 & 2017.
31 Cobbold 2019.
32 Question on notice, Supplementary Budget Estimates 2015–2016, Senate Select Committee on Education and Employment, Department of Education and Training Question No. SQ15-000888 (Schooling Resource Standard), 2014.
33 My School 2014 & 2017.
34 Senate Select Committee on Education and Employment 2014.
35 Senate Select Committee on Education and Employment 2014.
36 Australian Education Union – Federal, 'Schools Funding Review Submission', AEU, March 2011, p. 25.
37 D Gonski, K Greiner, K Boston, C Lawrence, P Tannock & B Scales, *Review of Funding for Schooling: Final report*, Federal Department of Education, Employment and Workplace Relations, Canberra, 2011, p. 181. <www.dese.gov.au/school-funding/resources/review-funding-schooling-final-report-december-2011>.
38 Gonski et al. 2011, p. 181.
39 Ken Boston, interview with the authors, 14 October 2020.
40 C Bonnor & R Wilson, 'The school money-go-round,' *EdMediaWatch*, 2021. <edmediawatch.com.au>.
41 Bonnor & Wilson 2021.
42 T Greenwell, 'Less choice, less affordability: The private school subsidy paradox', *Inside Story*, 24 January 2020. <insidestory.org.au/less-choice-less-affordability-the-private-school-subsidy-paradox/>.
43 Cobbold 2019, p. 16.
44 My School 2011 & 2017.
45 My School 2011 & 2017.
46 Paul Karp, 'Pisa results: Australian students' science, maths and reading in long-term decline', *The Guardian*, 6 December 2016. <www.theguardian.com/australia-

news/2016/dec/06/pisa-results-australian-students-science-maths-and-reading-in-long-term-decline>.

47 P Morgan, A Newman, B Roebuck & anonymous, written correspondence with the authors, October 2021.

48 Australian Education Union, 'Getting results: Gonski funding in Australian schools', AEU, 2016. <www.aeufederal.org.au/application/files/4814/8780/4156/GonskiGettingResults2.pdf>.

49 My School 2020.

50 AEU 2016.

51 AEU 2016.

52 My School 2012 & 2016.

7 Gonski's second coming (2017–21)

1 M Turnbull, *A Bigger Picture*, Hardie Grant Books, Melbourne, Vic., 2020, p. 521.

2 N Chrysanthos & A Carey, 'Growth in money for private school students outstrips public schools', *The Age*, 30 June 2020. <www.theage.com.au/national/nsw/growth-in-money-for-private-school-students-outstrips-public-schools-20200629-p557b9.html>.

3 ABC, 'Education, environment and equality', *Q&A*, September 2016. <www.abc.net.au/qanda/education-environment-and-equality/10652014>.

4 M Knott, 'Malcolm Turnbull's education revolution: End federal support for public schools', *Sydney Morning Herald*, 31 March 2016. <www.smh.com.au/politics/federal/malcolm-turnbulls-education-revolution-end-federal-support-for-public-schools-20160331-gnuo4l.html>.

5 Turnbull 2020, p. 523.

6 Correna Haythorpe, interview with the authors, 3 September 2020.

7 Turnbull 2020, p. 523.

8 Haythorpe 2020.

9 D Ashenden, 'Could Turnbull give a Gonski?', *Inside Story*, 24 September 2015. <insidestory.org.au/could-turnbull-give-a-gonski/>.

10 ABC, 'Prime Minister Malcolm Turnbull', *Q&A*, 20 June 2016. <www.abc.net.au/qanda/prime-minister-malcolm-turnbull/10652640>.

11 Ashenden 2015.

12 Turnbull 2020, p. 394.

13 Turnbull 2020, p 523.

14 M Grattan, 'Birmingham prepares for fundamental changes to Labor's Gonski funding model', *The Conversation*, 22 September 2016. <theconversation.com/birmingham-prepares-for-fundamental-changes-to-labors-gonski-funding-model-65828>.

15 P Goss, 'A simple and immediate fix for schools funding', Grattan Institute, 22 September 2016. <grattan.edu.au/news/a-simple-and-immediate-fix-for-schools-funding/>.

16 P Goss & J Sonnemann, 'Circuit breaker: A new compact on school funding', Grattan Institute, November 2016. <grattan.edu.au/wp-content/uploads/2016/11/881-Circuit-Breaker-New-Compact-replaced-3.pdf>.

17 Goss 22 September 2016.

18 Goss 22 September 2016.

19 Goss 22 September 2016.
20 Peter Goss, interview with the authors, 10 August 2020.
21 Goss 2020.
22 P Goss, 'Gonski 2.0: Is this the school funding plan we have been looking for? Finally, yes', *The Conversation*, 3 May 2017. <theconversation.com/gonski-2-0-is-this-the-school-funding-plan-we-have-been-looking-for-finally-yes-77081>.
23 Turnbull 2020, p. 527.
24 M Knott & M Koziol, 'Gonski 2.0: The story of how the government got it done', *Sydney Morning Herald*, 24 June 2017. <www.smh.com.au/politics/federal/gonski-20-the-story-of-how-the-government-got-it-done-20170623-gwwwuk.html>.
25 Turnbull 2020, p. 527.
26 Turnbull 2020, p. 521.
27 Tanya Plibersek, interview with the authors, 9 September 2020.
28 R Yosufzai, '"Gonski 2.0" school funding plan amounts to $22b cut: Plibersek', *SBS News*, 2 March 2017. <www.sbs.com.au/news/gonski-2-0-school-funding-plan-amounts-to-22b-cut-plibersek>.
29 ABC, 'Fact check: Has the Government cut $22 billion from schools?', RMIT *ABC Fact Check*, 5 June 2017. <www.abc.net.au/news/2017-06-05/fact-check-has-the-government-cut-22bn-from-schools/8526768?nw=0>.
30 ABC, 'Former education union chief urges all sides to back Gonski 2.0', *7:30*, 20 June 2017. <www.abc.net.au/7.30/former-education-union-chief-urges-all-sides-to/8636370>.
31 D Marin-Guzman, 'Inside the AEU: The union leading the Gonski attack on the Greens', *Australian Financial Review*, 23 June 2017. <www.afr.com/policy/economy/inside-the-aeu-the-union-leading-the-gonski-attack-on-the-greens-20170621-gwvfxx>.
32 Haythorpe 2020.
33 Australian Education Union – Federal Office, 'Turnbull's Gonski chaos will short change students', media release, AEU, 3 May 2017. <www.aeufederal.org.au/news-media/media-releases/2017/may/020517>.
34 Turnbull 2020, p. 532.
35 Plibersek 2020.
36 T Cobbold, 'Gonski 2.0 is the best special deal private schools have ever had', *Save our Schools*, 10 December 2017. <saveourschools.com.au/funding/new-figures-confirm-more-private-schools-will-be-over-funded-under-gonski-20/#more-37>.
37 T Cobbold, 'Public schools are defrauded by billions under new funding agreements', *Save our Schools*, 6 February 2019. <saveourschools.com.au/funding/public-schools-are-defrauded-by-billions-under-new-funding-agreements/>.
38 Cobbold 2017.
39 Peter Goss, interview with the authors, 10 August 2020.
40 Goss 2020.
41 P Goss & J Sonnemann, 'Submission to the Senate Inquiry into the Australian Education Amendment Bill 2017', Grattan Institute, May 2017, p. 10.
42 Goss & Sonnemann, 2017, p. 14.
43 Goss 2020.
44 Goss 2020.
45 M Knott, '"We have to face reality": Greens prepared to strike school funding deal with the Coalition', *Sydney Morning Herald*, 12 May 2017. <www.smh.com.

au/politics/federal/we-have-to-face-reality-greens-prepared-to-strike-school-funding-deal-with-the-coalition-20170512-gw3m31.html>.

46 Goss 2020.

47 M Harrington, 'Schools funding legislation passed by Parliament – an update on the amendments', FlagPost (Parliamentary Library), 28 June 2017. <parlinfo.aph.gov.au/parlInfo/download/library/prspub/5364824/upload_binary/5364824.pdf;fileType=application%2Fpdf#search=%22library/prspub/5364824%22>.

48 Goss 2020.

49 Goss 2020.

50 Harrington 2017.

51 Turnbull 2020, p. 530.

52 A Gavrielatos & S Hopgood, 'Schools Funding Review Submission', Australian Education Union, March 2011, p. 25.

53 Turnbull 2020, p. 531.

54 P Riordan, 'Labor hits out at Coalition for suggesting some private schools are over-funded', *Australian Financial Review*, 27 September 2016. <www.afr.com/politics/labor-hits-out-at-coalition-for-suggesting-some-private-schools-are-overfunded-20160927-grpgrm>.

55 G Chan, 'Labor accused of playing "bogeyman politics" over private school funding', *The Guardian*, 28 September 2016. <www.theguardian.com/australia-news/2016/sep/28/labor-accused-of-playing-bogeyman-politics-over-private-school-funding>.

56 M McGowan, 'Bill Shorten pledges extra $250m for Catholic schools if Labor elected', *The Guardian*, 9 March 2018. <www.theguardian.com/australia-news/2018/mar/09/bill-shorten-pledges-extra-250m-for-catholic-schools-if-labor-elected>.

57 J Ferguson, 'Labor fires Catholic funding war', *The Australian*, 9 March 2018.

58 S Benson, 'Labor victory fuelled by Catholic education backing', *The Australian*, 19 March 2018.

59 D Shanahan, 'Church campaign could reignite at next election', *The Australian*, 22 March 2018.

60 R Morton & R Baxendale, 'Scrutiny for Shorten's "special deal"', *The Australian*, 21 March 2018.

61 J Ferguson, 'PM's bid to appease furious Catholics', *The Australian*, 9 July 2018.

62 Turnbull 2020, p. 533.

63 P Karp, 'Catholic and independent schools given extra $4.6bn in funding peace deal', *The Guardian*, 20 September 2018. <www.theguardian.com/australia-news/2018/sep/20/catholic-and-independent-schools-given-extra-46bn-in-funding-peace-deal>.

64 R Lewis, 'Catholic swipe at "predictable complaints"', *The Australian*, 25 September 2018.

65 J Baker et al., 'Don't play favourites with Aussie kids' schools, Stokes tells Morrison', *Sydney Morning Herald*, 22 September 2018. <www.smh.com.au/national/don-t-play-favourites-with-aussie-kids-schools-stokes-tells-morrison-20180921-p505ab.html>.

66 T Cobbold, 'Public schools are defrauded by billions under new funding agreements', *Save our Schools*, 6 February 2019. <saveourschools.com.au/funding/public-schools-are-defrauded-by-billions-under-new-funding-agreements/>.

67 M McGowan, 'States seek public education deal after Coalition's Catholic school handout', *The Guardian*, 26 September 2018. <www.theguardian.com/australia-news/2018/sep/26/states-seek-public-education-deal-after-coalitions-catholic-school-handout>.

68 T Cobbold, 'The unwinding of Gonski Part 3: Morrison abandons needs based funding', *Save our Schools*, April 2021, pp. 29, 30. <saveourschools.com.au/wp-content/uploads/2021/04/Morrison-Abandons-Needs-Based-Funding.pdf>.

69 J Baker, 'Sleight of hand': Public schools get $3.5b less than original Gonski plan intended', *Sydney Morning Herald*, 4 September 2021. <http://www.smh.com.au/national/nsw/sleight-of-hand-public-schools-get-3-5b-less-than-original-gonski-plan-intended-20210903-p58oma.html>.

70 Cobbold 2019.

71 Cobbold 2021, p. 32.

72 P Goss, 'Lopsided funding gives more to private schools that need it least', *Sydney Morning Herald*, 16 May 2019. <www.smh.com.au/education/lopsided-funding-gives-more-to-private-schools-that-need-it-least-20190514-p51ndt.html>.

73 N Chrysanthos & A Carey, 'Growth in money for private school students outstrips public schools', *The Age*, 30 June 2020. <www.theage.com.au/national/nsw/growth-in-money-for-private-school-students-outstrips-public-schools-20200629-p557b9.html>.

8 The Gonski we got

1 S Thomson, '"Big five" education challenges: The "long tail" of underachievement in Australia', *Teacher Magazine*, 22 March 2021. <www.teachermagazine.com/au_en/articles/big-five-education-challenges-the-long-tail-of-underachievement-in-australia>.

2 Unless otherwise specified, the most recent figures and calculations are for 2020, derived from My School 2021 (<www.myschool.edu.au/>). A two-year time lag applies to finance data. Earlier My School data cited is derived from research completed prior to those dates.

3 Australian Curriculum, Assessment and Reporting Authority, My School, ACARA, 2011.

4 My School 2011 & 2020.

5 Australian Council for Educational Research, 'PISA 2018: Australian students' performance', ACER, 2018. <www.acer.org/au/discover/article/pisa-2018-australian-students-performance>.

6 Thomson 2021.

7 My School 2011 & 2020.

8 C Bonnor, 'Separating scholars: How Australia abandons its struggling schools', Centre for Policy Development, 2019. <cpd.org.au/wp-content/uploads/2019/01/Separating-Scholars.pdf>.

9 D Gonski et al., *Through Growth to Achievement: The Report of the Review to Achieve Educational Excellence in Australian Schools*, Commonwealth of Australia, 2018. <www.dese.gov.au/quality-schools-package/resources/through-growth-achievement-report-review-achieve-educational-excellence-australian-schools>.

10 A Tudge, 'Initial teacher education review launched', media release, 15 April 2021. <ministers.dese.gov.au/tudge/initial-teacher-education-review-launched>.

11 T Plibersek (ed.), *Upturn: A better normal after COVID-19*, NewSouth Publishing, Sydney, 2020, p. 145.
12 'Education Minister Bishop calls for higher standards in schools', Australian Politics.com, February 2007. <australianpolitics.com/2007/02/07/education-minister-calls-for-higher-standards.html>.
13 D Gonski, K Greiner, K Boston, C Lawrence, P Tannock & B Scales, *Review of Funding for Schooling: Final report*, Federal Department of Education, Employment and Workplace Relations, Canberra, 2011, p. 124. <www.dese.gov.au/school-funding/resources/review-funding-schooling-final-report-december-2011>.
14 S Thomson et al., 'Challenges for Australian Education: Results from PISA 2009', Australian Council for Educational Research, 2011, p. 72. <www.acer.org/files/PISA-Report-2009.pdf>.
15 C Bonnor, P Kidson, A Piccoli, P Sahlberg & R Wilson, *Structural Failure: Why Australia keeps falling short of our educational goals*, Gonski Institute for Education, 2021, p. 16.
16 Bonnor 2019.
17 Gonski et al. 2011, p. 105.
18 Australian Curriculum, Assessment and Reporting Authority, 'School income and capital expenditure for government and non-government schools (Calendar year), 2021'. <www.acara.edu.au/reporting/national-report-on-schooling-in-australia/national-report-on-schooling-in-australia-data-portal/school-funding/school-income-and-capital-expenditure-for-government-and-non-government-schools-(calendar-year)#view3>.
19 ACARA 2021.
20 T Cobbold, 'Gonski gone: Morrison abandons public school students', *Save our Schools*, 19 November 2020. <saveourschools.com.au/funding/gonski-gone-morrison-abandons-public-school-students/>.
21 My School 2017–20.
22 C Bonnor & B Shepherd, 'Institutionalised inequality', *Inside Story*, 21 September 2016. <insidestory.org.au/institutionalised-inequality/>.
23 P Goss, 'Education funding: We should be wary of simplistic arguments about money and outcomes', *The Guardian*, 3 August 2016. <www.theguardian.com/commentisfree/2016/aug/03/naplan-results-we-should-be-wary-of-simplistic-arguments-about-funding>.
24 T Cobbold, 'More school funding means better student outcomes', *Save our Schools*, 8 March 2021. <saveourschools.com.au/funding/more-school-funding-means-better-student-outcomes/>.
25 A Carey, 'Minister says quality teaching, not more school funding, key to better results', *Sydney Morning Herald*, 27 April 2021. <www.smh.com.au/national/minister-says-quality-teaching-not-more-school-funding-key-to-better-results-20210426-p57mfl.html?btis>.
26 Gonski et al. 2011, p. 15.
27 My School 2020.
28 My School 2011 & 2020.
29 Gonski et al. 2011, p. 196.
30 Tom Coll, interview with Chris Bonnor, 2021.

31 Better Education, 'VCE School Ranking'. <bettereducation.com.au/results/vce.aspx>.
32 S Wright & E Bagshaw, 'As cities grow, parts of regional Australia disappear and get angry', *Sydney Morning Herald*, 30 August 2019. <www.smh.com.au/politics/federal/as-cities-grow-parts-of-regional-australia-disappear-and-get-angry-20190829-p52m26.html>.
33 S Waslander, C Pater, & M Weide, 'Markets in education: An analytical review of empirical research on market mechanisms in education', OECD Education, Working Paper 52, OECD Publishing, 2010, pp. 54–55. <www.oecd-ilibrary.org/education/markets-in-education_5km4pskmkr27-en>.
34 Adelaide High School, 'Year 7 and 8 enrolment'. <www.adelaidehs.sa.edu.au/Enrolment/year-7-and-8-enrolment>.
35 L Novak & J David, 'Calls for education zoning system to be reviewed as popular schools run out of space', *The Advertiser*, 5 February 2012. <www.adelaidenow.com.au/ipad/calls-for-education-zoning-system-to-be-reviewed-as-popular-schools-run-out-of-space/news-story/412cfb6e14d0278032d2098aeedd8187>.
36 C Briggs, 'Almost half of Adelaide public high school students live outside their zone', *ABC News*, 24 July 2019. <www.abc.net.au/news/2019-07-24/new-figures-show-how-many-students-living-out-of-school-zones/11341622?nw=0>.
37 I Ting, A Palmer & N Scott, 'Rich school, poor school: Australia's great education divide', *ABC News*, 6 September 2019. <www.abc.net.au/news/2019-08-13/rich-school-poor-school-australias-great-education-divide/11383384>.
38 My School 2012 & 2018.
39 C Bonnor & B Shepherd, 'Uneven playing field: The state of Australia's schools', Centre for Policy Development, 2016, p. 37. <cpd.org.au/wp-content/uploads/2016/05/The-State-of-Australias-Schools.pdf>.
40 OECD, 'Equity in education: Breaking down barriers to social mobility', OECD Publishing, Paris, 2018, p. 121. <www.oecd-ilibrary.org/education/equity-in-education_9789264073234-en>.
41 B Preston, 'The social make-up of schools: A report prepared for the Australian Education Union', Barbara Preston Research, Canberra, 2018, p. 1. <www.aeufederal.org.au/application/files/7115/2090/2405/Preston2018.pdf>.
42 C Bonnor, 'Institutionalised separation', discussion paper, Centre for Policy Development, 2018. <cpd.org.au/2018/07/institutionalised-separation/>.
43 J Baker, 'Sydney to get its first new selective high school in 25 years', *Sydney Morning Herald*, 22 June 2021. <http://www.smh.com.au/politics/nsw/sydney-to-get-its-first-new-selective-high-school-in-25-years-20210622-p5839h.html>.
44 C Bonnor, C Ho & G Richards, 'A creeping Indigenous separation', discussion paper, Centre for Policy Development, 2018. <cpd.org.au/2018/02/creeping-indigenous-separation-discussion-paper-february-2018/>.
45 J Baker, 'How COVID-19 exposed the fault lines in Australian education', *Sydney Morning Herald*, 16 May 2020. <www.smh.com.au/national/how-covid-19-exposed-the-fault-lines-in-australian-education-20200514-p54t5v.html>.
46 J Baker, 'NSW schools struggle to find teachers as supply collapses', *Sydney Morning Herald*, 23 June 2021. <http://www.smh.com.au/national/nsw/nsw-schools-struggle-to-find-teachers-as-supply-collapses-20210621-p582w5.html>.

47 S Lansdown, '2021 NAPLAN scores not impacted by COVID-19 pandemic in Australia', *Canberra Times*, 25 August 2021. <www.canberratimes.com.au/story/7398363/pleasant-surprise-in-this-years-naplan-scores/>.
48 J Sonnemann & P Goss, 'Disadvantaged students may have lost 1 month of learning during COVID-19 shutdown. But the government can fix it', *The Conversation*, 15 June 2020. <theconversation.com/disadvantaged-students-may-have-lost-1-month-of-learning-during-covid-19-shutdown-but-the-government-can-fix-it-140540>.
49 Education Endowment Foundation (UK), 'Best evidence on impact of Covid-19 on pupil attainment', 27 June 2021. <educationendowmentfoundation.org.uk/eef-support-for-schools/covid-19-resources/best-evidence-on-impact-of-school-closures-on-the-attainment-gap/>.
50 Office of Civil Rights, 'Education in a pandemic: The disparate impacts of COVID-19 on America's students', Department of Education, USA, 9 June 2021. <www2.ed.gov/about/offices/list/ocr/docs/20210608-impacts-of-covid19.pdf>.
51 J Baker, 'NSW schools struggle to find teachers as supply collapses', *Sydney Morning Herald*, 23 June 2021. <http://www.smh.com.au/national/nsw/nsw-schools-struggle-to-find-teachers-as-supply-collapses-20210621-p582w5.html>.
52 I Muller, 'Teachers ditching school at alarming rate offered chance to instead excel at Victorian academy', *ABC News*, 22 July 2021. <www.abc.net.au/news/2021-07-22/victoria-contracts-workloads-teacher-shortage/100307708>.
53 B Roebuck, J Frew & anonymous, written correspondence with the authors, October 2021.
54 Gonski et al. 2011, p. 107.
55 Bonnor & Shepherd 2016, p. 25.
56 OECD 2018.
57 J Chesters & A Daly, 'Do peer effects mediate the association between family socio-economic status and educational achievement?', *Australian Journal of Social Issues*, vol. 52, 2017, pp. 63–77.
58 OECD 2018, p. 122.
59 Preston 2018, p. 17.
60 L Perry, 'To reduce inequality in Australian schools, make them less socially segregated', *The Conversation*, 20 April 2018. <theconversation.com/to-reduce-inequality-in-australian-schools-make-them-less-socially-segregated-95034>.

9 Gonski, a post-mortem

1 S Marginson, 'Re-assessing Karmel: Results of the 1973 Education Settlement', *Progress in Political Economy*, no. 16, March 1984, pp. 15–33. <www.ppesydney.net/content/uploads/2020/04/Reassessing-Karmel-results-of-the-1973-education-settlement.pdf>.
2 R Millar & H Cook, 'Batman robocalls spark formal complaints', *Sydney Morning Herald*, 1 April 2018. <www.smh.com.au/politics/federal/batman-robocalls-spark-formal-complaints-20180401-p4z7aj.html>.
3 Australian Curriculum, Assessment and Reporting Authority, My School, ACARA, 2011.

4 L Connors & J McMorrow, *New Directions in Schools Funding: A proposed model*, Faculty of Education and Social Work, The University of Sydney, Sydney, 2010, p. 41.
5 C Bonnor & R Wilson, 'The school money-go-round', *EdMediaWatch*, 2021. <drive.google.com/file/d/1rnn0w1nWYreOMRSsDfzt4n8KXHaGbw2h/view>.
6 Connors & McMorrow 2010, p. 53.
7 Ken Boston, interview with the authors, 1 June 2021.
8 Marginson 1984.
9 C Armitage, 'Private schools likely to cut fees', *The Australian*, 13 May 1999.
10 N Craig, 'Our richest schools raise fees by 91%', *The Age*, 16 January 2011. <www.theage.com.au/national/victoria/our-richest-schools-raise-fees-by-91-percent-20110115-19s1g.html>.
11 David Kemp 'Major reform of non-government school funding', media release, 11 May, 1999.
12 Commonwealth of Australia, Questions, House of Representatives, Canberra, 13 May 1999, p. 5397.
13 D Kemp, 'Major reform of non-government school funding', media release, 11 May 1999.
14 A Probyn, 'Wesley funding windfall', *Herald Sun*, 31 August 2000.
15 Craig 2011.
16 G Healy, 'Fees not linked to schools handout', *The Australian*, 30 September 2000.
17 G Whitlam, *The Whitlam Government*, Viking, Ringwood, 1985, p. 309.
18 I Wilkinson, B Caldwell, R Selleck, J Harris & P Dettman, *A History of State Aid to Non-Government Schools in Australia*, Educational Transformations Pty Ltd, Canberra, 2006, p. 63.
19 Wilkinson et al. 2006, p. 63.
20 Catholic Education Commission of Victoria, *The Affordability of Catholic Schools in Victoria*, Monash University-ACER, February 2004.
21 Editorial, 'Labor's private school hit list', *The Age*, 15 September 2004. <www.theage.com.au/national/labors-private-school-hit-list-20040915-gdymvq.html>.
22 S Davis & F Sewell, 'Gillard says "education revolution" is keeping Far Northerners in work', *ABC News*, 20 May 2010. <www.abc.net.au/local/audio/2010/05/20/2904722.htm>.

10 Levelling the playing field

1 A Piccoli, 'There's a way to fix the biggest structural problem in Australian education', *Sydney Morning Herald*, 11 August 2020. <www.smh.com.au/national/there-s-a-way-to-fix-the-biggest-structural-problem-in-australian-education-20200808-p55jv4.html>.
2 Piccoli 2020.
3 D Ashenden, 'Political games hide hard facts of Gonski education reform', *Crikey*, 21 August 2012. <www.crikey.com.au/2012/08/21/political-games-hide-hard-facts-of-gonski-education-reform/>.
4 L Perry & A McConney, 'School socioeconomic status and student outcomes in reading and mathematics: A comparison of Australia and Canada', *Australian Journal of Education*, vol. 57, no. 2, August 2013, pp. 124–40.

5 Perry & McConney 2013.
6 S Thomson, 'Aussie students are a year behind students 10 years ago in science, maths and reading', *The Conversation*, 3 December 2019. <theconversation.com/aussie-students-are-a-year-behind-students-10-years-ago-in-science-maths-and-reading-127013>.
7 S Thomson, L De Bortoli, C Underwood & M Schmid, PISA 2018, 'Pisa in Brief I: Student performance', Australian Council for Educational Research, Canberra, 2019. <research.acer.edu.au/cgi/viewcontent.cgi?article=1036&context=ozpisa>.
8 OECD, 'PISA 2018 Results: Combined Executive Summaries volume I, II & III', OECD Publishing, Paris, 2019. <www.oecd.org/pisa/Combined_Executive_Summaries_PISA_2018.pdf>.
9 T Greenwell, 'Why do Canada's schools outperform Australia's?,' *Inside Story*, 9 April 2020. <insidestory.org.au/why-do-canadas-schools-outperform-australias/>.
10 Greenwell 2020.
11 Gonski et al. 2011, p. 186.
12 Bonnor & Wilson, 2021.
13 My School, 2021.
14 Bonnor & Wilson, 2021.
15 OECD, 'Balancing school choice and equity: An international perspective based on PISA', OECD Publishing, Paris, 2019, p. 84. <www.oecd-ilibrary.org/docserver/2592c974-en.pdf?expires=1636317028&id=id&accname=guest&checksum=8899BD0A19AD8D627994B69EF73FDAB3>.
16 Big Picture Education Australia (BPEA), <www.bigpicture.org.au/>.
17 H Shams, 'Big Picture Education Australia program helps students enter university without ATAR score', *ABC Radio Sydney*, 19 April 2021. <www.abc.net.au/news/2021-04-19/hsc-alternative-pathway-big-picture-education-australia-no-atar/100075440>.
18 A Smith, 'Student login: Aurora College is the first virtual high school in NSW', *Sydney Morning Herald*, 5 March 2017. <www.smh.com.au/education/student-login-aurora-college-is-the-first-virtual-high-school-in-nsw-20170303-gupyrl.html>; <aurora.nsw.edu.au/>.
19 T Greenwell, 'Inside Australia's first virtual school', *Inside Story*, 28 September 2017. <insidestory.org.au/inside-australias-first-virtual-school/>.
20 A Patty, 'Catholic leader dismisses school funding reform as a "flight of fantasy"', *Sydney Morning Herald*, 10 February 2021. <http://www.smh.com.au/national/nsw/catholic-leader-dismisses-school-funding-reform-as-flight-of-fantasy-20210217-p573a2.html>.
21 T Cobbold, 'Integration of private schools in the public system would deepen structural failure', *Save our Schools*, 22 February 2021. <saveourschools.com.au/funding/integration-of-private-schools-in-the-public-system-would-deepen-structural-failure>.
22 Jacinta Collins, interview with the authors, 10 September 2020.
23 Collins 2020.
24 Mark Spencer, interview with the authors, 4 June 2021.
25 Cobbold 2021.

26 B Schneiders and R Millar, 'Australia's top private schools are growing richer and faster than ever', *Sydney Morning Herald*, 18 June 2021. <www.smh.com.au/national/australia-s-top-private-schools-are-growing-richer-and-faster-than-ever-20210615-p5814b.html>.

27 Cobbold 2021.

28 Commonwealth of Australia, Parliamentary Debates, Canberra, 14 September 2011. <parlinfo.aph.gov.au/parlInfo/genpdf/chamber/hansardr/db12227e-c808-4b45-8e11-e59ca86f689e/0036/hansard_frag.pdf;fileType=application/pdf>.

29 D Barber, 'Labor's frontbench, too, is a mostly private-school affair', *Crikey*, 30 December 2013. <www.crikey.com.au/2013/12/20/labors-frontbench-too-is-a-mostly-private-school-affair/>.

30 Tanya Plibersek, interview with the authors, 9 September 2020.

31 A Rorris, 'Australian schooling – the price of failure and reward for success', Australian Education Union, April 2016. <apo.org.au/sites/default/files/resource-files/2016-04/apo-nid63526.pdf>.

32 D Hetherington, 'What price the gap? Education and inequity in Australia', issues paper, Public Education Foundation, 2018. <publiceducationfoundation.org.au/wp-content/uploads/2018/04/Issues-Paper_What-Price-The-Gap.pdf>.

33 Bonnor & Wilson 2021.

34 C Bonnor, P Kidson, A Piccoli, P Sahlberg & R Wilson, *Structural Failure: Why Australia keeps falling short of its educational goals*, UNSW Gonski Institute, Sydney, 2021. <www.gie.unsw.edu.au/sites/default/files/documents/Structural%20Failure_final.pdf>.

35 S Macklin & S Pilcher, 'One quarter of Australian 11–12-year-olds don't have the literacy and numeracy skills they need', *The Conversation*, 28 October 2020. <theconversation.com/one-quarter-of-australian-11-12-year-olds-dont-have-the-literacy-and-numeracy-skills-they-need-148912>.

36 S Thomson, 'Many Australian school students feel they "don't belong" in school: New research', *The Conversation*, 6 June 2018. <theconversation.com/many-australian-school-students-feel-they-dont-belong-in-school-new-research-97866>.

37 S Waslander, C Pater & M Weide, 'Markets in education: An analytical review of empirical research on market mechanisms in education', *OECD Education Working Paper*, no. 52, OECD Publishing, 2010. <www.oecd-ilibrary.org/education/markets-in-education_5km4pskmkr27-en>.

38 J Keating, G Savage & J Polesel, 'Letting schools off the hook? Exploring the role of Australian secondary schools in the COAG Year 12 attainment agenda', *Journal of Education Policy*, vol. 28, no. 2, 2010, pp. 268–86.

39 C Lubienski, 'Do quasi-markets foster innovation in education? A comparative perspective', *OECD Education Working Papers*, no. 25, OECD Publishing, 2009. <files.eric.ed.gov/fulltext/ED530731.pdf>.

40 Pallavi Singhal, 'The factors holding back Australia's most disadvantaged students', *Sydney Morning Herald*, 31 January 2018. <www.smh.com.au/education/the-factors-holding-back-australias-most-disadvantaged-students-20180130-h0qdgx.html>.

Index

Locators in *italics* refer to tables and figures. Locators in **bold** refer to Glossary definitions for those headings. This index uses letter-by-letter alphabetisation and set-out style. The Timeline is not indexed.

Index

Index

Index

Index

Index

FSC
www.fsc.org
MIX
Papier | Fördert
gute Waldnutzung
FSC® C083411

Zeitfracht Medien GmbH
Ferdinand-Jühlke-Straße 7
99095 Erfurt, Deutschland
produktsicherheit@kolibri360.de